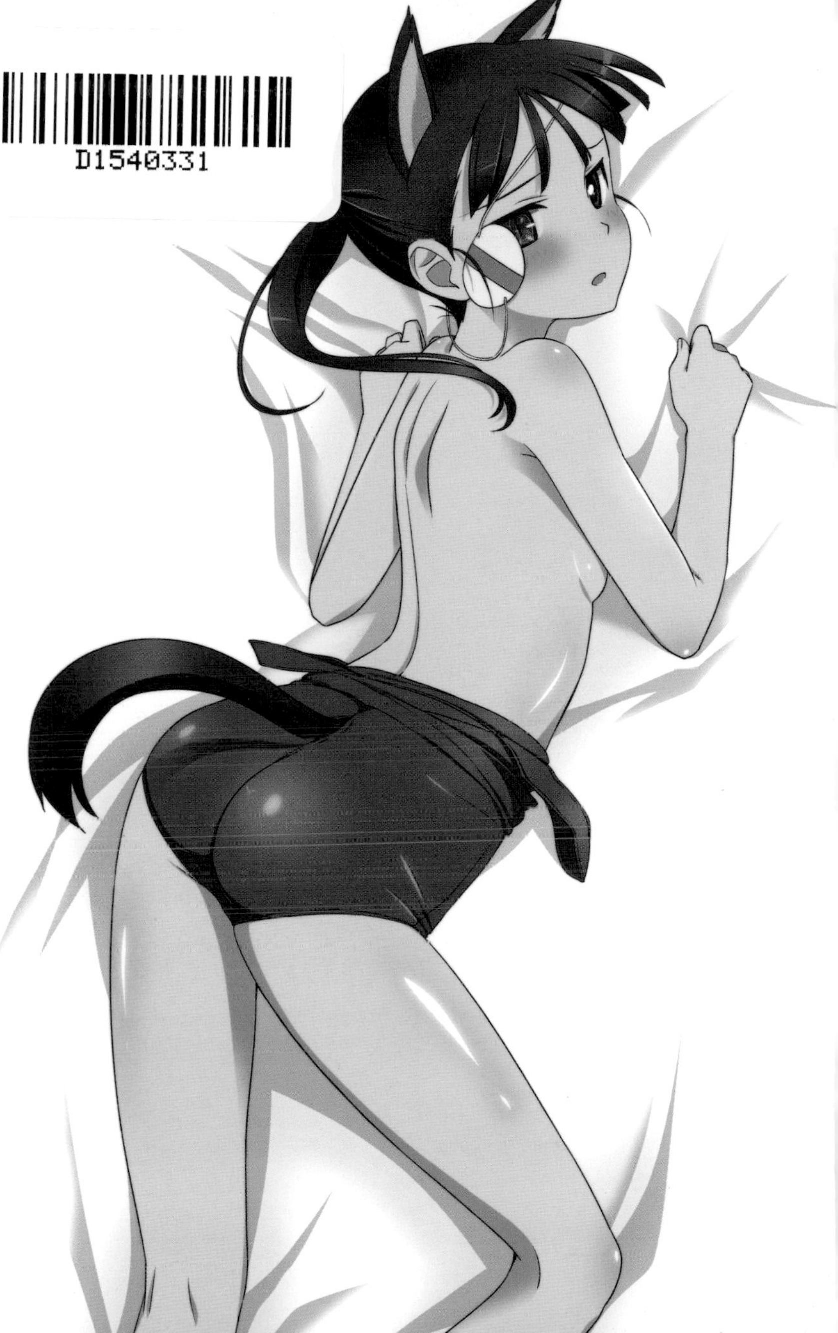

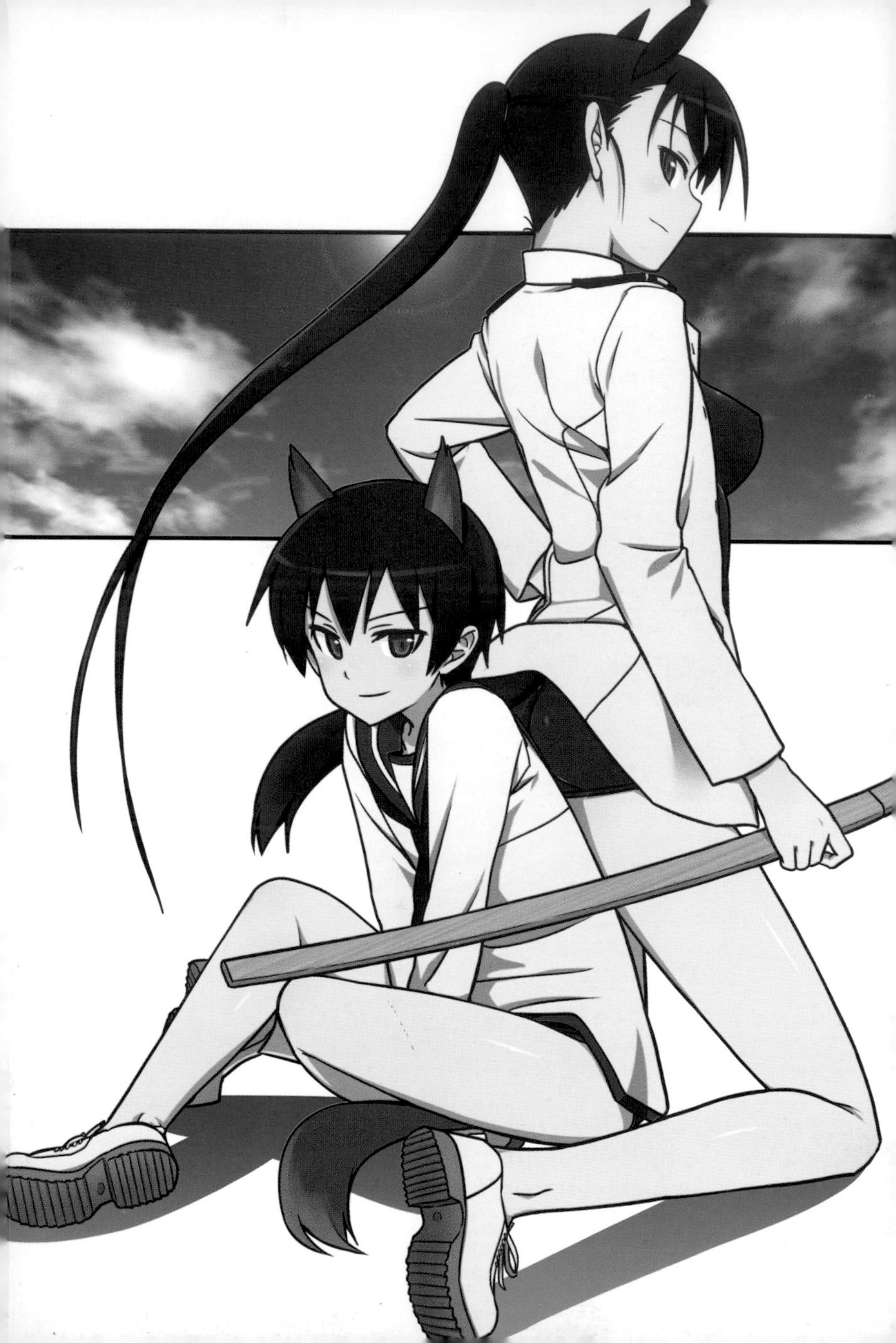

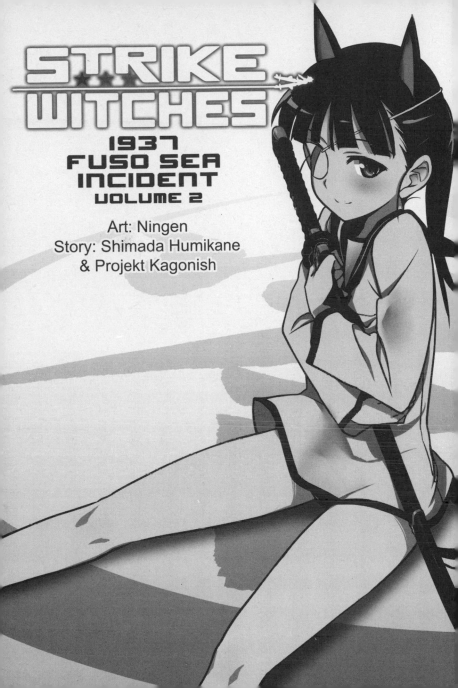

STRIKE WITCHES

1937 FUSO SEA INCIDENT
VOLUME 2

Art: Ningen
Story: Shimada Humikane
& Projekt Kagonish

CHAPTER 7:
TWO WITCHES

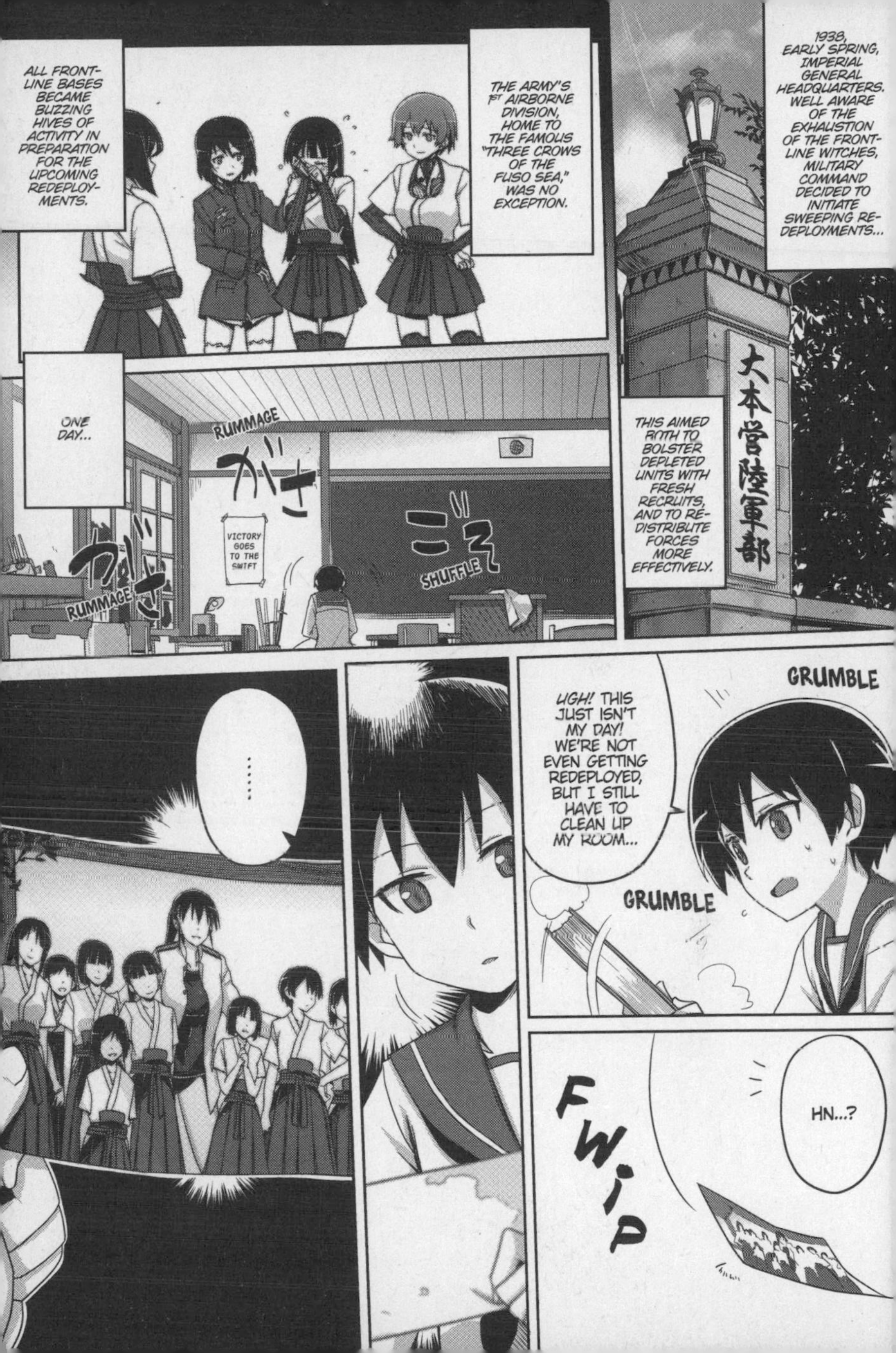
1938, EARLY SPRING, IMPERIAL GENERAL HEADQUARTERS. WELL AWARE OF THE EXHAUSTION OF THE FRONT-LINE WITCHES, MILITARY COMMAND DECIDED TO INITIATE SWEEPING RE-DEPLOYMENTS...
大本営陸軍部
THIS AIMED BOTH TO BOLSTER DEPLETED UNITS WITH FRESH RECRUITS, AND TO RE-DISTRIBUTE FORCES MORE EFFECTIVELY.
THE ARMY'S 1ST AIRBORNE DIVISION, HOME TO THE FAMOUS "THREE CROWS OF THE FUSO SEA," WAS NO EXCEPTION.
ALL FRONT-LINE BASES BECAME BUZZING HIVES OF ACTIVITY IN PREPARATION FOR THE UPCOMING REDEPLOY-MENTS.
ONE DAY...
ごそ
SHUFFLE
がさ
RUMMAGE
VICTORY GOES TO THE SWIFT
がさ
RUMMAGE
GRUMBLE
UGH! THIS JUST ISN'T MY DAY! WE'RE NOT EVEN GETTING REDEPLOYED, BUT I STILL HAVE TO CLEAN UP MY ROOM...
GRUMBLE
HN...?
FWIP
......

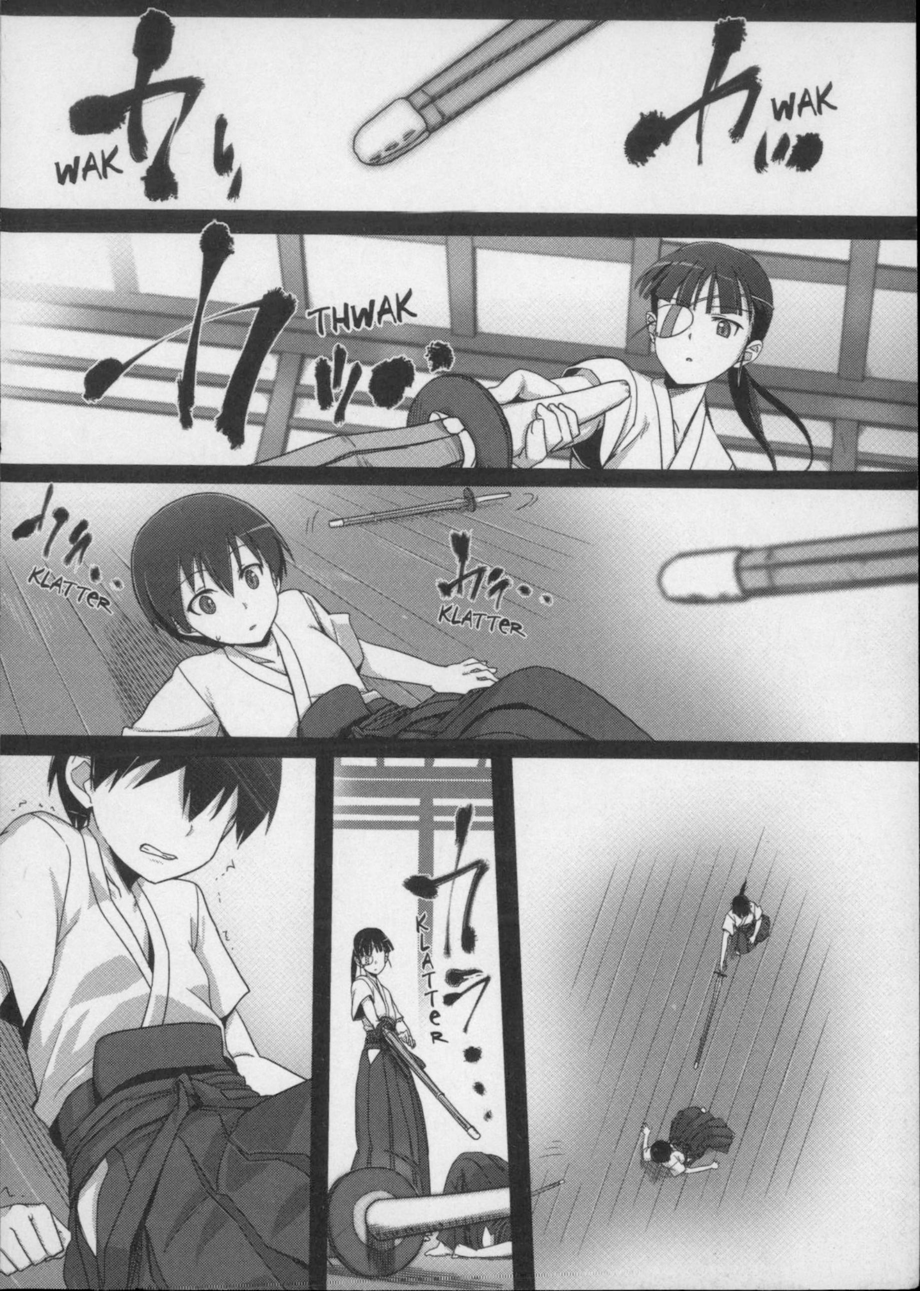
WAK
WAK
THWAK
KLATTER
KLATTER
KLATTER

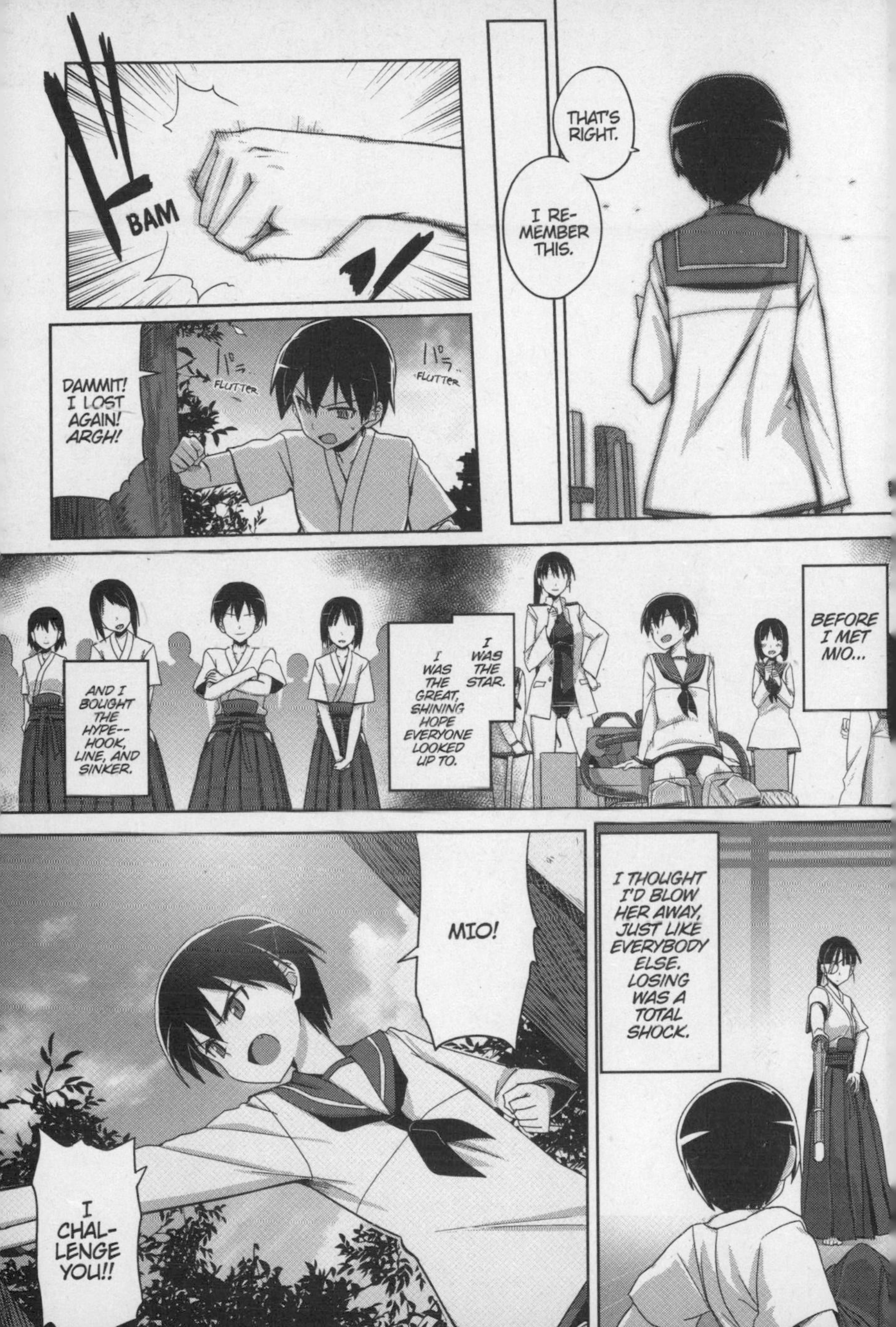
THAT'S RIGHT.
I RE-MEMBER THIS.
BAM
DAMMIT! I LOST AGAIN! ARGH!
FLUTTER
FLUTTER
BEFORE I MET MIO...
I WAS THE STAR.
I WAS THE GREAT, SHINING HOPE EVERYONE LOOKED UP TO.
AND I BOUGHT THE HYPE--HOOK, LINE, AND SINKER.
I THOUGHT I'D BLOW HER AWAY, JUST LIKE EVERYBODY ELSE. LOSING WAS A TOTAL SHOCK.
MIO!
I CHAL-LENGE YOU!!

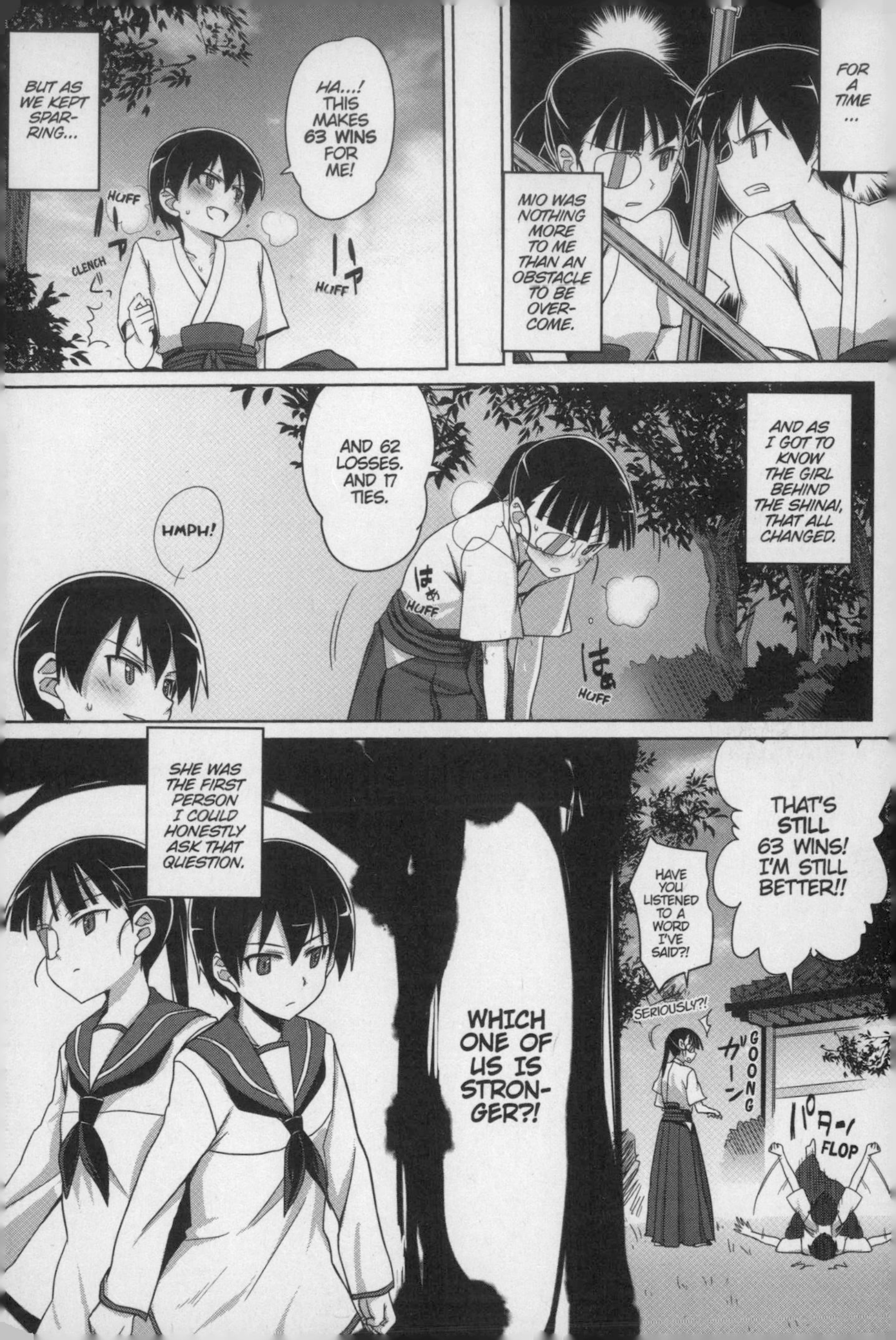
FOR A TIME...
MIO WAS NOTHING MORE TO ME THAN AN OBSTACLE TO BE OVERCOME.
BUT AS WE KEPT SPARRING...
HA...! THIS MAKES 63 WINS FOR ME!
HUFF
CLENCH
HUFF
AND AS I GOT TO KNOW THE GIRL BEHIND THE SHINAI, THAT ALL CHANGED.
AND 62 LOSSES. AND 17 TIES.
HUFF
HUFF
HMPH!
THAT'S STILL 63 WINS! I'M STILL BETTER!!
HAVE YOU LISTENED TO A WORD I'VE SAID?!
SERIOUSLY?!
GOONG
FLOP
SHE WAS THE FIRST PERSON I COULD HONESTLY ASK THAT QUESTION.
WHICH ONE OF US IS STRONGER?!

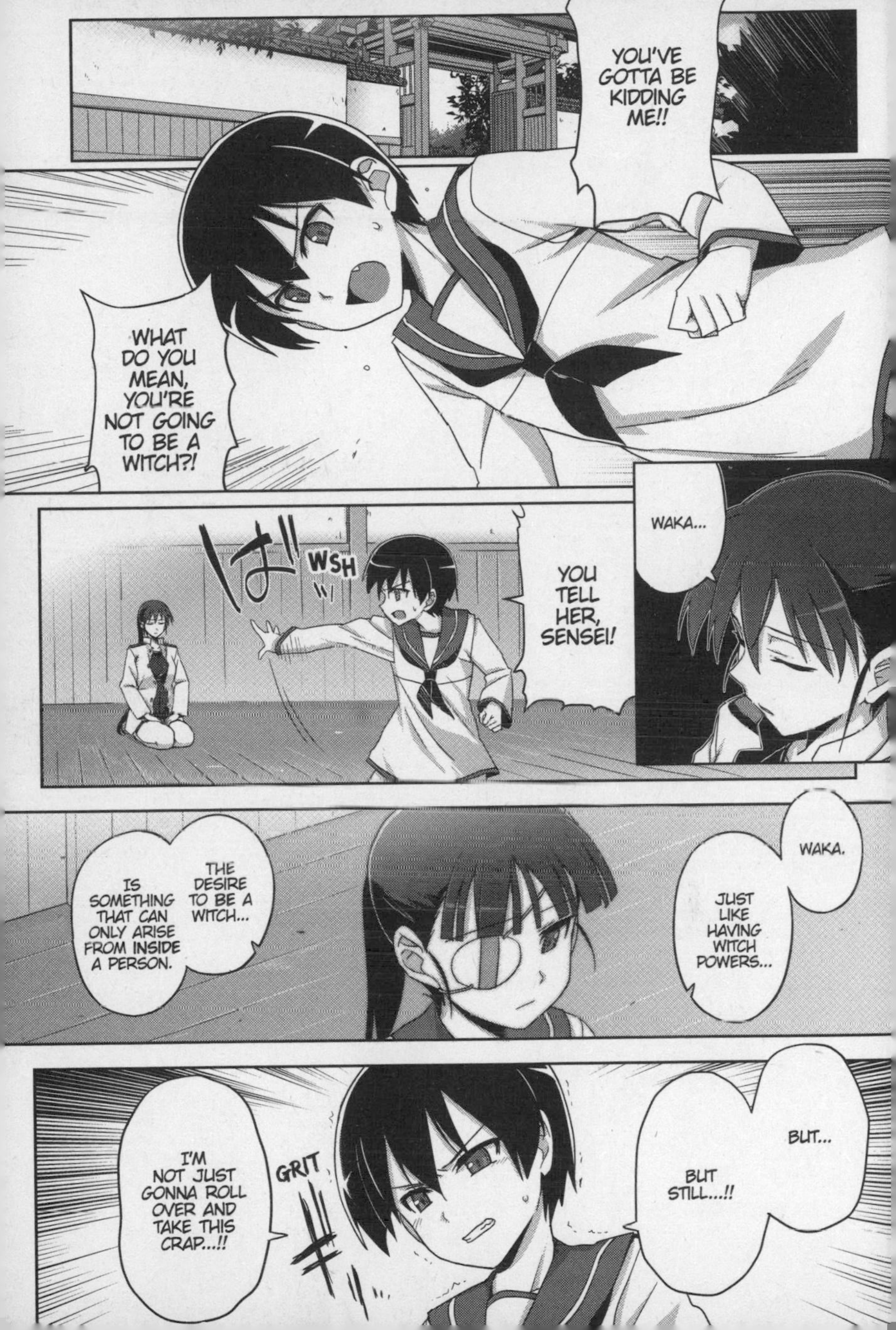
YOU'VE GOTTA BE KIDDING ME!!
WHAT DO YOU MEAN, YOU'RE NOT GOING TO BE A WITCH?!
WAKA...
YOU TELL HER, SENSEI!
WSH
は!!
WAKA.
JUST LIKE HAVING WITCH POWERS...
THE DESIRE TO BE A WITCH...
IS SOMETHING THAT CAN ONLY ARISE FROM INSIDE A PERSON.
BUT...
BUT STILL...!!
GRIT
I'M NOT JUST GONNA ROLL OVER AND TAKE THIS CRAP...!!

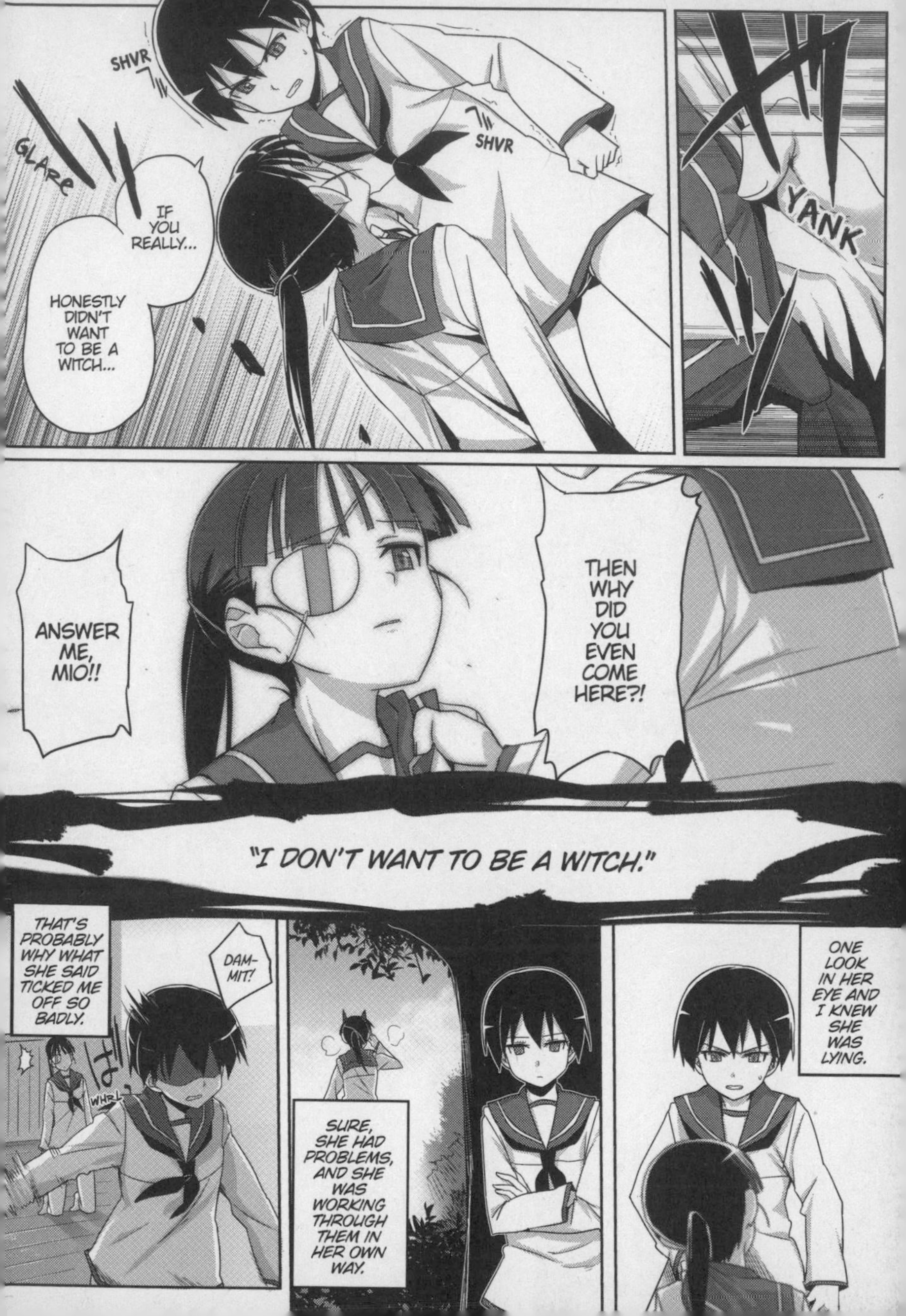
YANK
SHVR
SHVR
GLARE
IF YOU REALLY...
HONESTLY DIDN'T WANT TO BE A WITCH...
THEN WHY DID YOU EVEN COME HERE?!
ANSWER ME, MIO!!
"I DON'T WANT TO BE A WITCH."
ONE LOOK IN HER EYE AND I KNEW SHE WAS LYING.
SURE, SHE HAD PROBLEMS, AND SHE WAS WORKING THROUGH THEM IN HER OWN WAY.
THAT'S PROBABLY WHY WHAT SHE SAID TICKED ME OFF SO BADLY.
DAM-MIT!
WHRL

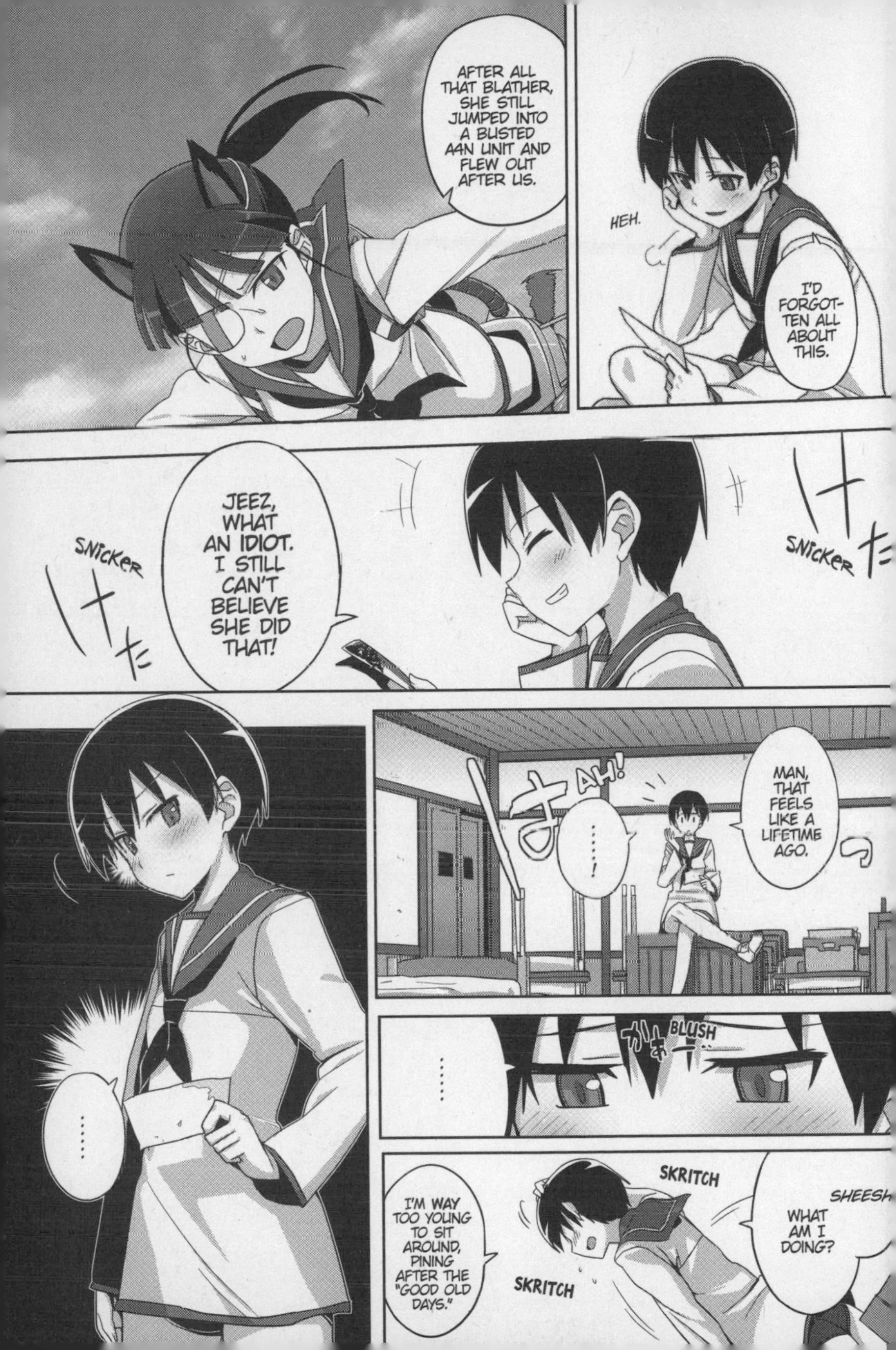
HEH.
I'D FORGOTTEN ALL ABOUT THIS.
AFTER ALL THAT BLATHER, SHE STILL JUMPED INTO A BUSTED A4N UNIT AND FLEW OUT AFTER US.
SNICKER
JEEZ, WHAT AN IDIOT. I STILL CAN'T BELIEVE SHE DID THAT!
SNICKER
MAN, THAT FEELS LIKE A LIFETIME AGO.
AH!
......!
BLUSH
......
SHEESH
WHAT AM I DOING?
SKRITCH
I'M WAY TOO YOUNG TO SIT AROUND, PINING AFTER THE "GOOD OLD DAYS."
SKRITCH
......

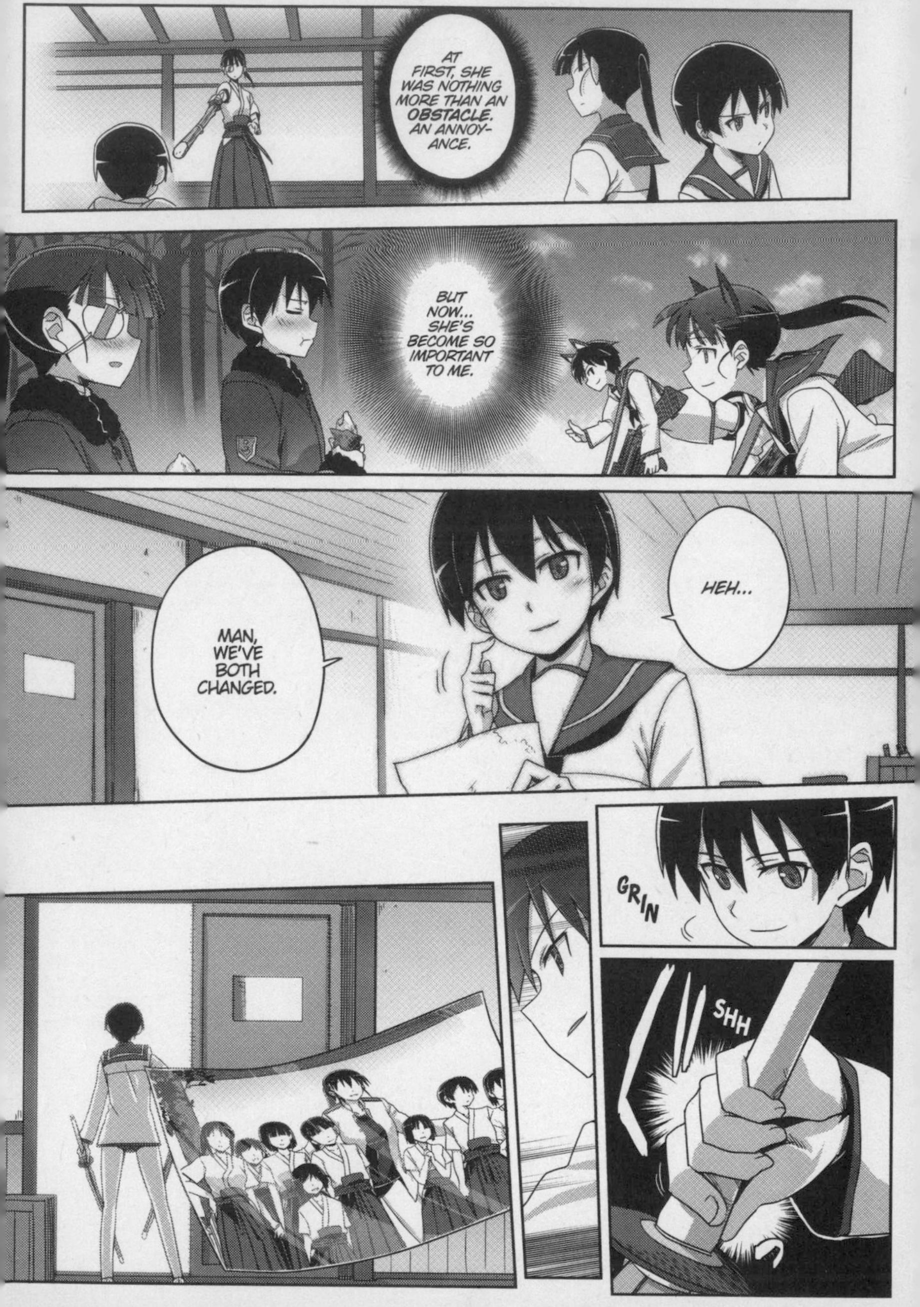
AT FIRST, SHE WAS NOTHING MORE THAN AN OBSTACLE. AN ANNOY-ANCE.
BUT NOW... SHE'S BECOME SO IMPORTANT TO ME.
HEH...
MAN, WE'VE BOTH CHANGED.
GRIN
SHH

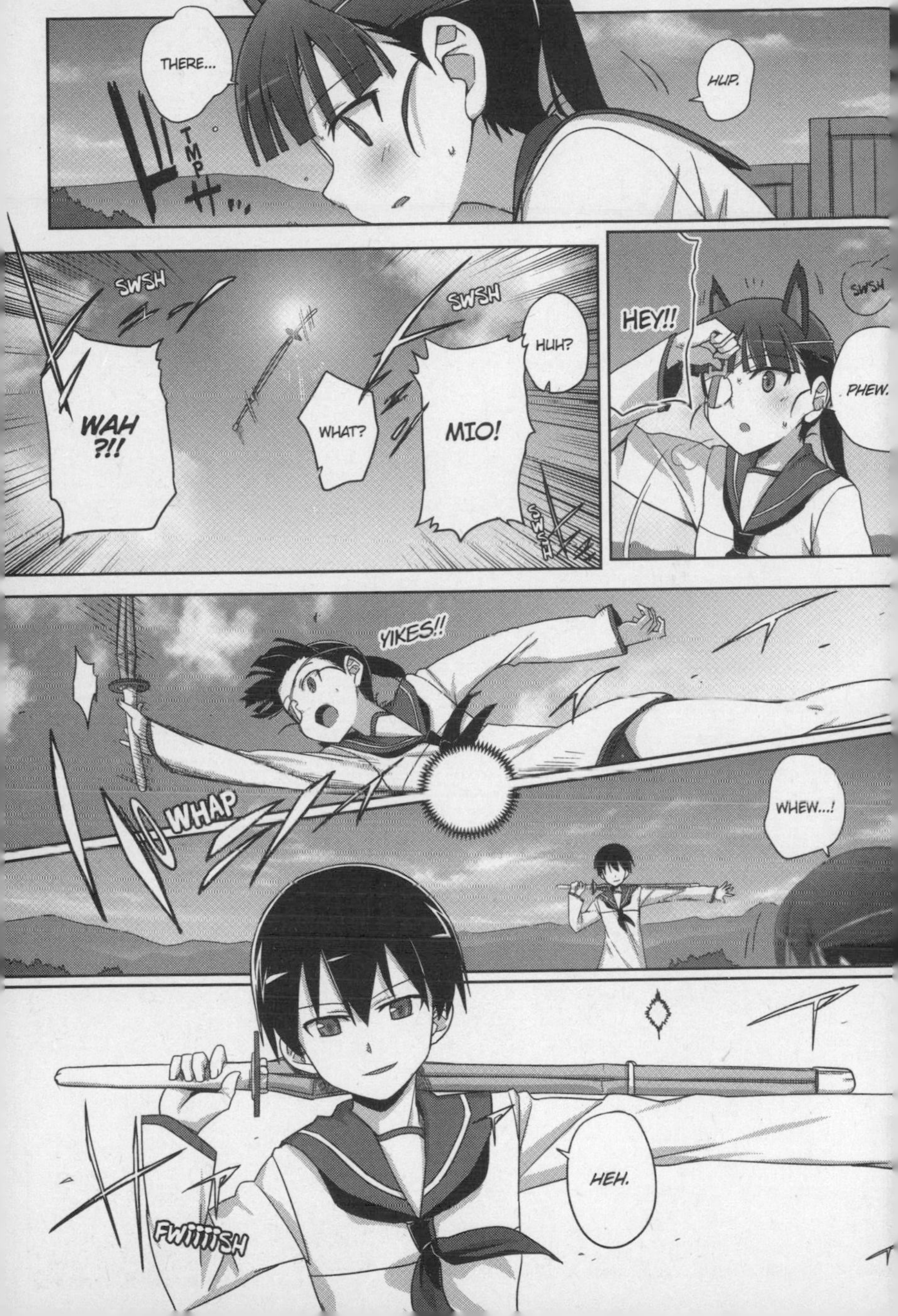
HUP.
THERE...
TMP
SWSH
PHEW.
HEY!!
SWSH
HUH?
MIO!
WHAT?
SWSH
WAH ?!!
SWSH
YIKES!!
WHEW...!
WHAP
HEH.
FWIIIISH

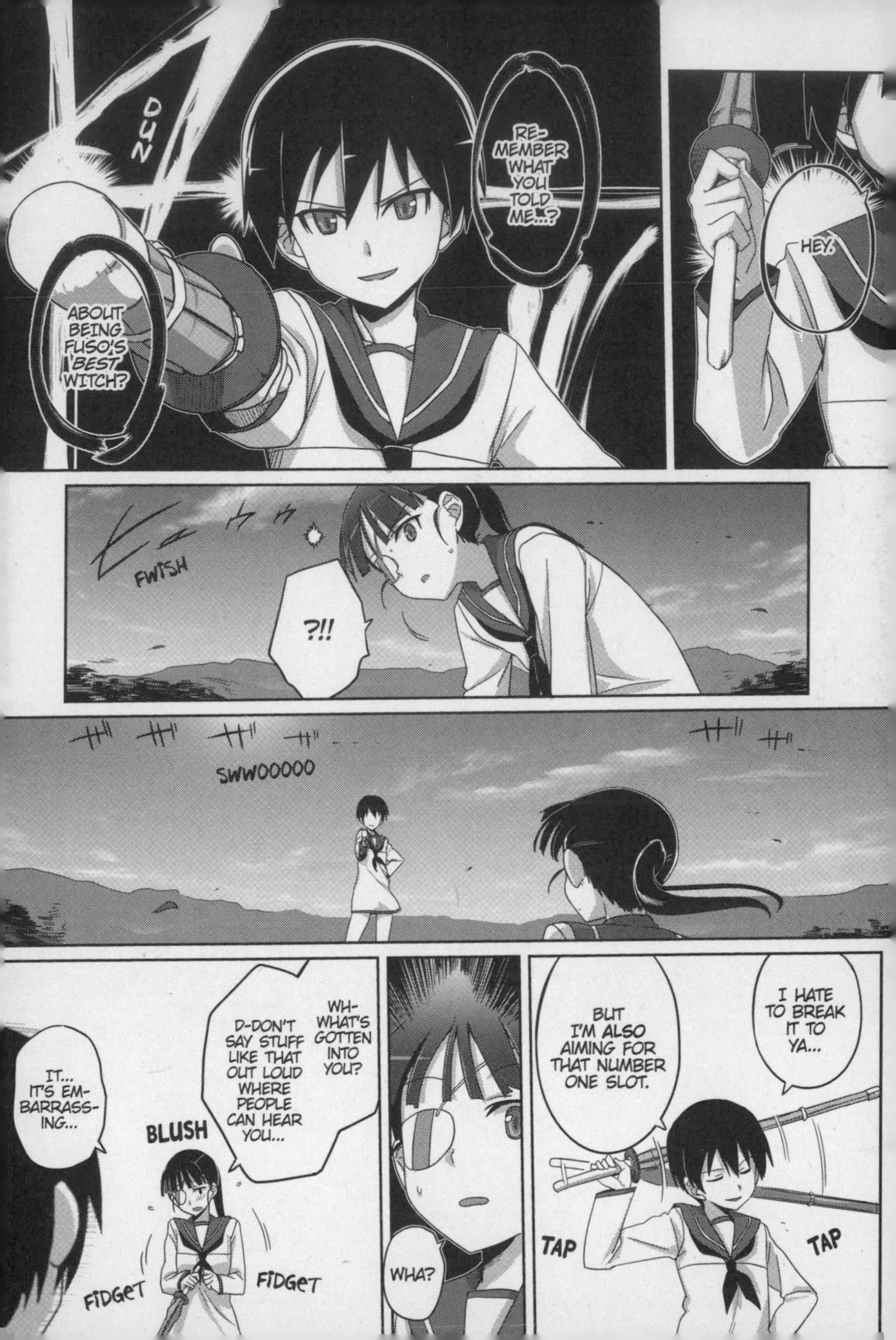
HEY.
RE-MEMBER WHAT YOU TOLD ME...?
DUN
ABOUT BEING FUSO'S 'BEST WITCH'?
FWISH
?!!
SWWOOOOO
I HATE TO BREAK IT TO YA...
BUT I'M ALSO AIMING FOR THAT NUMBER ONE SLOT.
TAP
TAP
WHA?
WH- WHAT'S GOTTEN INTO YOU?
D-DON'T SAY STUFF LIKE THAT OUT LOUD WHERE PEOPLE CAN HEAR YOU...
IT... IT'S EM-BARRASS-ING...
BLUSH
FIDGET
FIDGET

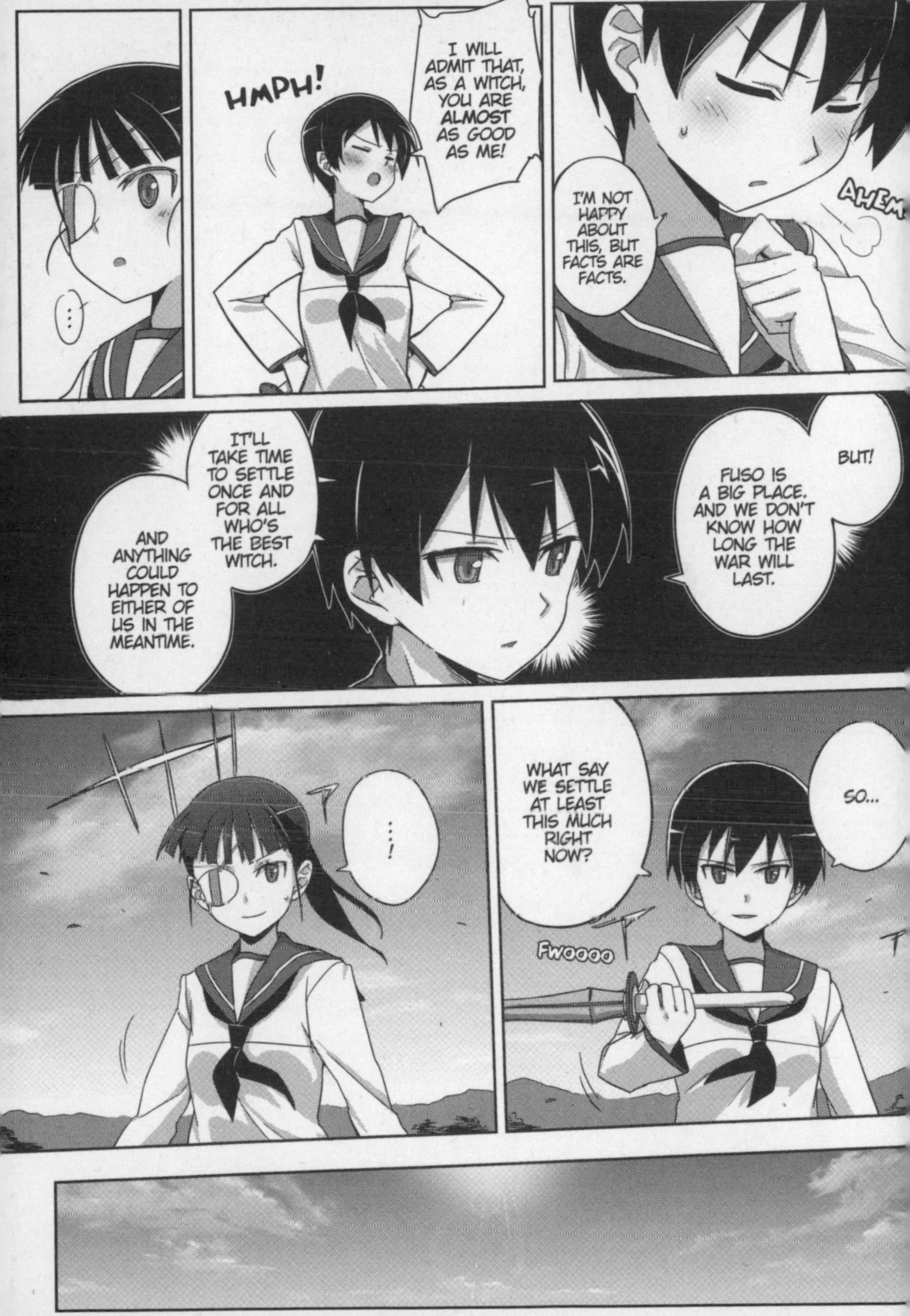
AHEM
I'M NOT HAPPY ABOUT THIS, BUT FACTS ARE FACTS.
I WILL ADMIT THAT, AS A WITCH, YOU ARE ALMOST AS GOOD AS ME!
HMPH!
...
BUT!
FUSO IS A BIG PLACE. AND WE DON'T KNOW HOW LONG THE WAR WILL LAST.
IT'LL TAKE TIME TO SETTLE ONCE AND FOR ALL WHO'S THE BEST WITCH.
AND ANYTHING COULD HAPPEN TO EITHER OF US IN THE MEANTIME.
SO...
WHAT SAY WE SETTLE AT LEAST THIS MUCH RIGHT NOW?
FWOOOO
...!

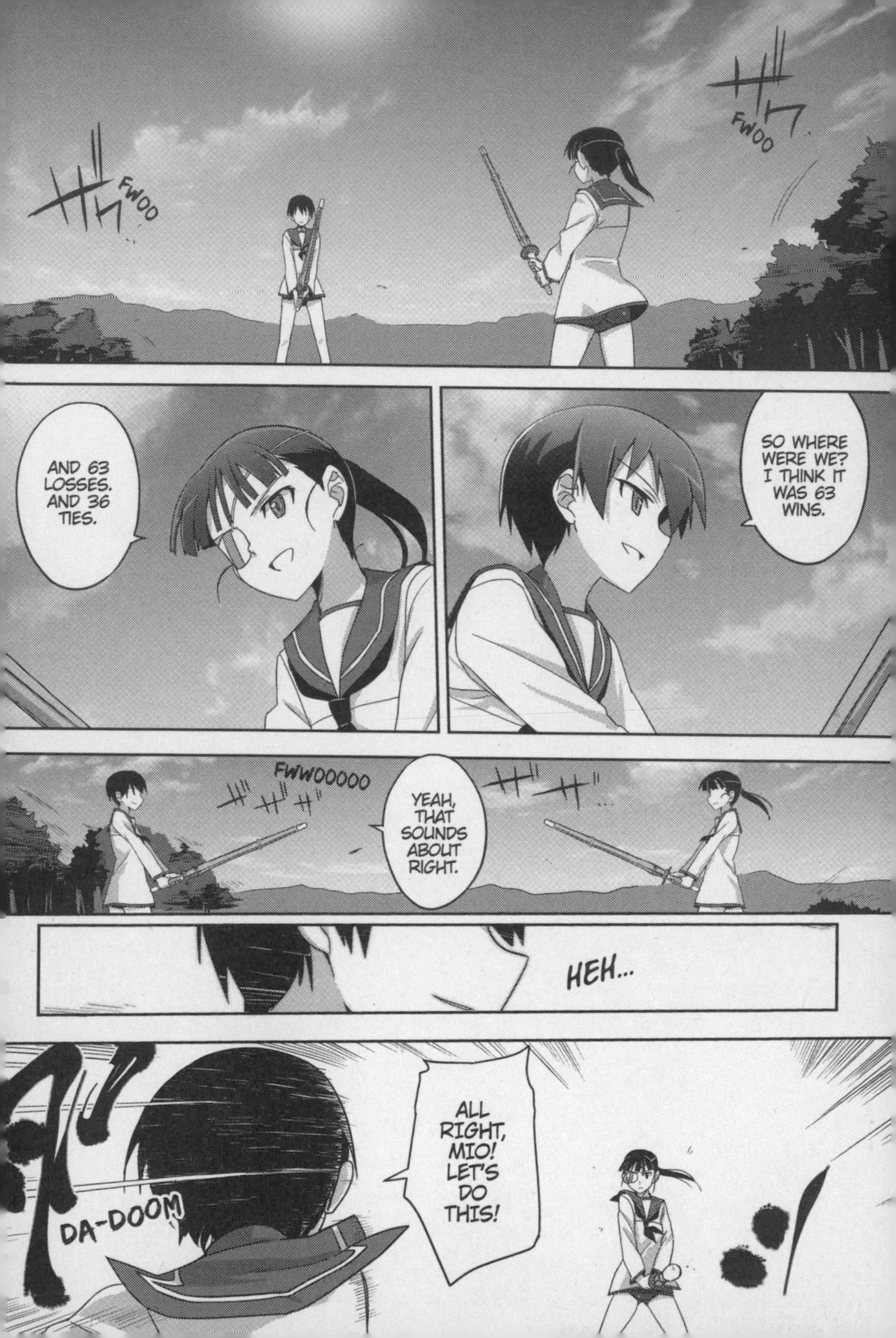
FWOO
FWOO
SO WHERE WERE WE? I THINK IT WAS 63 WINS.
AND 63 LOSSES. AND 36 TIES.
FWWOOOOO
YEAH, THAT SOUNDS ABOUT RIGHT.
HEH...
ALL RIGHT, MIO! LET'S DO THIS!
DA-DOOM

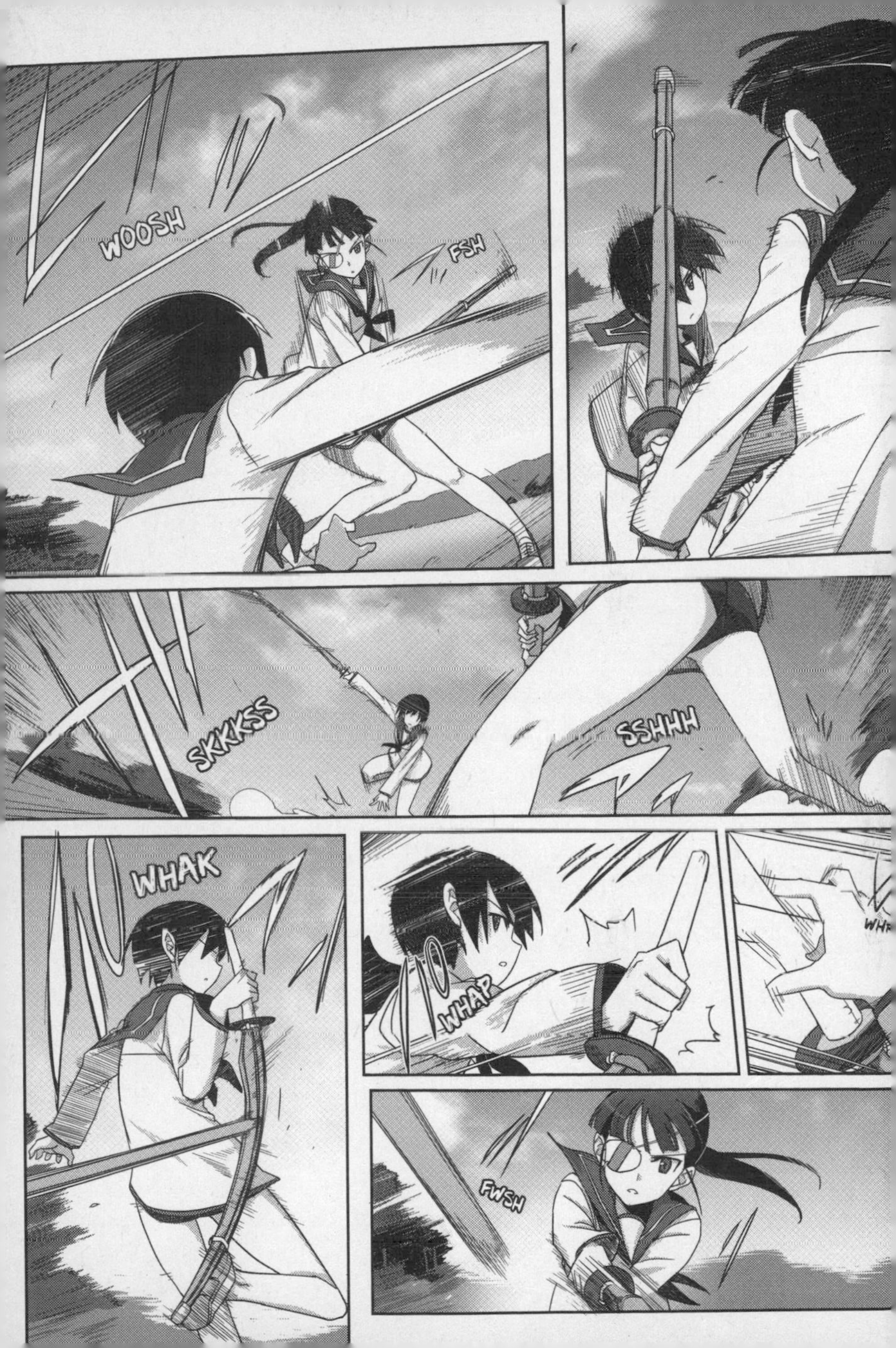
FSH
WOOSH
SSHHH
SKKKSS
WHAP
FWSH
WHAK

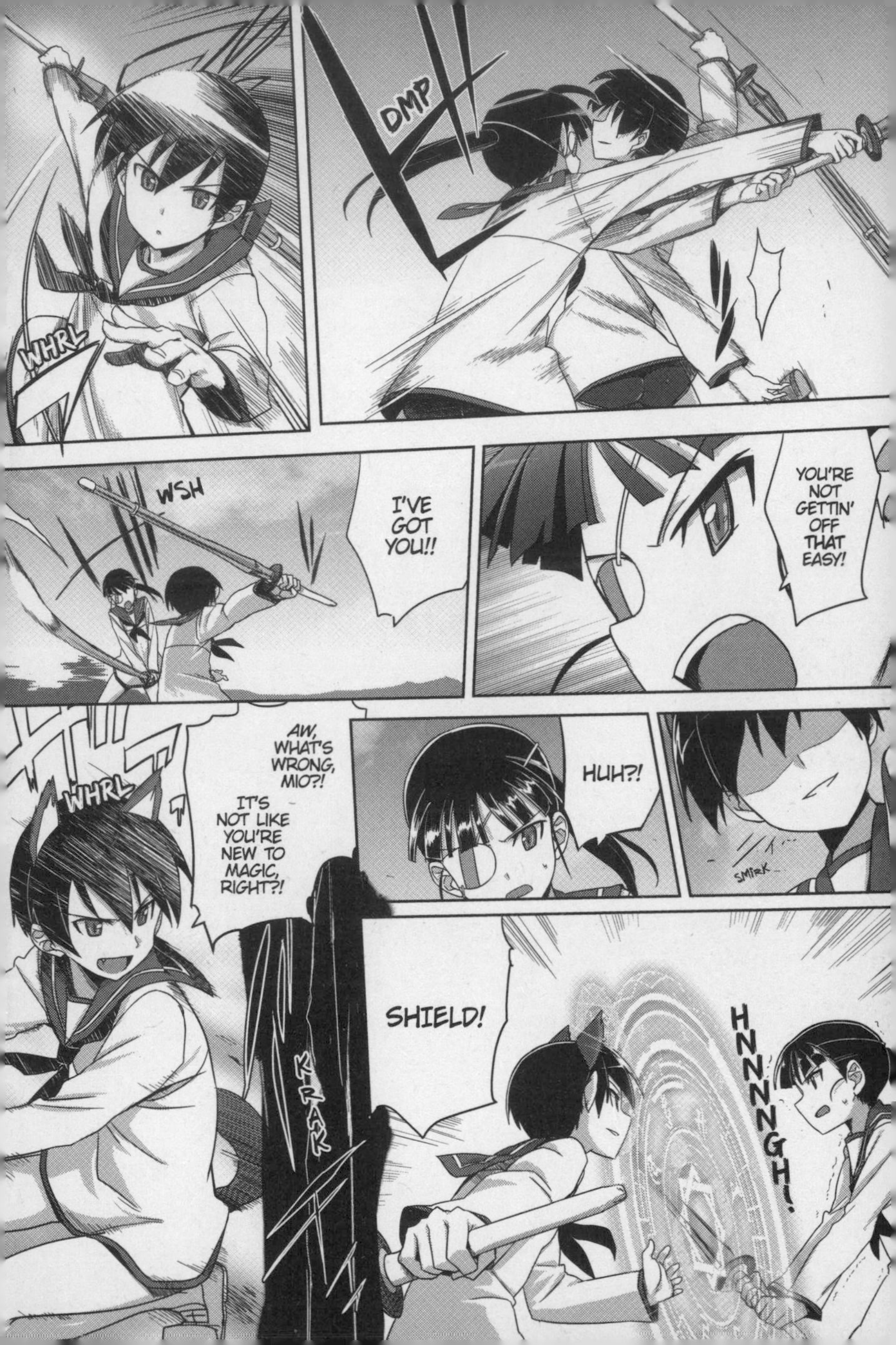
DMP
WHRL
YOU'RE NOT GETTIN' OFF THAT EASY!
I'VE GOT YOU!!
WSH
SMIRK
HUH?!
SHIELD!
HNNNNGH!
KRAK
WHRL
AW, WHAT'S WRONG, MIO?!
IT'S NOT LIKE YOU'RE NEW TO MAGIC, RIGHT?!

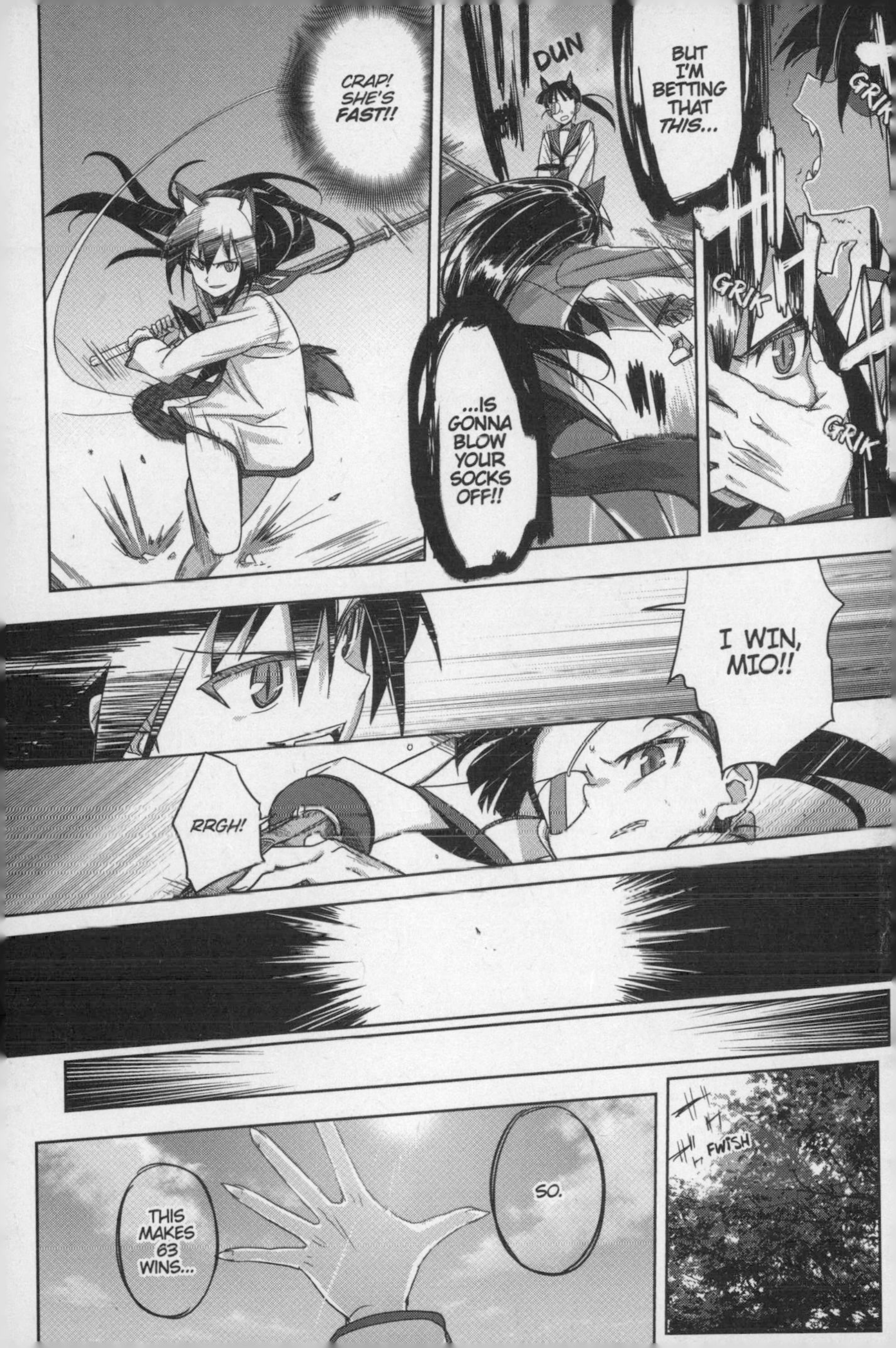
GRIK
GRIK
GRIK
DUN
BUT I'M BETTING THAT THIS...
...IS GONNA BLOW YOUR SOCKS OFF!!
CRAP! SHE'S FAST!!
I WIN, MIO!!
RRGH!
FWISH
SO.
THIS MAKES 63 WINS...

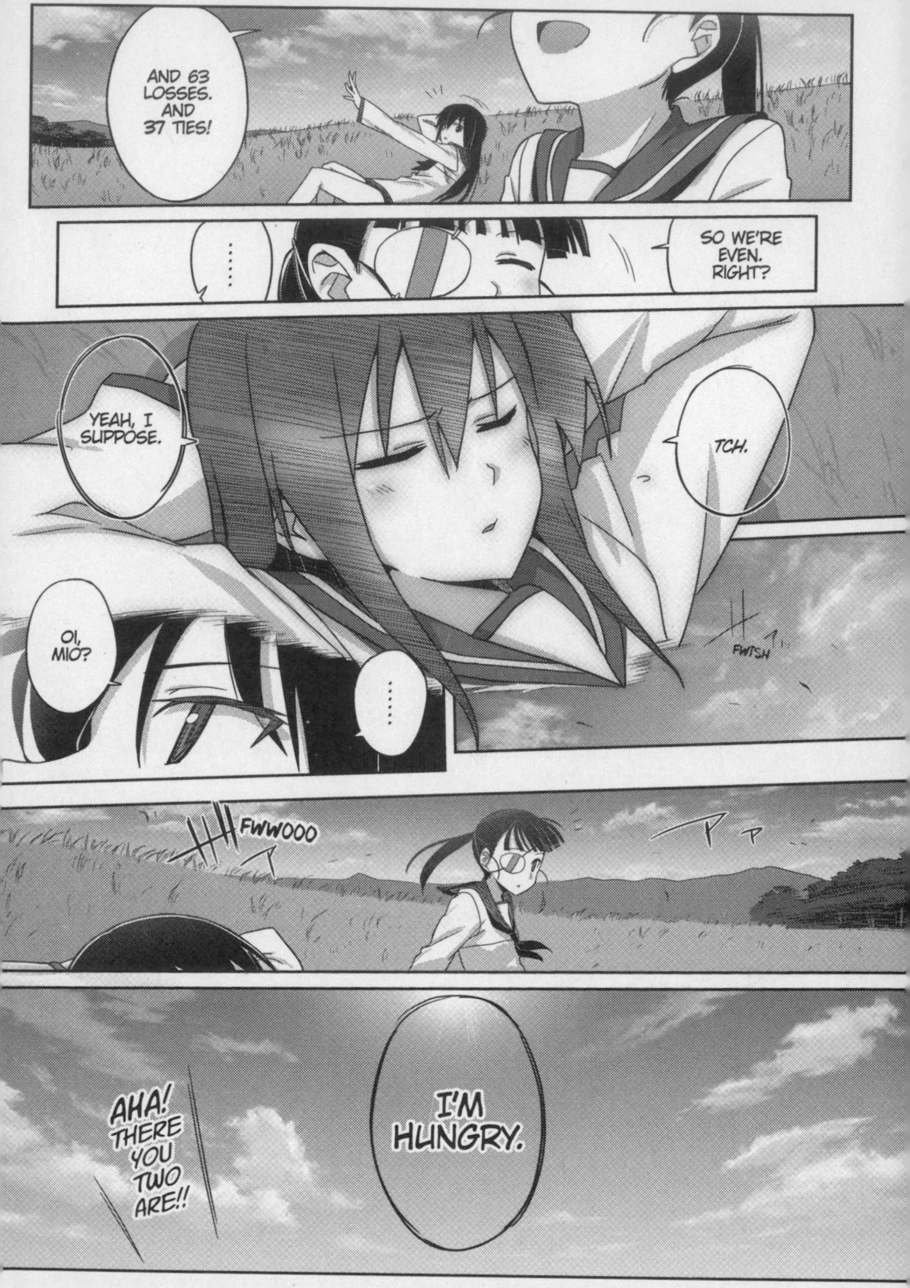
AND 63 LOSSES. AND 37 TIES!
SO WE'RE EVEN. RIGHT?
......
TCH.
YEAH, I SUPPOSE.
FWISH
......
OI, MIO?
FWWOOO
I'M HUNGRY.
AHA! THERE YOU TWO ARE!!

Chapter 7:
The Best Witch
[Mission Complete]

CHAPTER 8:
FALLEN CHERRY BLOSSOMS

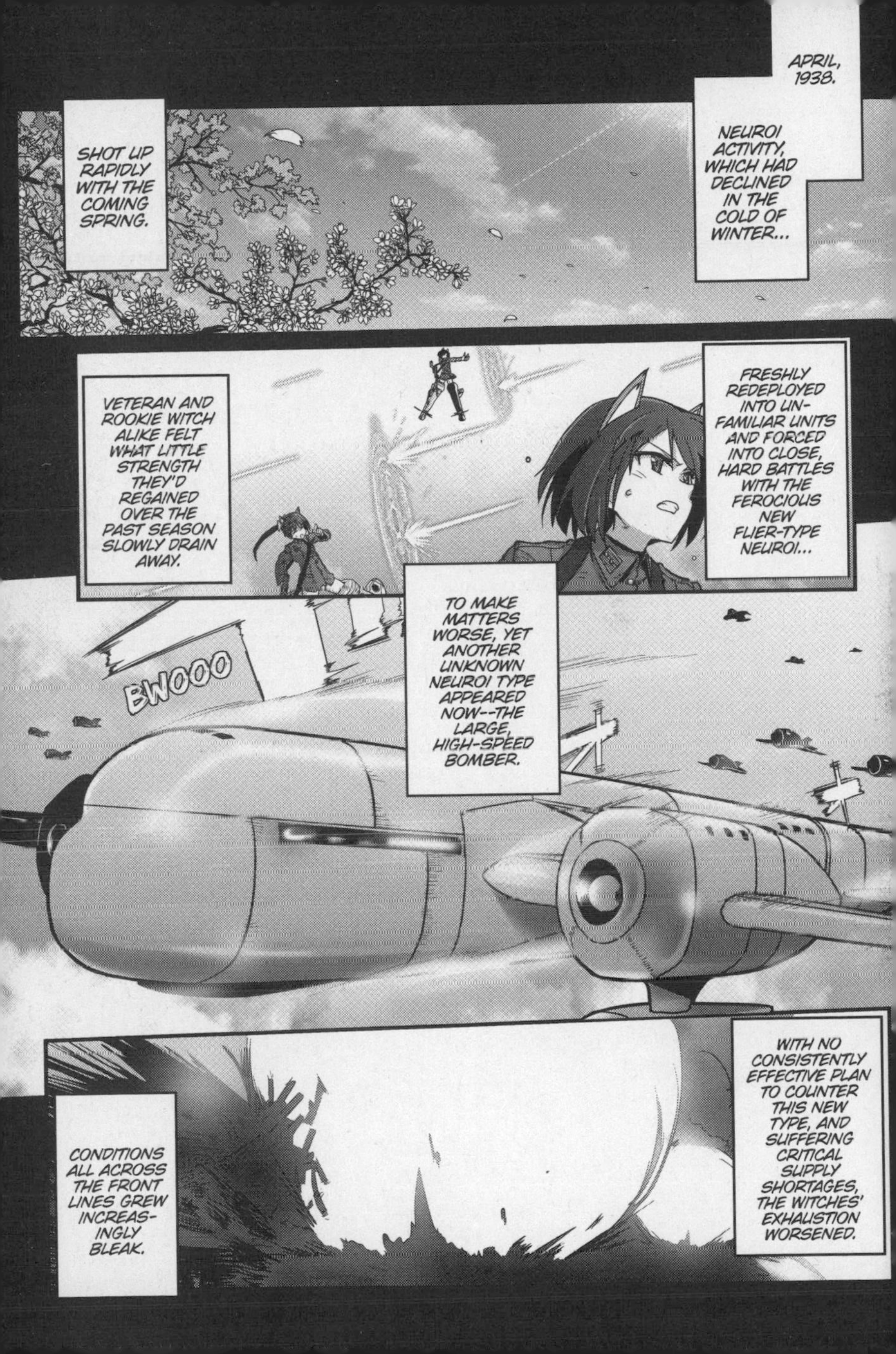
APRIL, 1938.
NEUROI ACTIVITY, WHICH HAD DECLINED IN THE COLD OF WINTER...
SHOT UP RAPIDLY WITH THE COMING SPRING.
FRESHLY REDEPLOYED INTO UN-FAMILIAR UNITS AND FORCED INTO CLOSE, HARD BATTLES WITH THE FEROCIOUS NEW FLIER-TYPE NEUROI...
VETERAN AND ROOKIE WITCH ALIKE FELT WHAT LITTLE STRENGTH THEY'D REGAINED OVER THE PAST SEASON SLOWLY DRAIN AWAY.
TO MAKE MATTERS WORSE, YET ANOTHER UNKNOWN NEUROI TYPE APPEARED NOW--THE LARGE, HIGH-SPEED BOMBER.
BWOOO
WITH NO CONSISTENTLY EFFECTIVE PLAN TO COUNTER THIS NEW TYPE, AND SUFFERING CRITICAL SUPPLY SHORTAGES, THE WITCHES' EXHAUSTION WORSENED.
CONDITIONS ALL ACROSS THE FRONT LINES GREW INCREAS-INGLY BLEAK.

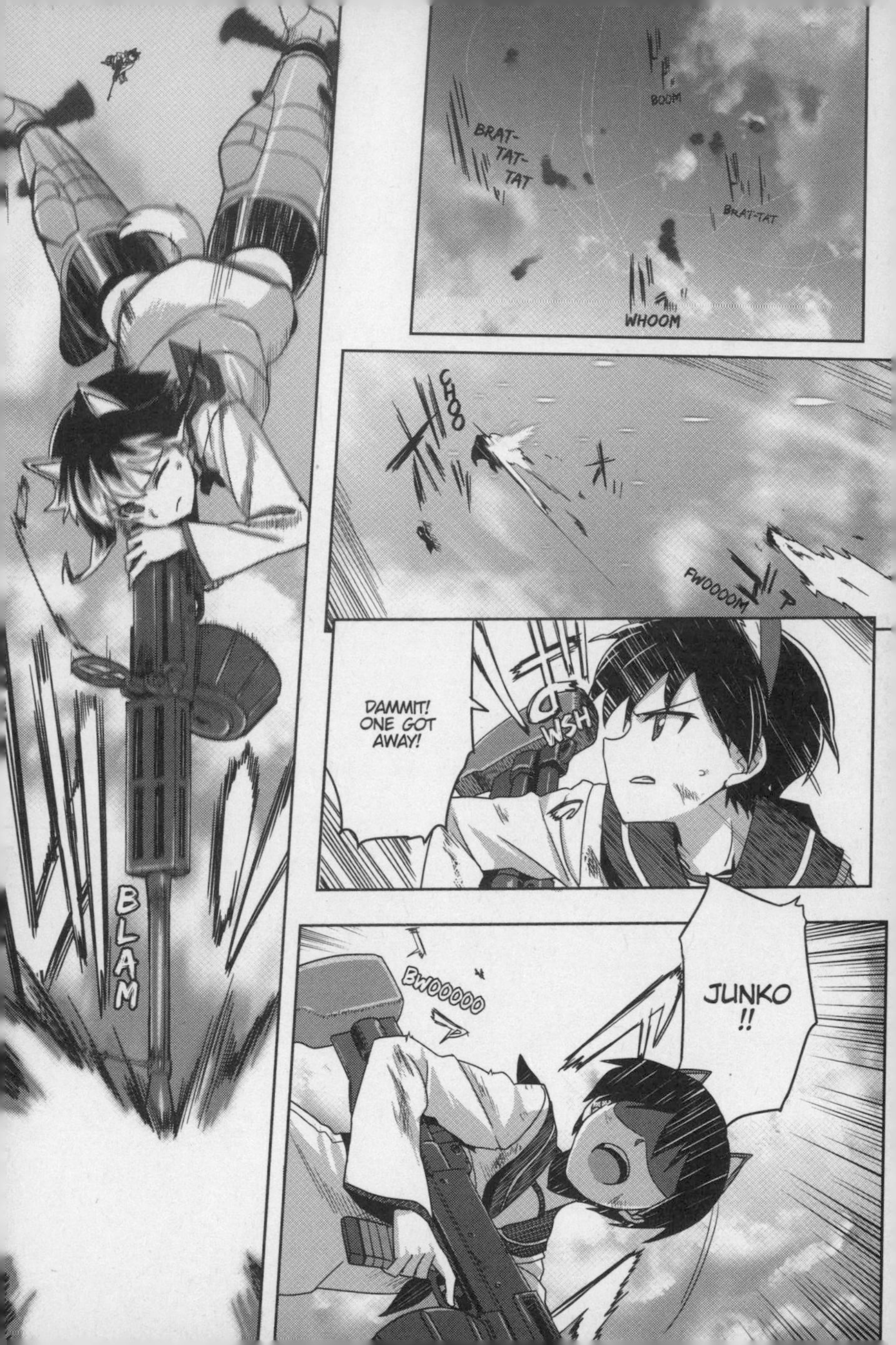
BOOM
BRAT-TAT-TAT
BRAT-TAT
WHOOM
CHOO
FWOOOOM
DAMMIT! ONE GOT AWAY!
WSH
JUNKO!!
BWOOOOOO
BLAM

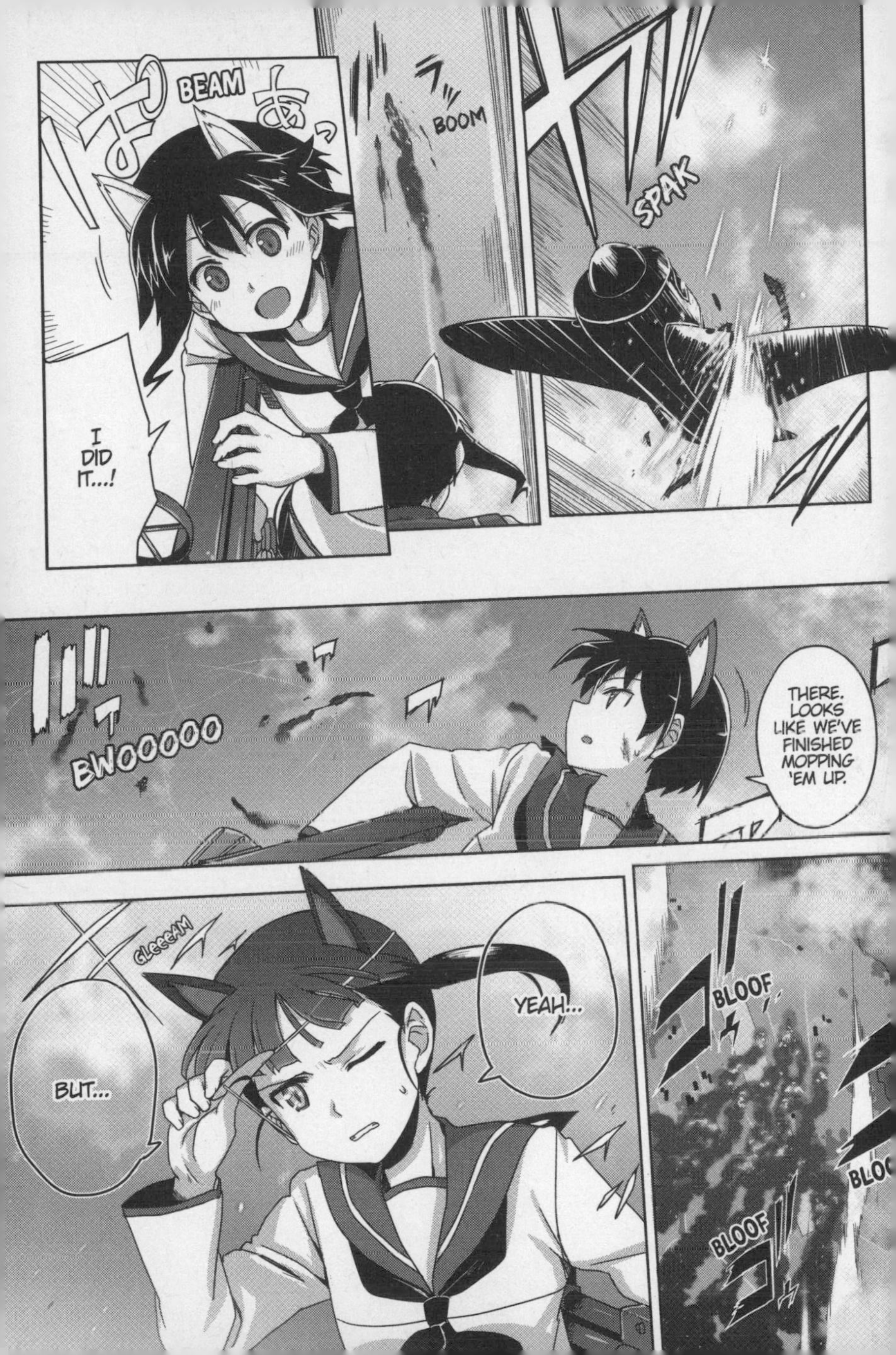
SPAK
BOOM
BEAM
あっ
I DID IT...!
THERE. LOOKS LIKE WE'VE FINISHED MOPPING 'EM UP.
BWOOOOO
BLOOF
BLOO
BLOOF
YEAH...
GLEEEAM
BUT...

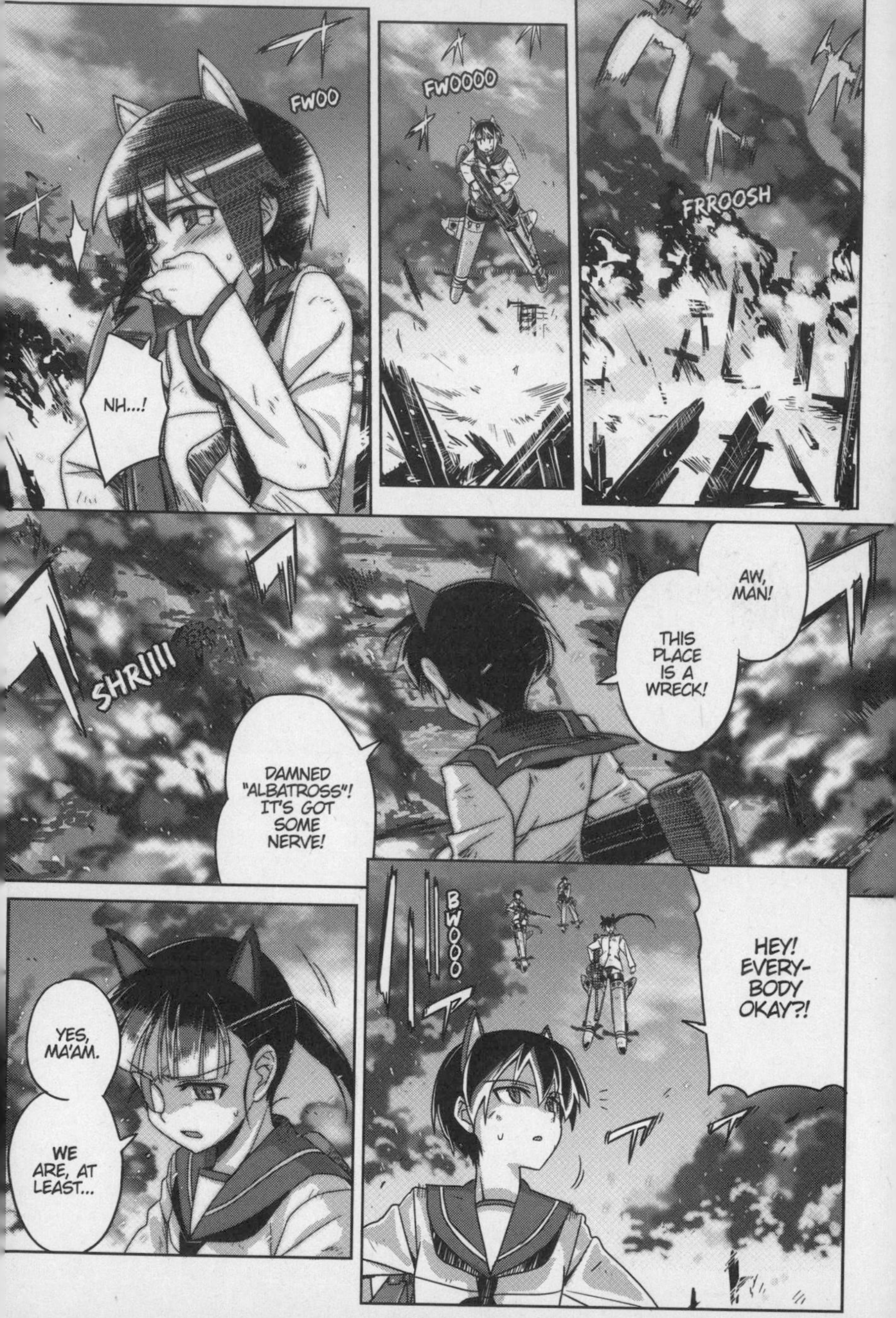
FRROOSH
FWOOOO
FWOO
NH...!
AW, MAN!
THIS PLACE IS A WRECK!
DAMNED "ALBATROSS"! IT'S GOT SOME NERVE!
SHRIIII
HEY! EVERY-BODY OKAY?!
BWOOO
YES, MA'AM.
WE ARE, AT LEAST...

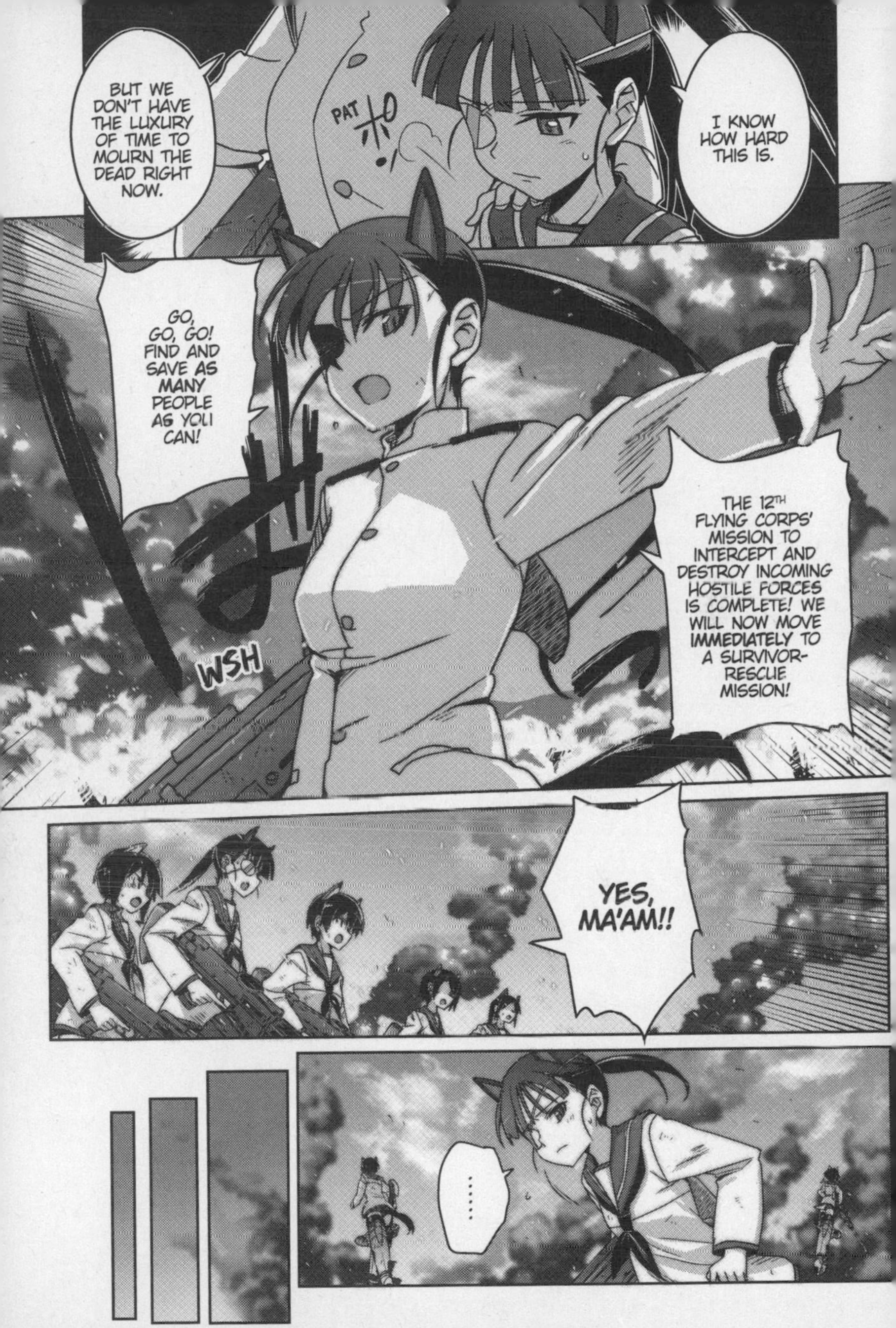
I KNOW HOW HARD THIS IS.
BUT WE DON'T HAVE THE LUXURY OF TIME TO MOURN THE DEAD RIGHT NOW.
PAT
THE 12TH FLYING CORPS' MISSION TO INTERCEPT AND DESTROY INCOMING HOSTILE FORCES IS COMPLETE! WE WILL NOW MOVE IMMEDIATELY TO A SURVIVOR-RESCUE MISSION!
GO, GO, GO! FIND AND SAVE AS MANY PEOPLE AS YOU CAN!
WSH
YES, MA'AM!!
......

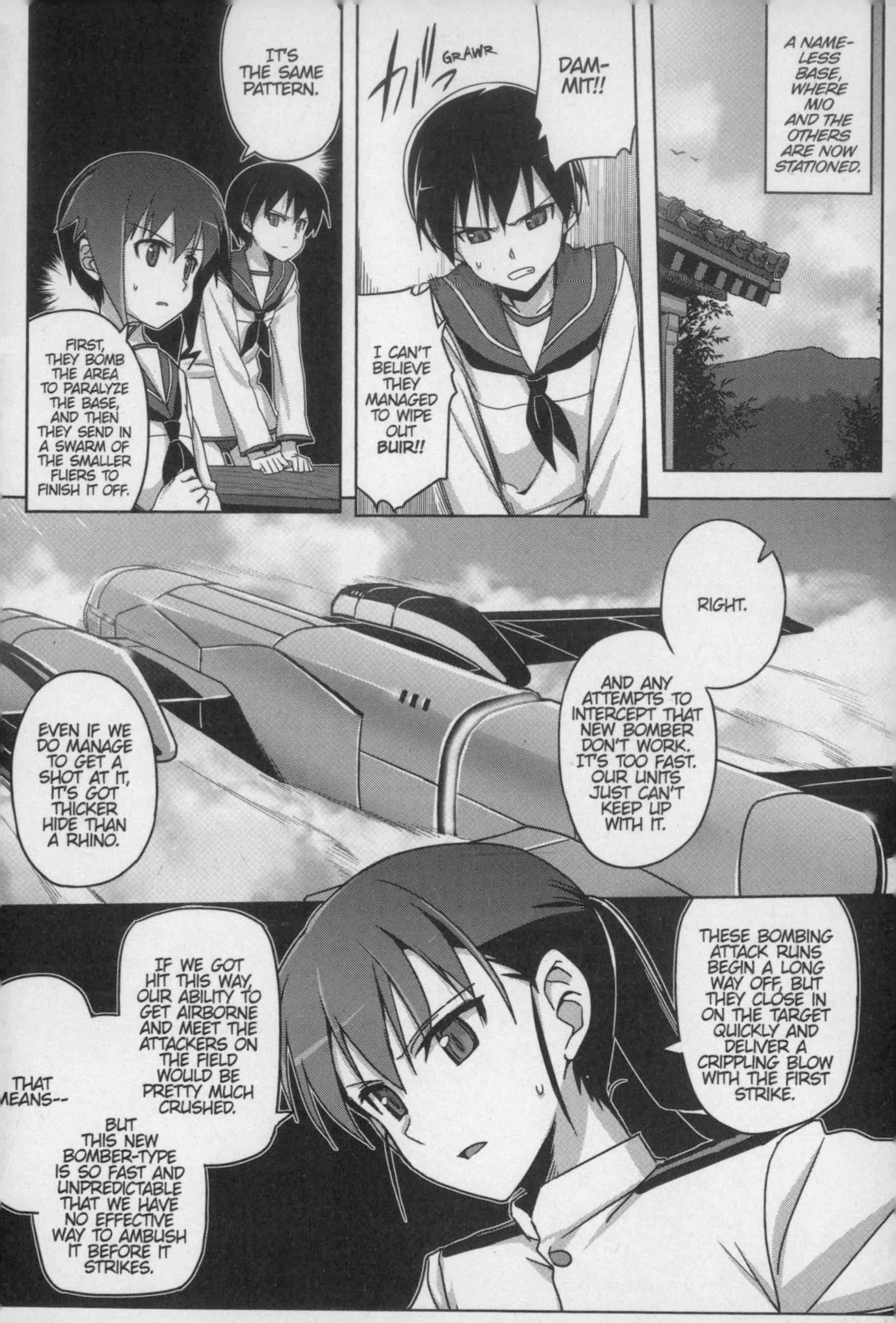
A NAMELESS BASE, WHERE MIO AND THE OTHERS ARE NOW STATIONED.
GRAWR
DAM-MIT!!
I CAN'T BELIEVE THEY MANAGED TO WIPE OUT BUIR!!
IT'S THE SAME PATTERN.
FIRST, THEY BOMB THE AREA TO PARALYZE THE BASE, AND THEN THEY SEND IN A SWARM OF THE SMALLER FLIERS TO FINISH IT OFF.
RIGHT.
AND ANY ATTEMPTS TO INTERCEPT THAT NEW BOMBER DON'T WORK. IT'S TOO FAST. OUR UNITS JUST CAN'T KEEP UP WITH IT.
EVEN IF WE DO MANAGE TO GET A SHOT AT IT, IT'S GOT THICKER HIDE THAN A RHINO.
THESE BOMBING ATTACK RUNS BEGIN A LONG WAY OFF, BUT THEY CLOSE IN ON THE TARGET QUICKLY AND DELIVER A CRIPPLING BLOW WITH THE FIRST STRIKE.
IF WE GOT HIT THIS WAY, OUR ABILITY TO GET AIRBORNE AND MEET THE ATTACKERS ON THE FIELD WOULD BE PRETTY MUCH CRUSHED.
BUT THIS NEW BOMBER-TYPE IS SO FAST AND UNPREDICTABLE THAT WE HAVE NO EFFECTIVE WAY TO AMBUSH IT BEFORE IT STRIKES.
THAT MEANS--

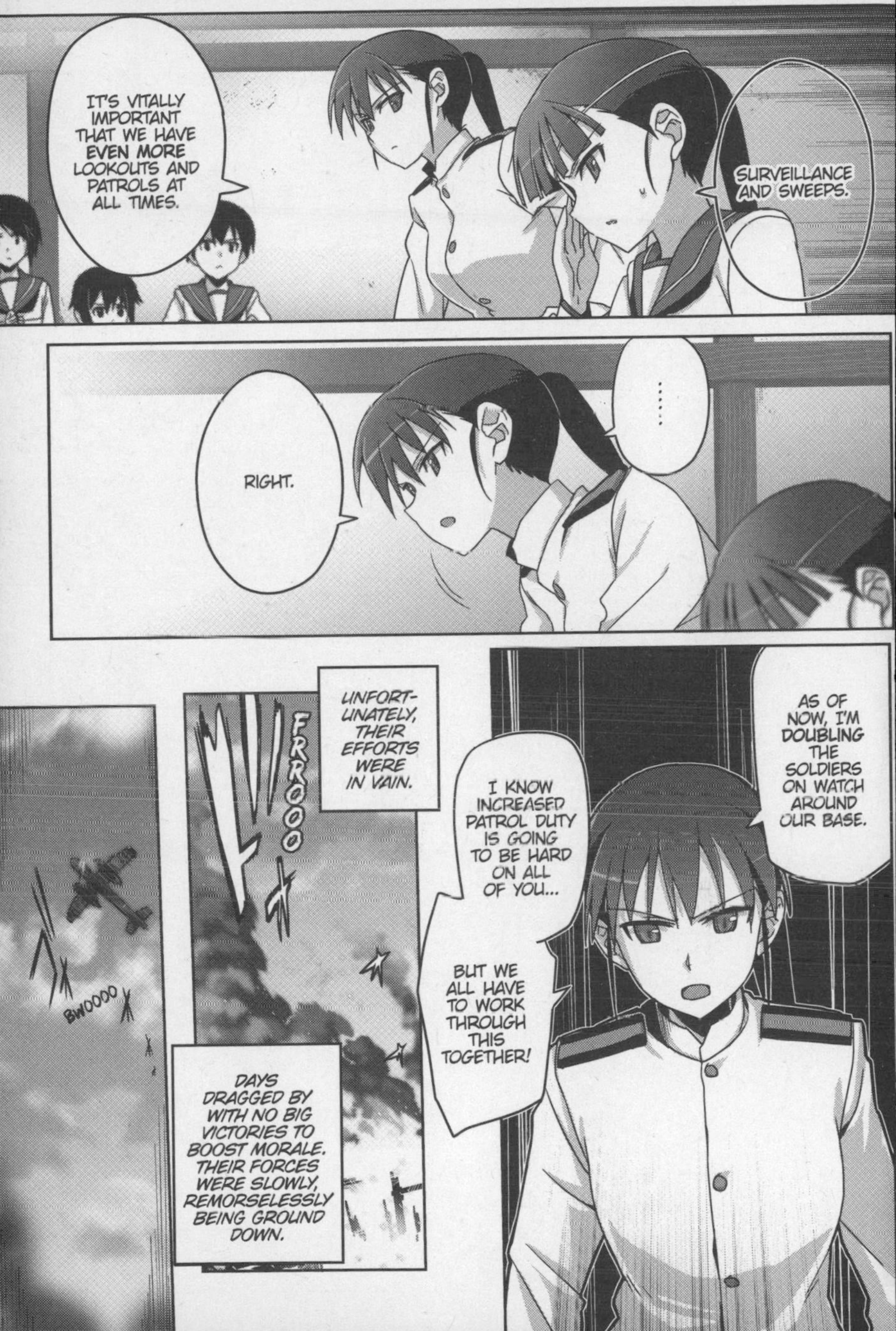
SURVEILLANCE AND SWEEPS.
IT'S VITALLY IMPORTANT THAT WE HAVE EVEN MORE LOOKOUTS AND PATROLS AT ALL TIMES.
......
RIGHT.
AS OF NOW, I'M DOUBLING THE SOLDIERS ON WATCH AROUND OUR BASE.
I KNOW INCREASED PATROL DUTY IS GOING TO BE HARD ON ALL OF YOU...
BUT WE ALL HAVE TO WORK THROUGH THIS TOGETHER!
UNFORTUNATELY, THEIR EFFORTS WERE IN VAIN.
FRROOO
DAYS DRAGGED BY WITH NO BIG VICTORIES TO BOOST MORALE. THEIR FORCES WERE SLOWLY, REMORSELESSLY BEING GROUND DOWN.
BWOOOO

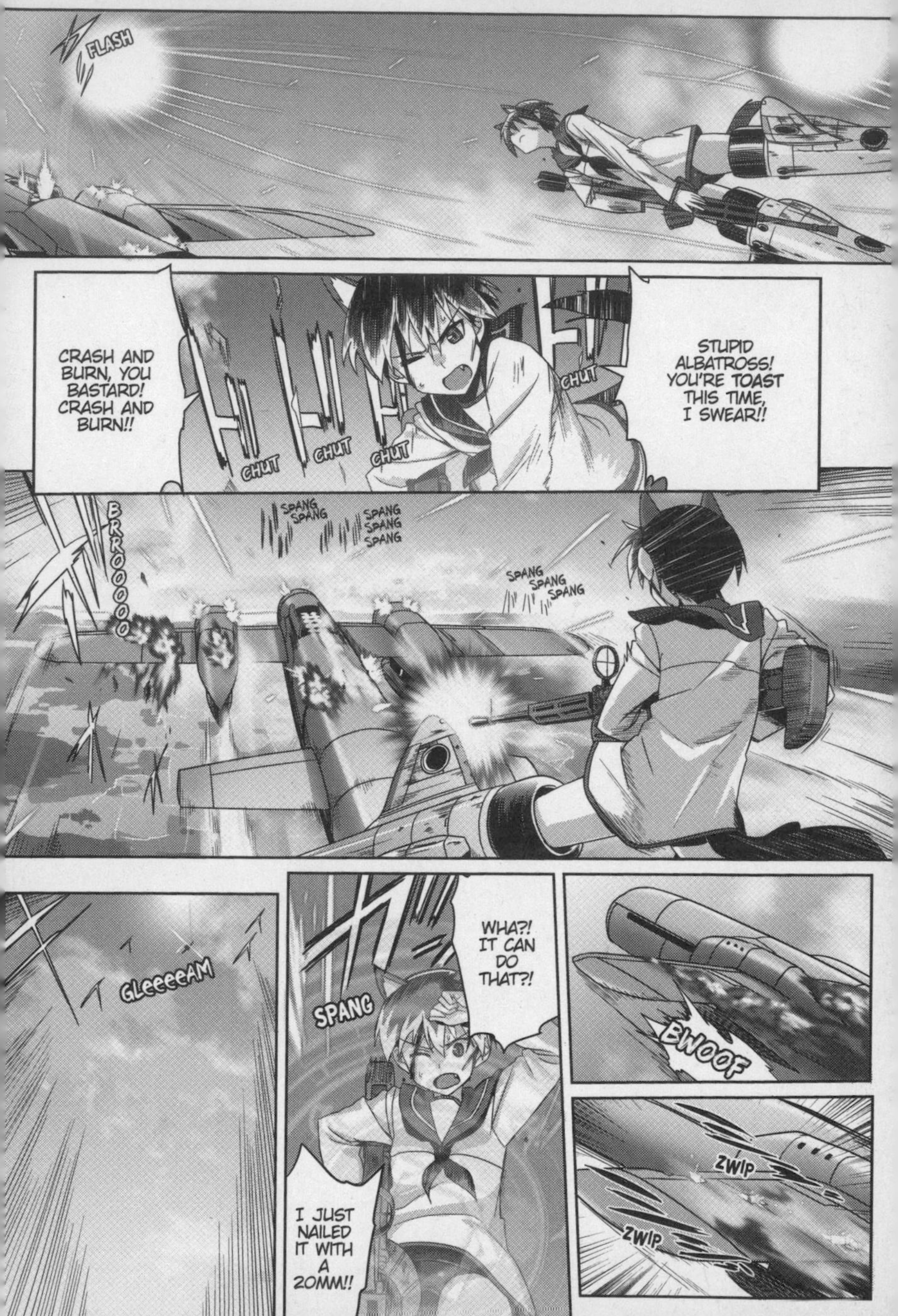

FLASH
STUPID ALBATROSS! YOU'RE TOAST THIS TIME, I SWEAR!!
CHUT
CRASH AND BURN, YOU BASTARD! CRASH AND BURN!!
CHUT CHUT CHUT
SPANG SPANG SPANG
SPANG SPANG SPANG
SPANG SPANG
BRROOOOOO
BWOOF
ZWIP
ZWIP
WHA?! IT CAN DO THAT?!
SPANG
I JUST NAILED IT WITH A 20MM!!
GLEEEEAM

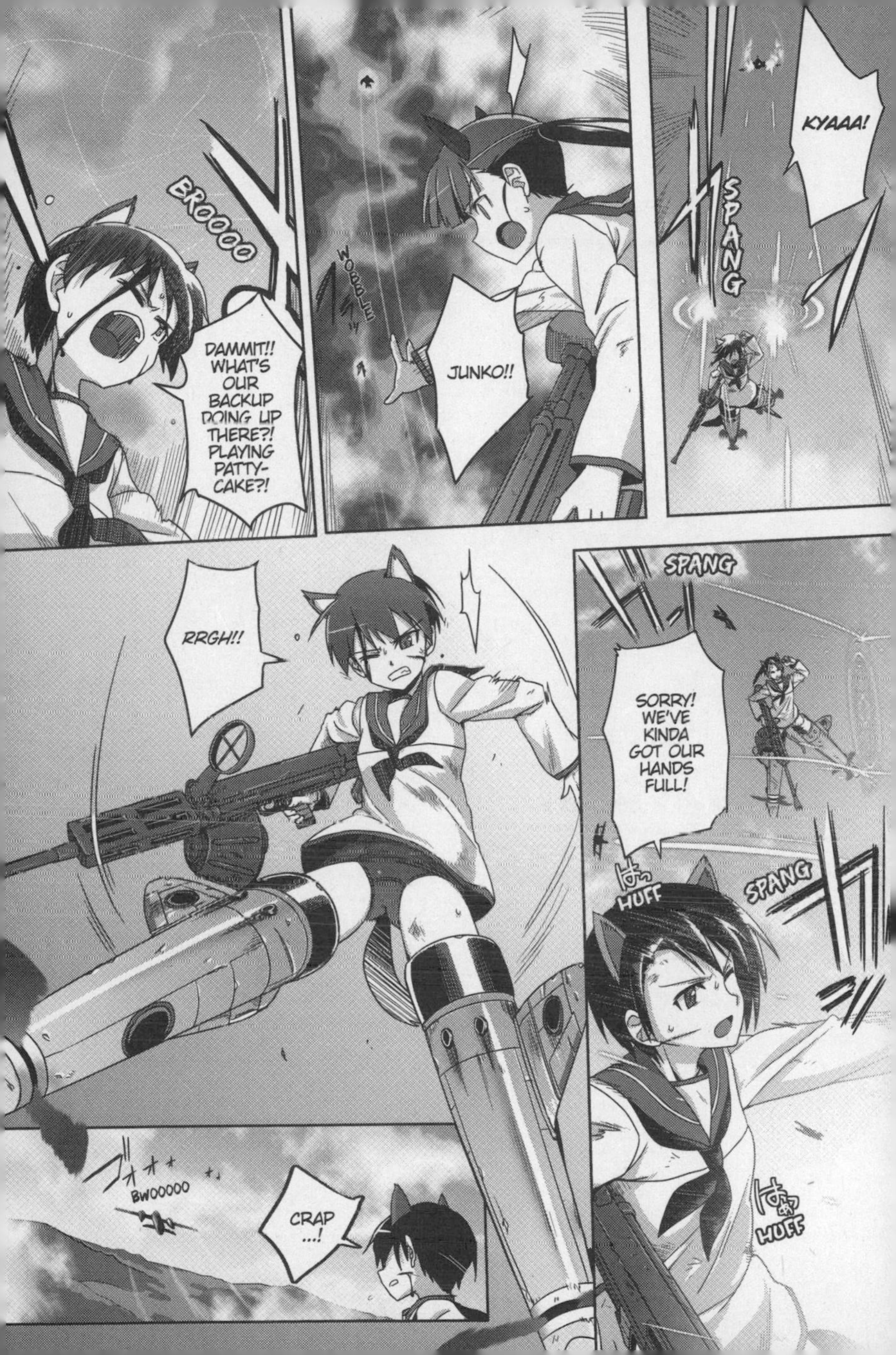
KYAAA!
SPANG
SPANG
JUNKO!!
WOBBLE
BROOOOO
DAMMIT!! WHAT'S OUR BACKUP DOING UP THERE?! PLAYING PATTY-CAKE?!
SPANG
SORRY! WE'VE KINDA GOT OUR HANDS FULL!
HUFF
SPANG
HUFF
RRGH!!
CRAP ...!
BWOOOOO

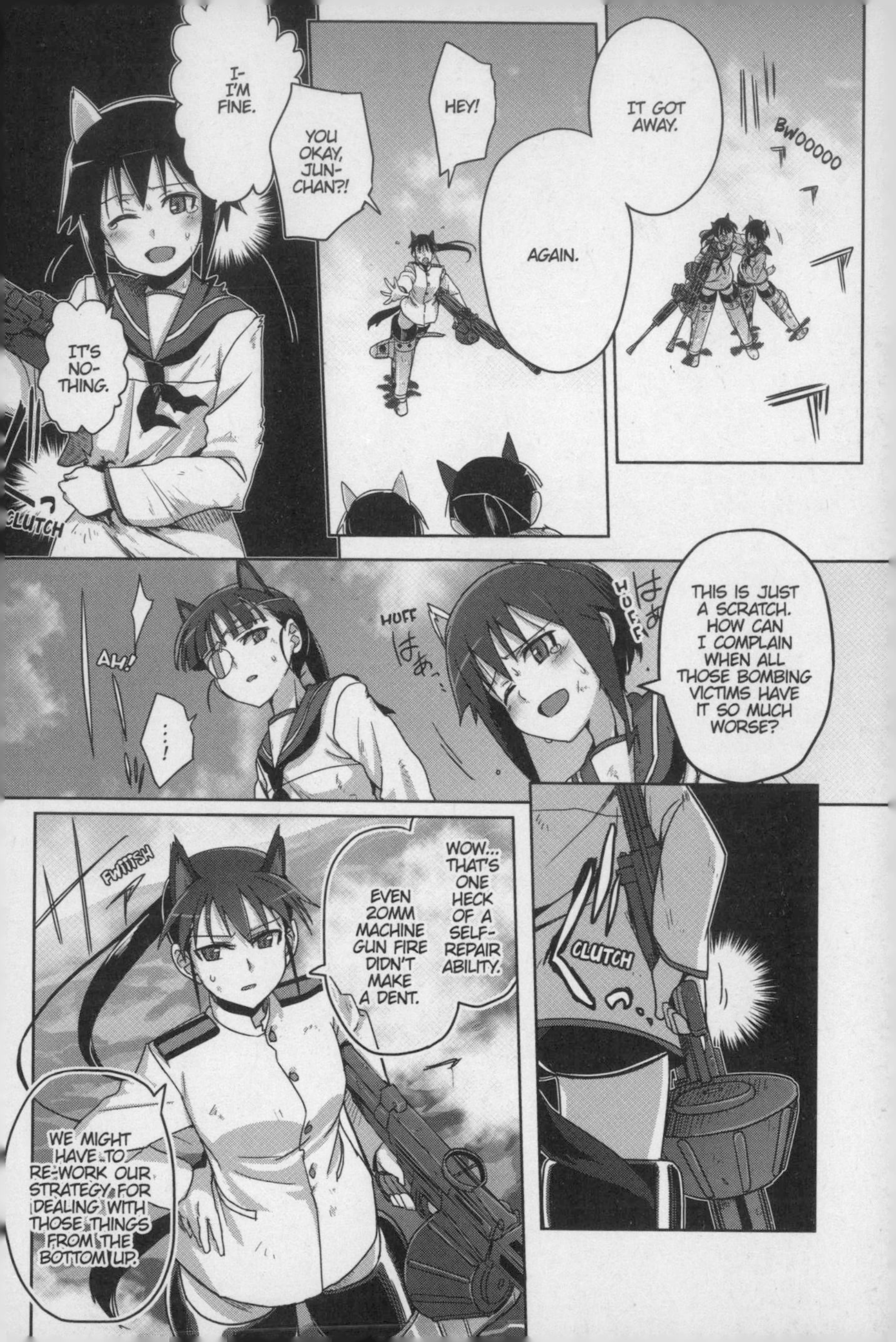
BWOOOOO
IT GOT AWAY.
AGAIN.
HEY!
YOU OKAY, JUN-CHAN?!
I- I'M FINE.
IT'S NO-THING.
CLUTCH
HUFF はぁ
THIS IS JUST A SCRATCH. HOW CAN I COMPLAIN WHEN ALL THOSE BOMBING VICTIMS HAVE IT SO MUCH WORSE?
HUFF はぁっ
AH!
...!
CLUTCH
FWIIISH
WOW... THAT'S ONE HECK OF A SELF-REPAIR ABILITY.
EVEN 20MM MACHINE GUN FIRE DIDN'T MAKE A DENT.
WE MIGHT HAVE TO RE-WORK OUR STRATEGY FOR DEALING WITH THOSE THINGS FROM THE BOTTOM UP.

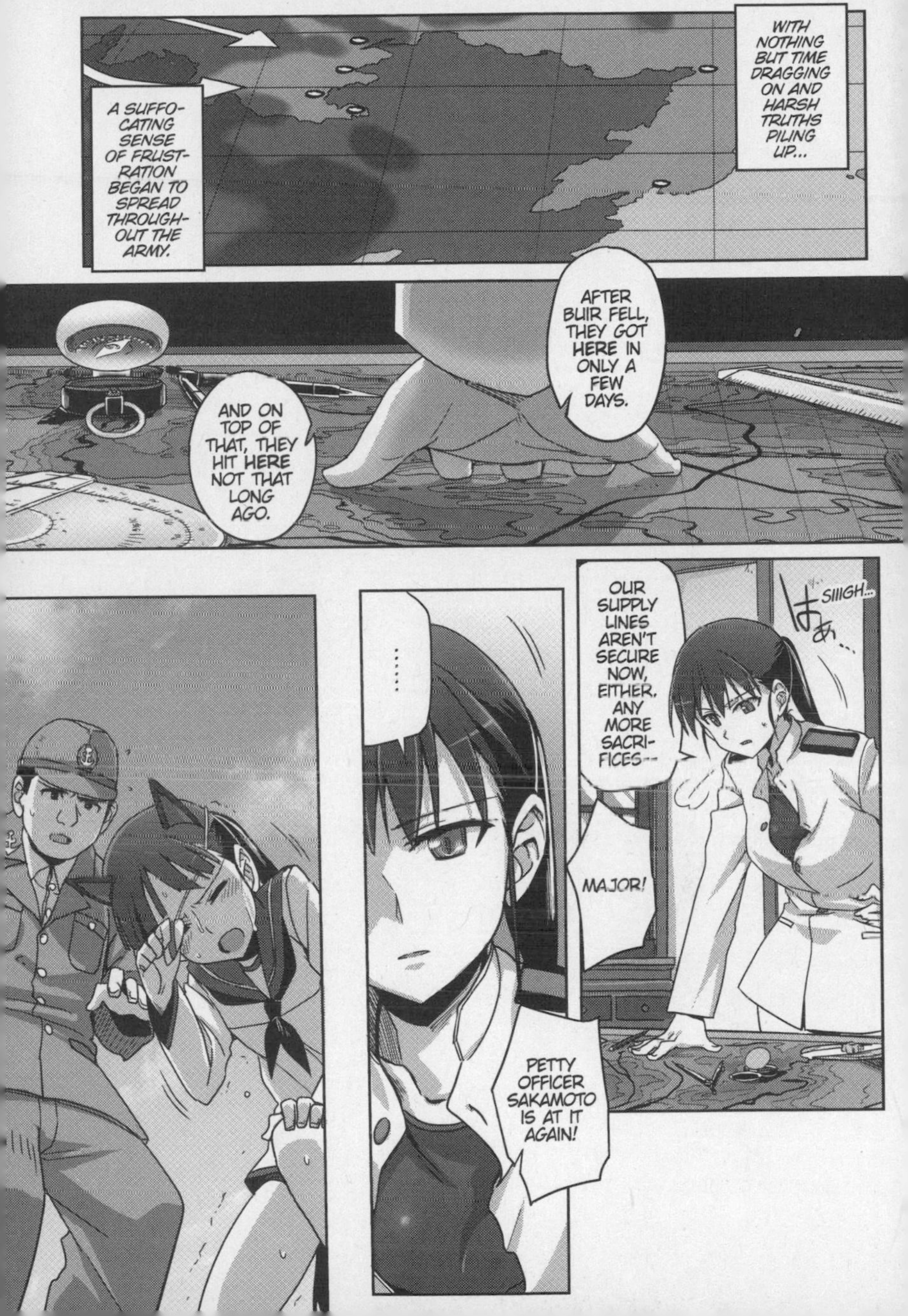
WITH NOTHING BUT TIME DRAGGING ON AND HARSH TRUTHS PILING UP...
A SUFFOCATING SENSE OF FRUSTRATION BEGAN TO SPREAD THROUGHOUT THE ARMY.
AFTER BUIR FELL, THEY GOT HERE IN ONLY A FEW DAYS.
AND ON TOP OF THAT, THEY HIT HERE NOT THAT LONG AGO.
はあ…
SIIIGH...
OUR SUPPLY LINES AREN'T SECURE NOW, EITHER. ANY MORE SACRIFICES--
......
MAJOR!
PETTY OFFICER SAKAMOTO IS AT IT AGAIN!

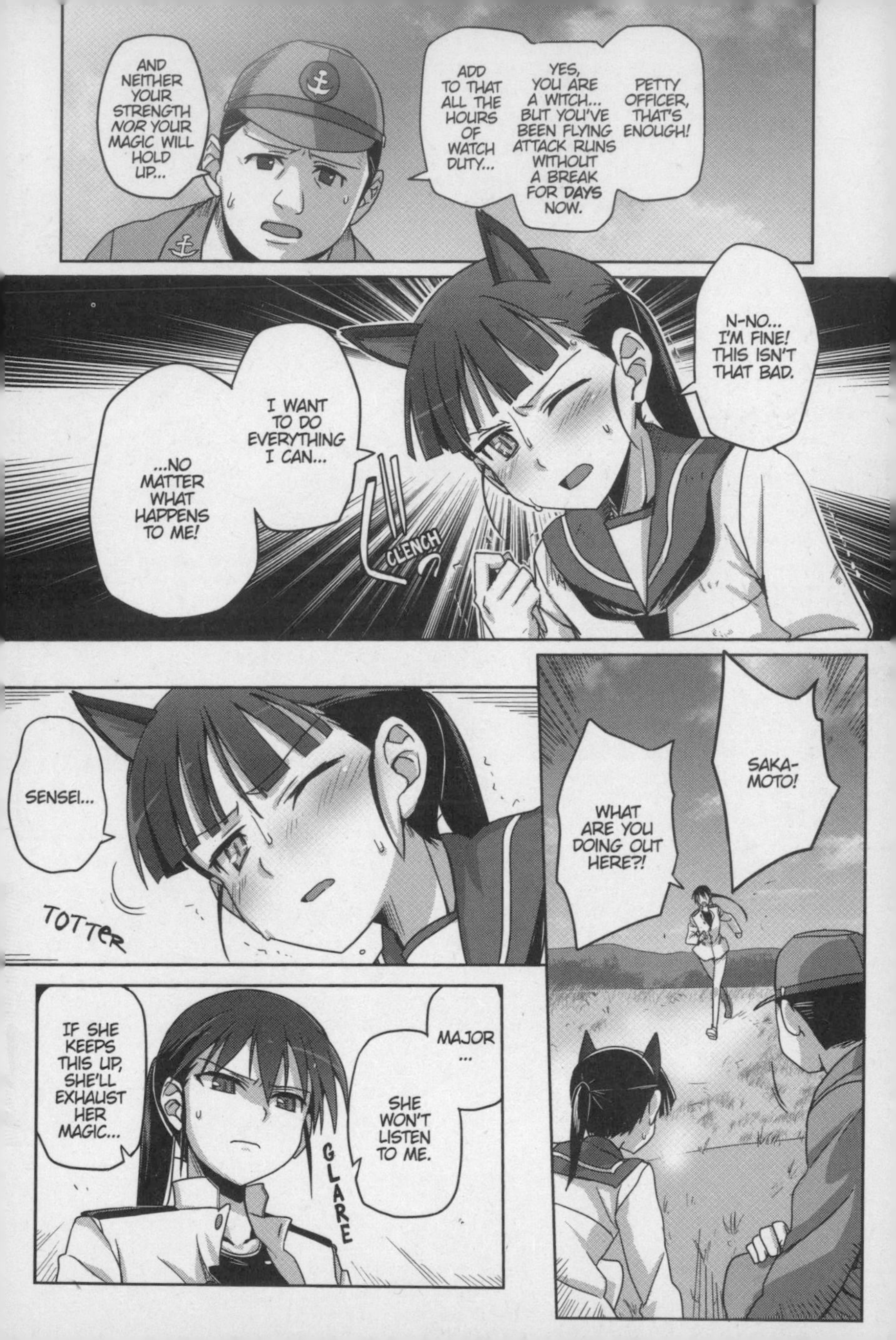
PETTY OFFICER, THAT'S ENOUGH!
YES, YOU ARE A WITCH... BUT YOU'VE BEEN FLYING ATTACK RUNS WITHOUT A BREAK FOR DAYS NOW.
ADD TO THAT ALL THE HOURS OF WATCH DUTY...
AND NEITHER YOUR STRENGTH NOR YOUR MAGIC WILL HOLD UP...
N-NO... I'M FINE! THIS ISN'T THAT BAD.
I WANT TO DO EVERYTHING I CAN...
...NO MATTER WHAT HAPPENS TO ME!
CLENCH
SAKA-MOTO!
WHAT ARE YOU DOING OUT HERE?!
SENSEI...
TOTTER
MAJOR...
SHE WON'T LISTEN TO ME.
GLARE
IF SHE KEEPS THIS UP, SHE'LL EXHAUST HER MAGIC...

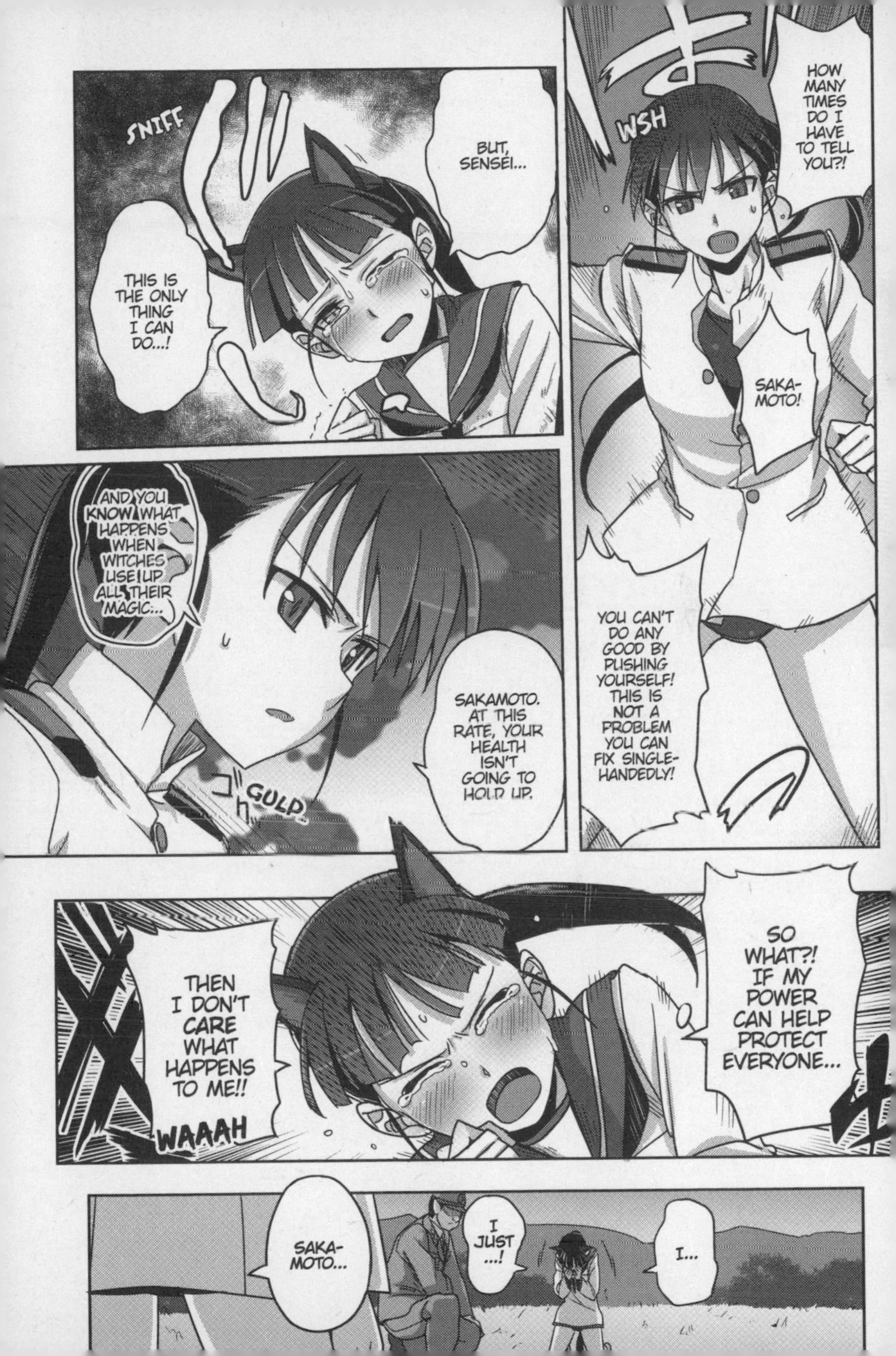
HOW MANY TIMES DO I HAVE TO TELL YOU?!
WSH
SAKA-MOTO!
YOU CAN'T DO ANY GOOD BY PUSHING YOURSELF! THIS IS NOT A PROBLEM YOU CAN FIX SINGLE-HANDEDLY!
BUT, SENSEI...
SNIFF
THIS IS THE ONLY THING I CAN DO...!
SAKAMOTO. AT THIS RATE, YOUR HEALTH ISN'T GOING TO HOLD UP.
GULP
AND YOU KNOW WHAT HAPPENS WHEN WITCHES USE UP ALL THEIR MAGIC...
SO WHAT?! IF MY POWER CAN HELP PROTECT EVERYONE...
THEN I DON'T CARE WHAT HAPPENS TO ME!!
WAAAH
I...
I JUST ...!
SAKA-MOTO...

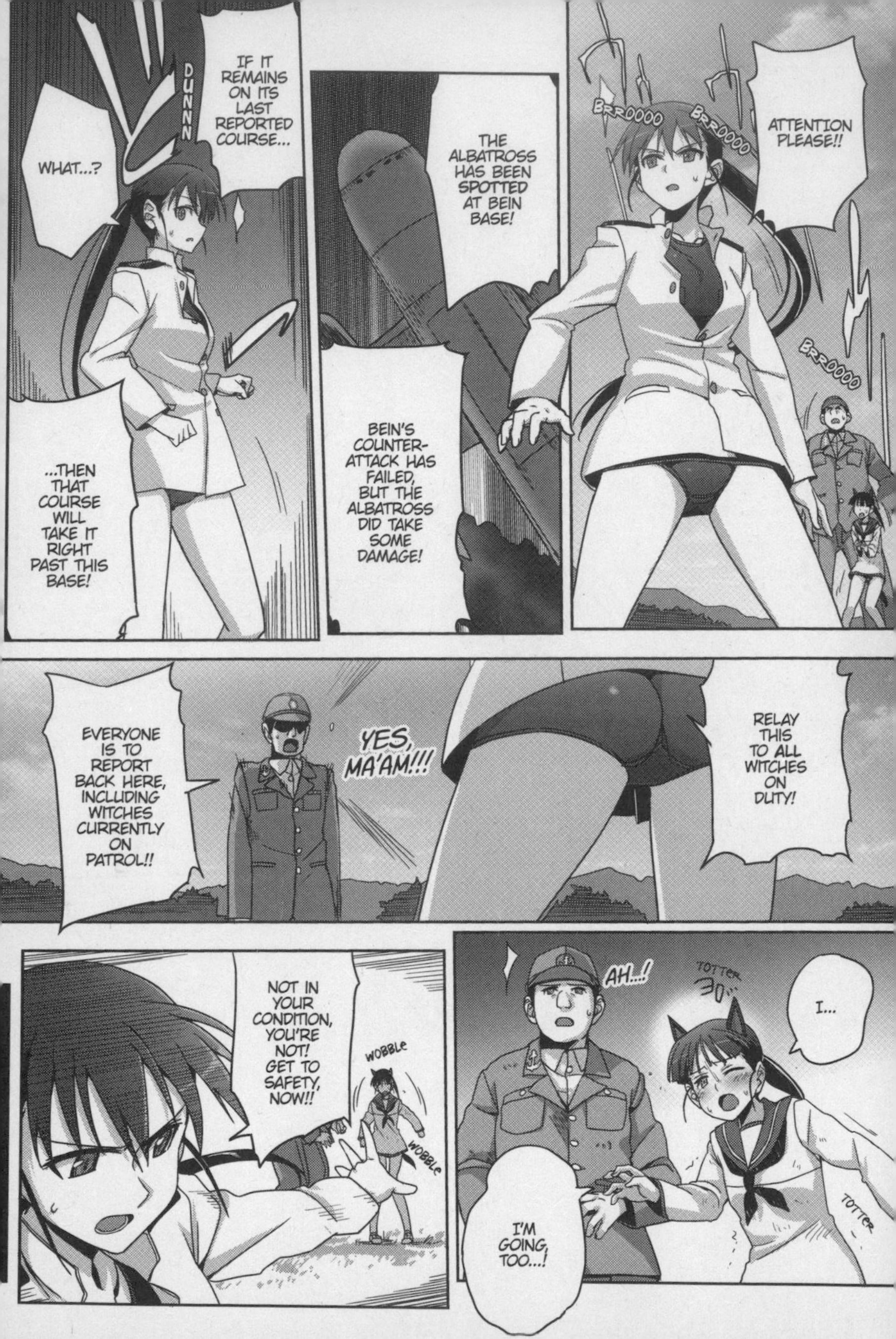

ATTENTION PLEASE!!
BRROOOO
BRROOOO
BRROOOO
THE ALBATROSS HAS BEEN SPOTTED AT BEIN BASE!
BEIN'S COUNTER-ATTACK HAS FAILED, BUT THE ALBATROSS DID TAKE SOME DAMAGE!
IF IT REMAINS ON ITS LAST REPORTED COURSE...
DUNNN
WHAT...?
...THEN THAT COURSE WILL TAKE IT RIGHT PAST THIS BASE!
RELAY THIS TO ALL WITCHES ON DUTY!
YES, MA'AM!!!
EVERYONE IS TO REPORT BACK HERE, INCLUDING WITCHES CURRENTLY ON PATROL!!
I...
TOTTER
AH...!
TOTTER
I'M GOING, TOO...!
NOT IN YOUR CONDITION, YOU'RE NOT! GET TO SAFETY, NOW!!
WOBBLE
WOBBLE

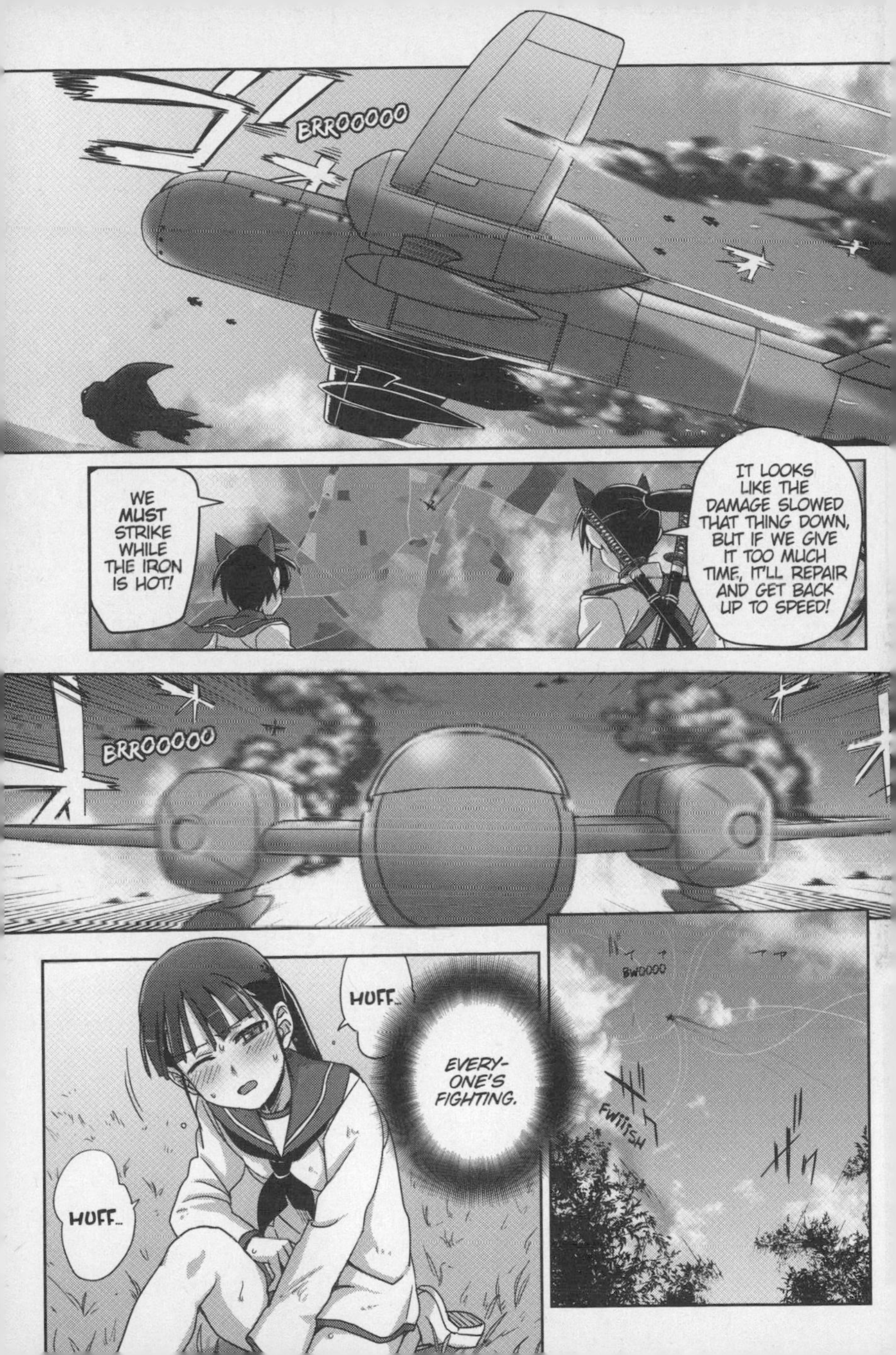
BRROOOOO
IT LOOKS LIKE THE DAMAGE SLOWED THAT THING DOWN, BUT IF WE GIVE IT TOO MUCH TIME, IT'LL REPAIR AND GET BACK UP TO SPEED!
WE MUST STRIKE WHILE THE IRON IS HOT!
BRROOOOO
BWOOOO
FWIIISH
HUFF...
EVERY-ONE'S FIGHTING.
HUFF...

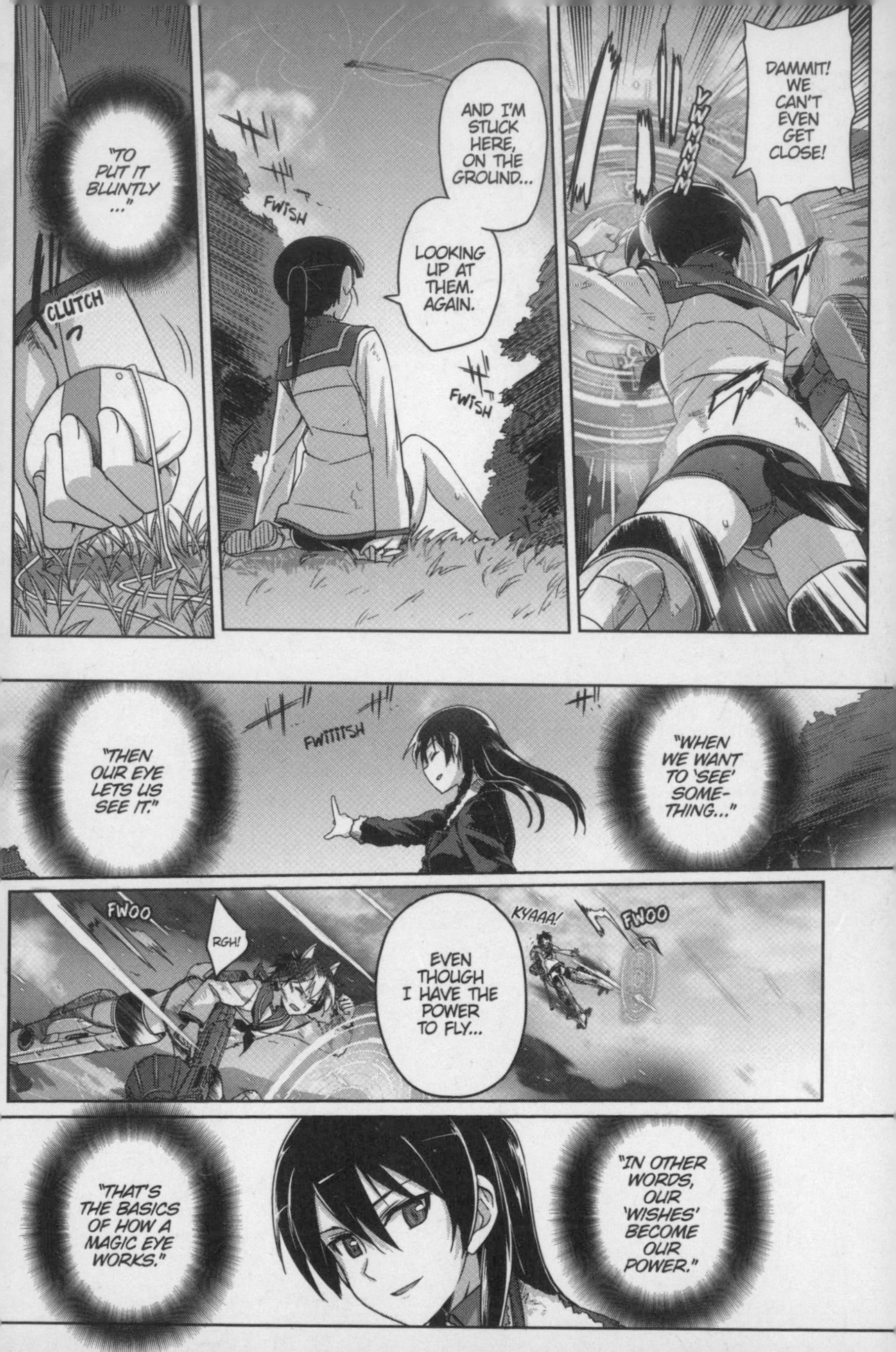

DAMMIT! WE CAN'T EVEN GET CLOSE!
VWMMMM
AND I'M STUCK HERE, ON THE GROUND...
FWISH
LOOKING UP AT THEM. AGAIN.
FWISH
"TO PUT IT BLUNTLY..."
CLUTCH
"WHEN WE WANT TO 'SEE' SOMETHING..."
FWIIIISH
"THEN OUR EYE LETS US SEE IT."
FWOO
KYAAA!
EVEN THOUGH I HAVE THE POWER TO FLY...
RGH!
FWOO
"IN OTHER WORDS, OUR 'WISHES' BECOME OUR POWER."
"THAT'S THE BASICS OF HOW A MAGIC EYE WORKS."

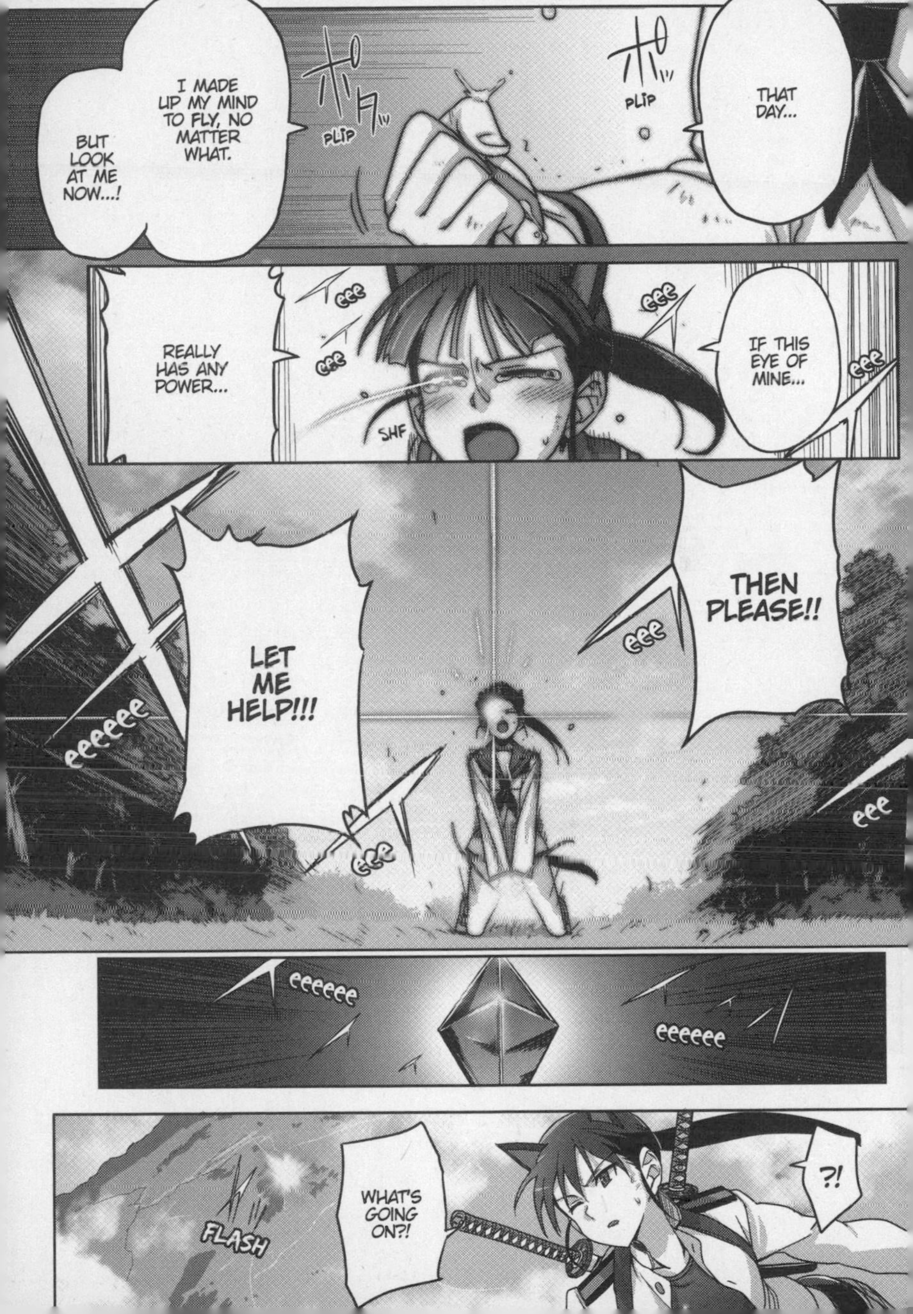
THAT DAY...
ポ
PLIP
I MADE UP MY MIND TO FLY, NO MATTER WHAT.
BUT LOOK AT ME NOW...!
ポタ
PLIP
IF THIS EYE OF MINE...
eee
eee
REALLY HAS ANY POWER...
eee
eee
SHF
THEN PLEASE!!
eee
eee
LET ME HELP!!!
eee
eeeeee
eeeeee
eeeeee
?!
WHAT'S GOING ON?!
FLASH

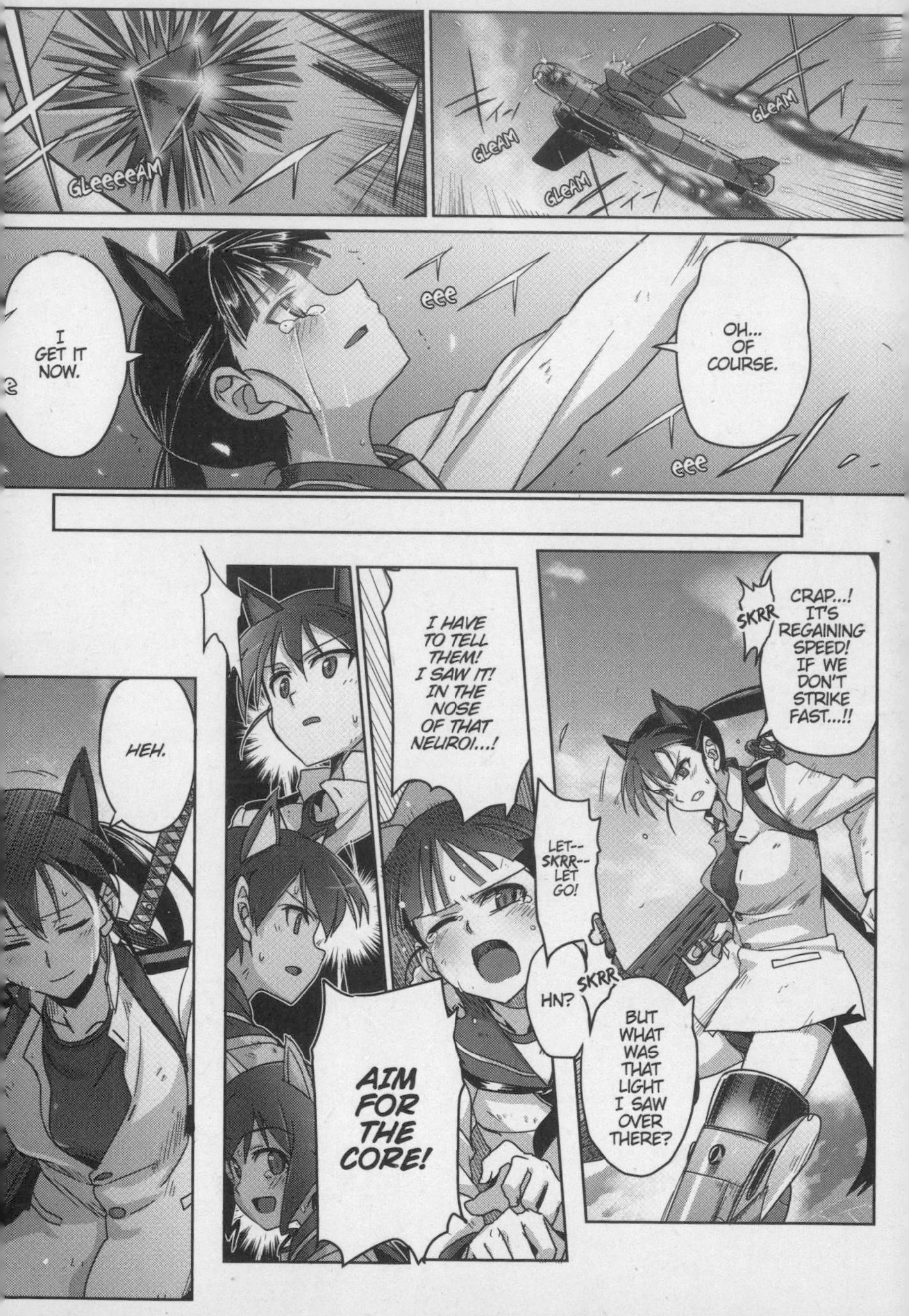
GLEAM
GLEAM
GLEAM
GLEEEEAM
eee
OH... OF COURSE.
I GET IT NOW.
eee
SKRR
CRAP...! IT'S REGAINING SPEED! IF WE DON'T STRIKE FAST...!!
LET-- SKRR-- LET GO!
SKRR
HN?
BUT WHAT WAS THAT LIGHT I SAW OVER THERE?
I HAVE TO TELL THEM! I SAW IT! IN THE NOSE OF THAT NEUROI...!
AIM FOR THE CORE!
HEH.

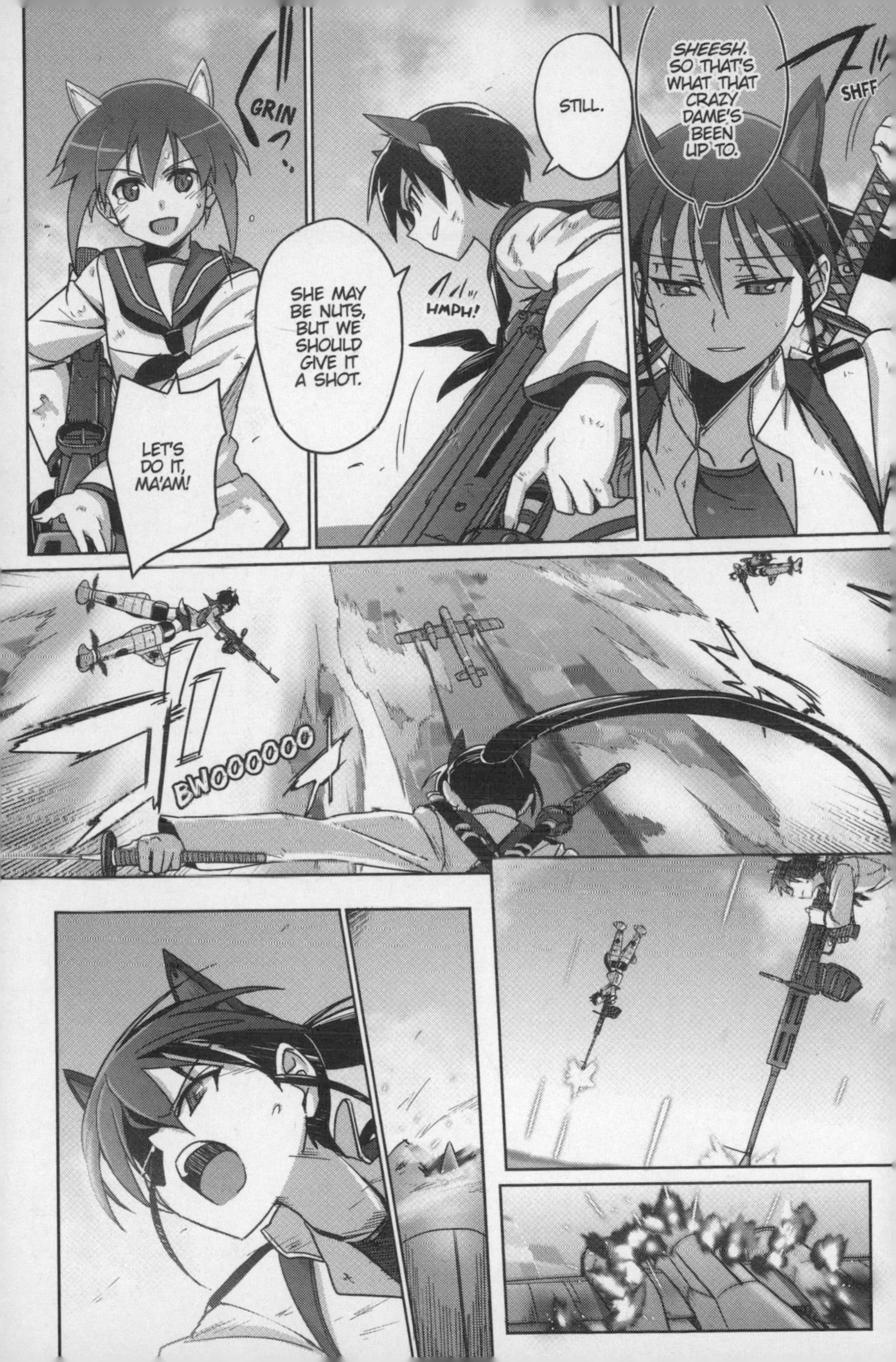
SHEESH. SO THAT'S WHAT THAT CRAZY DAME'S BEEN UP TO.
SHFF
STILL.
SHE MAY BE NUTS, BUT WE SHOULD GIVE IT A SHOT.
HMPH!
GRIN
LET'S DO IT, MA'AM!
BWOOOOOO

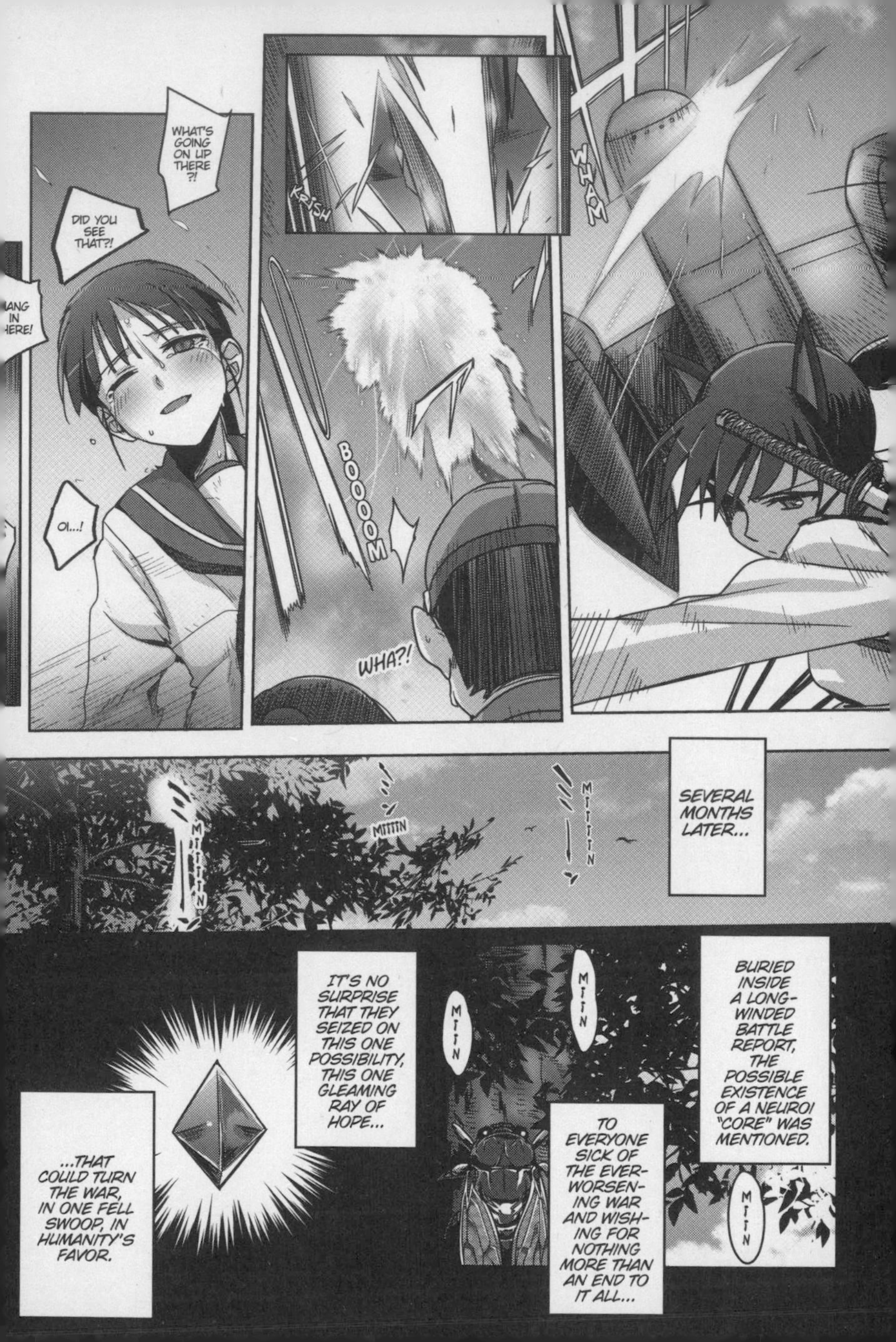
WHAM
KRISH
BOOOOOM
WHA?!
WHAT'S GOING ON UP THERE ?!
DID YOU SEE THAT?!
OI...!
SEVERAL MONTHS LATER...
MIIIIN
MIIIIN
MIIIIN
BURIED INSIDE A LONG-WINDED BATTLE REPORT, THE POSSIBLE EXISTENCE OF A NEUROI "CORE" WAS MENTIONED.
MIIN
MIIN
MIIN
TO EVERYONE SICK OF THE EVER-WORSENING WAR AND WISHING FOR NOTHING MORE THAN AN END TO IT ALL...
IT'S NO SURPRISE THAT THEY SEIZED ON THIS ONE POSSIBILITY, THIS ONE GLEAMING RAY OF HOPE...
...THAT COULD TURN THE WAR, IN ONE FELL SWOOP, IN HUMANITY'S FAVOR.

Chapter 8:
Fallen Cherry Blossoms
[Mission Complete]

CHAPTER 8.5:
CALM BEFORE THE STORM

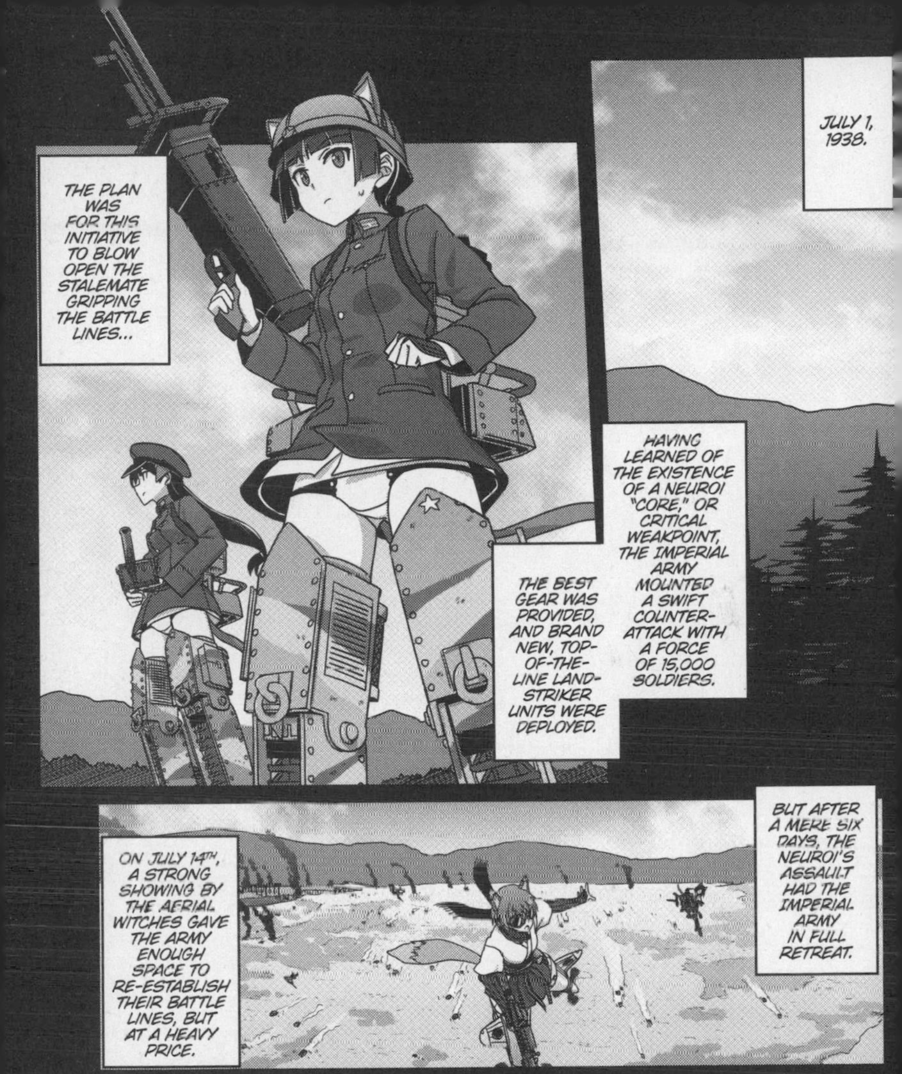

JULY 1, 1938.
HAVING LEARNED OF THE EXISTENCE OF A NEUROI "CORE," OR CRITICAL WEAKPOINT, THE IMPERIAL ARMY MOUNTED A SWIFT COUNTER-ATTACK WITH A FORCE OF 15,000 SOLDIERS.
THE BEST GEAR WAS PROVIDED, AND BRAND NEW, TOP-OF-THE-LINE LAND-STRIKER UNITS WERE DEPLOYED.
THE PLAN WAS FOR THIS INITIATIVE TO BLOW OPEN THE STALEMATE GRIPPING THE BATTLE LINES...
BUT AFTER A MERE SIX DAYS, THE NEUROI'S ASSAULT HAD THE IMPERIAL ARMY IN FULL RETREAT.
ON JULY 14TH, A STRONG SHOWING BY THE AERIAL WITCHES GAVE THE ARMY ENOUGH SPACE TO RE-ESTABLISH THEIR BATTLE LINES, BUT AT A HEAVY PRICE.
BY JULY 25TH, JUST A LITTLE OVER THREE WEEKS SINCE THE START OF THE COUNTER-ATTACK...
THE ARMY REGISTERED 5,000 CASUALTIES, A THIRD OF ITS FORCE. REDEPLOYMENT WAS DEEMED NECESSARY.

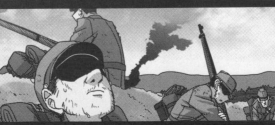

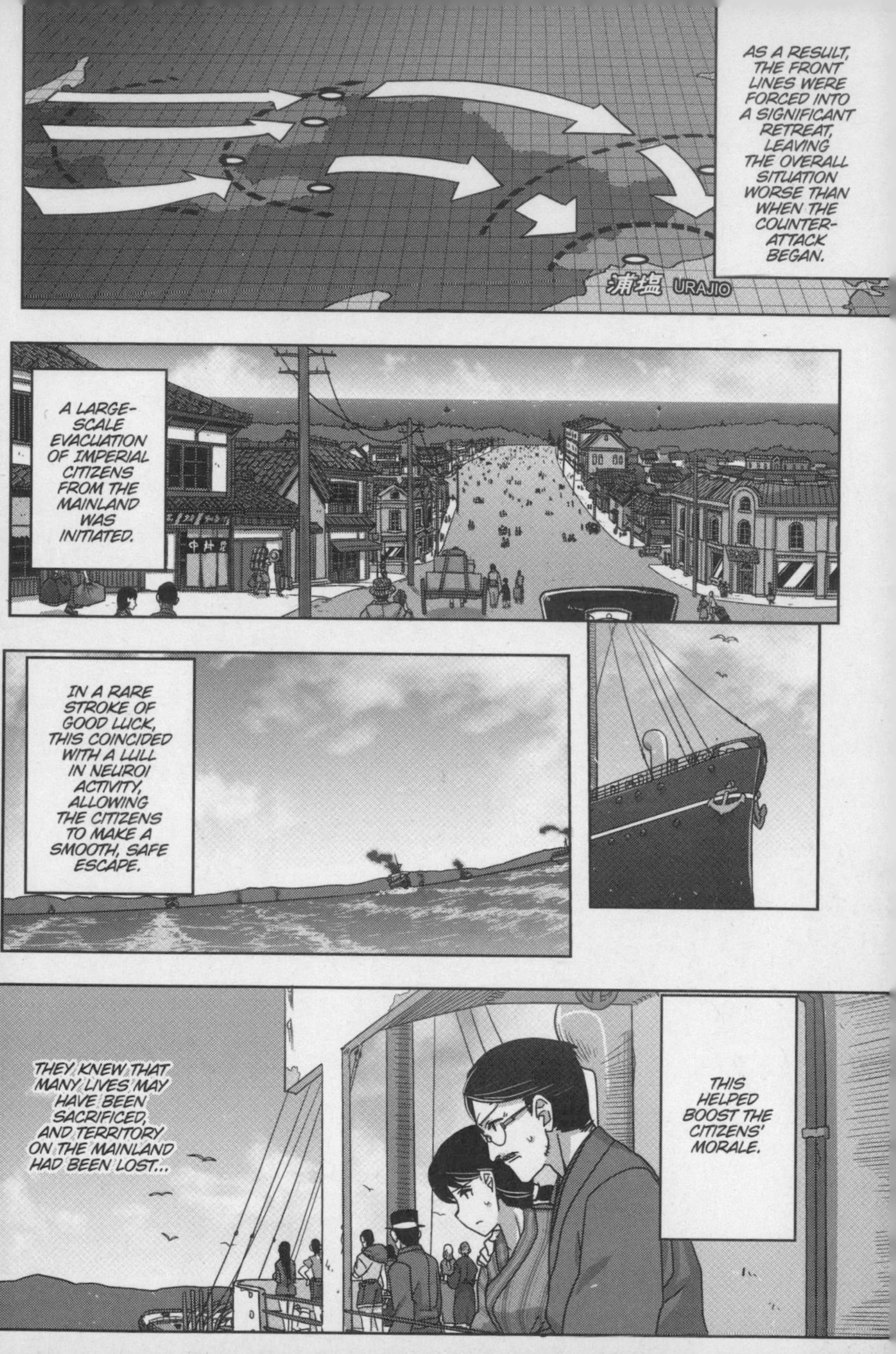
AS A RESULT, THE FRONT LINES WERE FORCED INTO A SIGNIFICANT RETREAT, LEAVING THE OVERALL SITUATION WORSE THAN WHEN THE COUNTER-ATTACK BEGAN.
浦塩 URAJIO
A LARGE-SCALE EVACUATION OF IMPERIAL CITIZENS FROM THE MAINLAND WAS INITIATED.
IN A RARE STROKE OF GOOD LUCK, THIS COINCIDED WITH A LULL IN NEUROI ACTIVITY, ALLOWING THE CITIZENS TO MAKE A SMOOTH, SAFE ESCAPE.
THIS HELPED BOOST THE CITIZENS' MORALE.
THEY KNEW THAT MANY LIVES MAY HAVE BEEN SACRIFICED, AND TERRITORY ON THE MAINLAND HAD BEEN LOST...

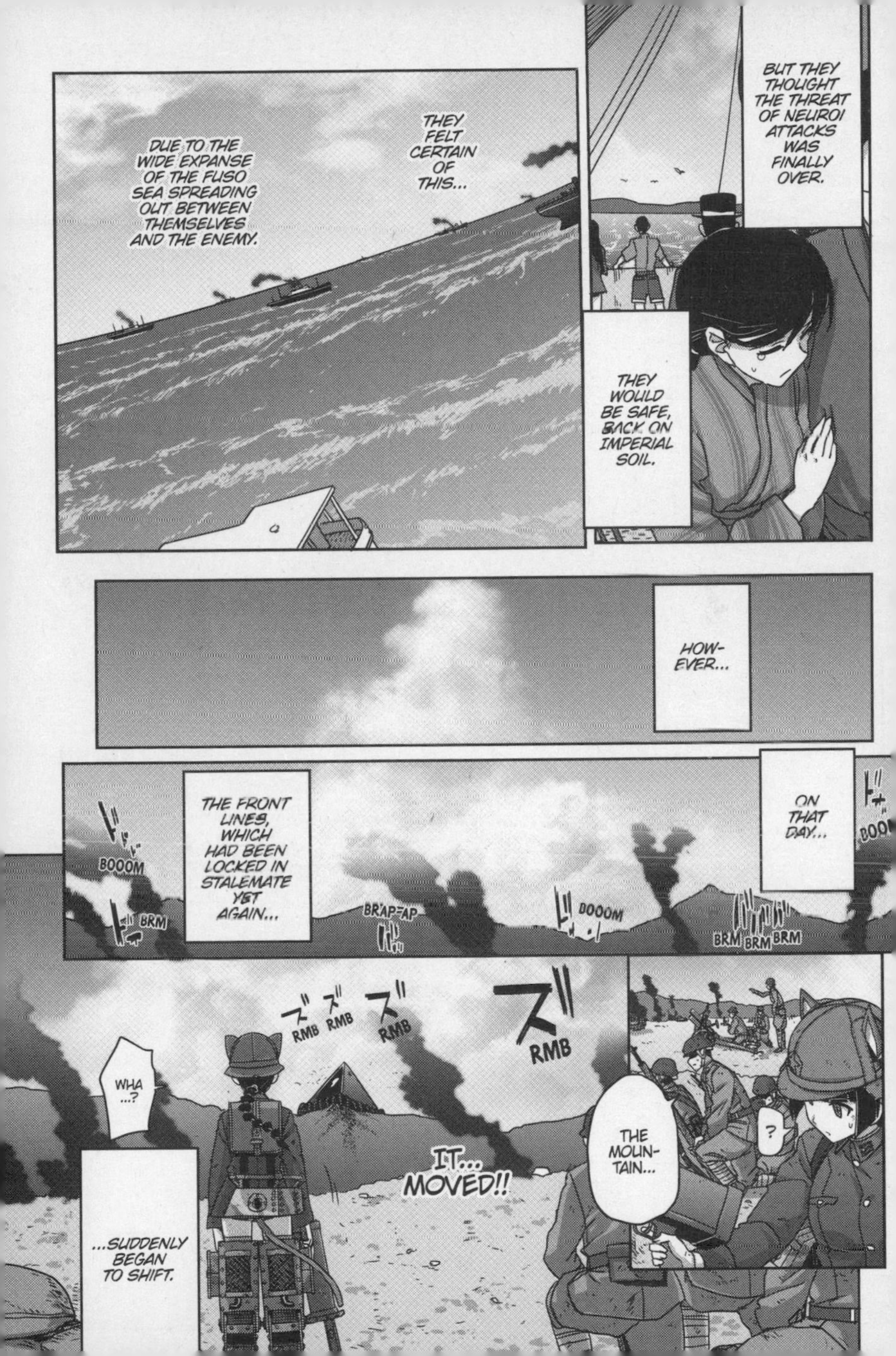

BUT THEY THOUGHT THE THREAT OF NEUROI ATTACKS WAS FINALLY OVER.
THEY WOULD BE SAFE, BACK ON IMPERIAL SOIL.
THEY FELT CERTAIN OF THIS...
DUE TO THE WIDE EXPANSE OF THE FUSO SEA SPREADING OUT BETWEEN THEMSELVES AND THE ENEMY.
HOW-EVER...
ON THAT DAY...
BOOM
BRM BRM BRM
BOOOM
BRAPFAP
THE FRONT LINES, WHICH HAD BEEN LOCKED IN STALEMATE YET AGAIN...
BOOOM
BRM
THE MOUN-TAIN...
?
RMB
RMB
RMB RMB
IT... MOVED!!
WHA ...?
...SUDDENLY BEGAN TO SHIFT.

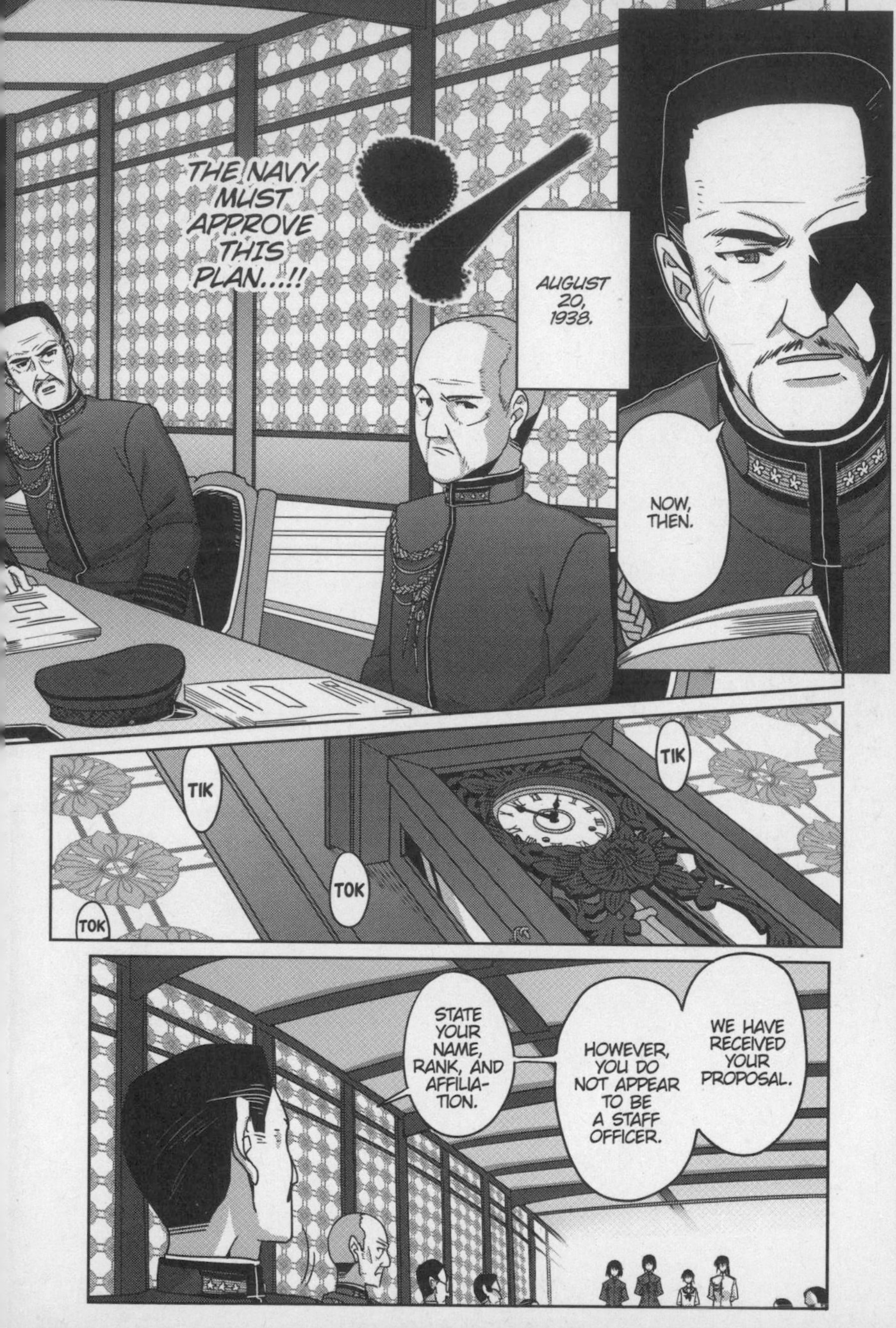
NOW, THEN.
AUGUST 20, 1938.
THE NAVY MUST APPROVE THIS PLAN...!!
TIK
TIK
TOK
TOK
WE HAVE RECEIVED YOUR PROPOSAL.
HOWEVER, YOU DO NOT APPEAR TO BE A STAFF OFFICER.
STATE YOUR NAME, RANK, AND AFFILIATION.

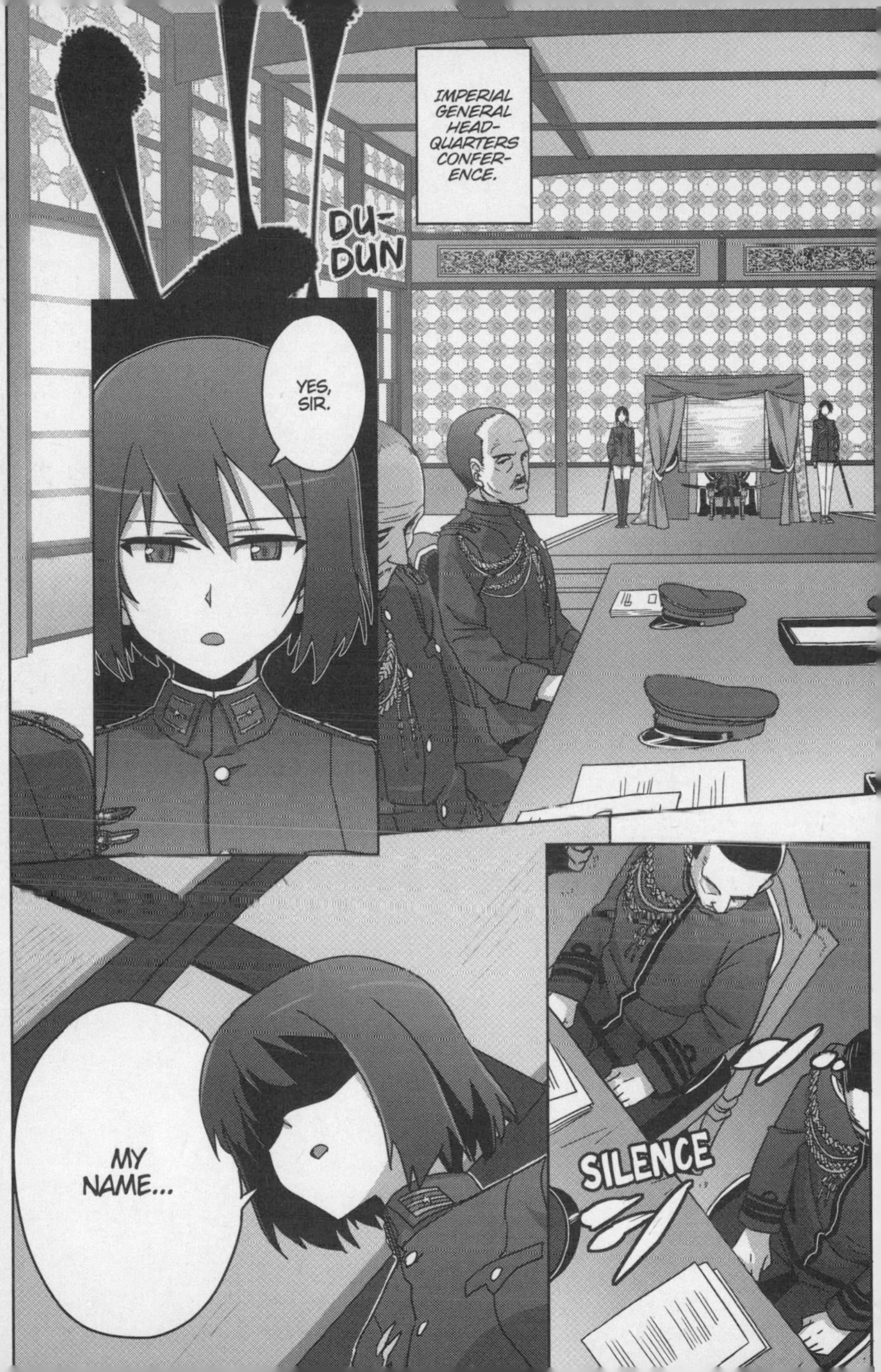
IMPERIAL GENERAL HEAD-QUARTERS CONFER-ENCE.
DU-DUN
YES, SIR.
SILENCE
MY NAME...

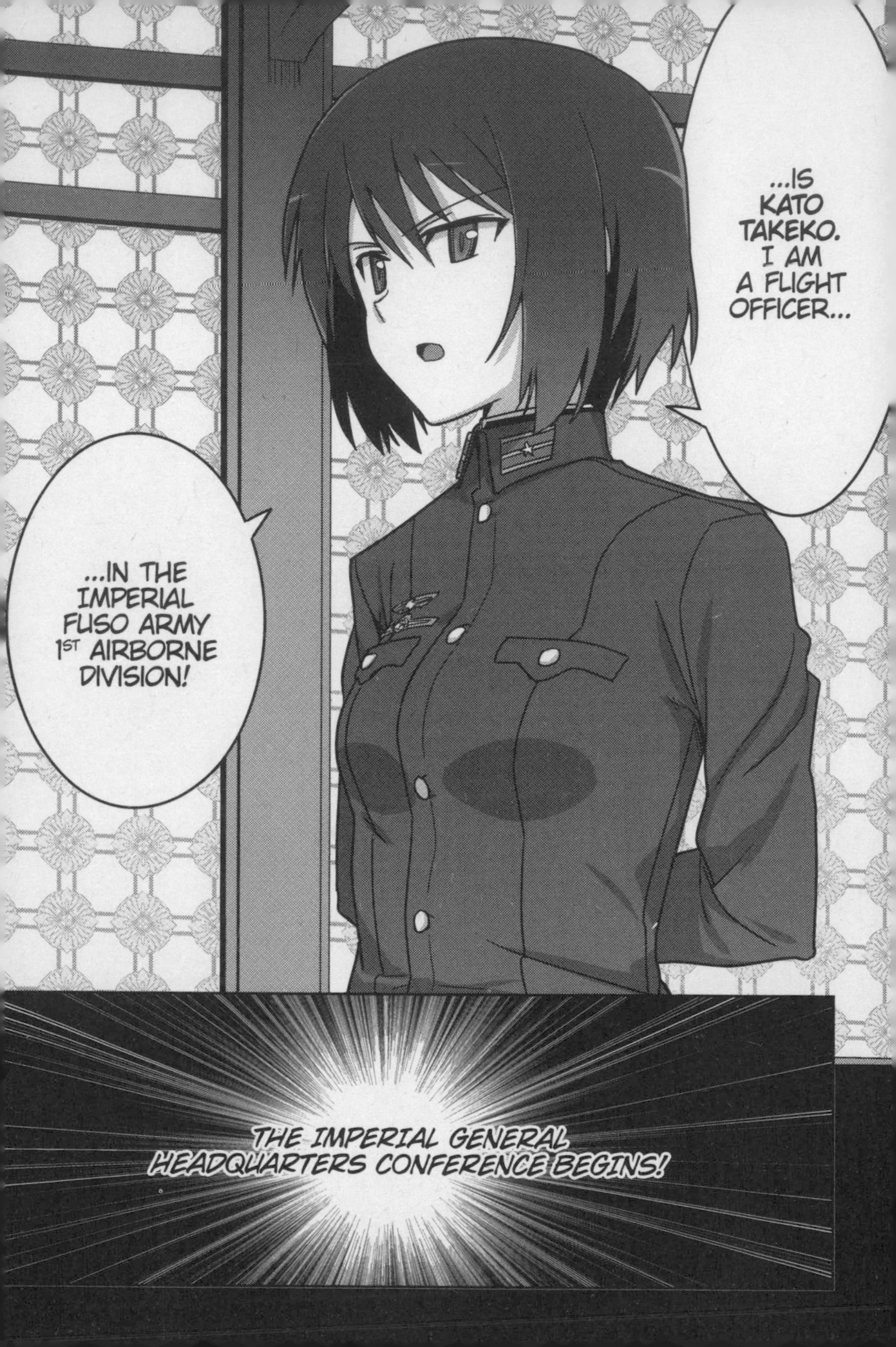
...IS KATO TAKEKO. I AM A FLIGHT OFFICER...
...IN THE IMPERIAL FUSO ARMY 1ST AIRBORNE DIVISION!
THE IMPERIAL GENERAL HEADQUARTERS CONFERENCE BEGINS!

Chapter 8.5:
Calm Before the Storm
[Mission Complete]

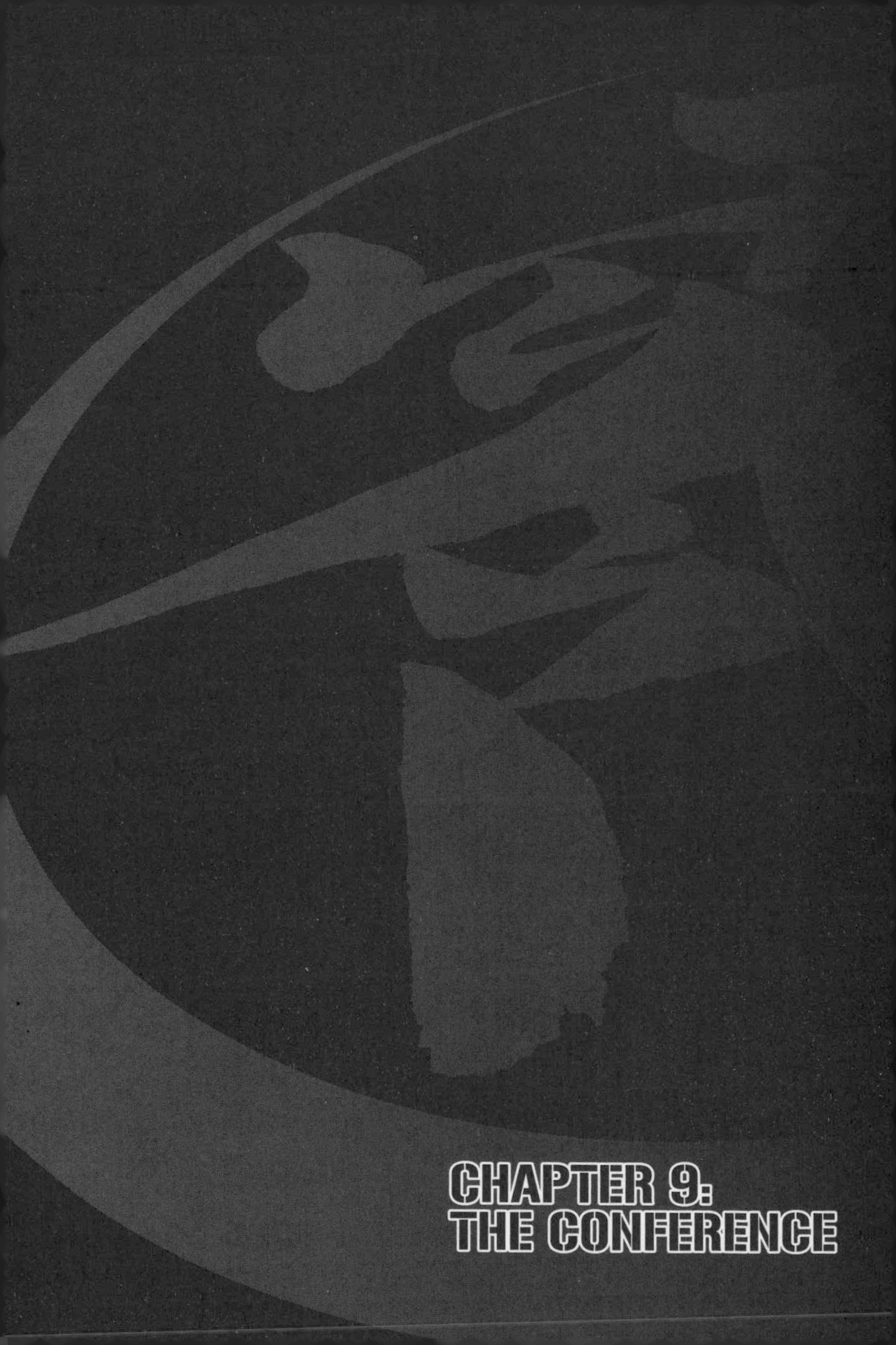

CHAPTER 9: THE CONFERENCE

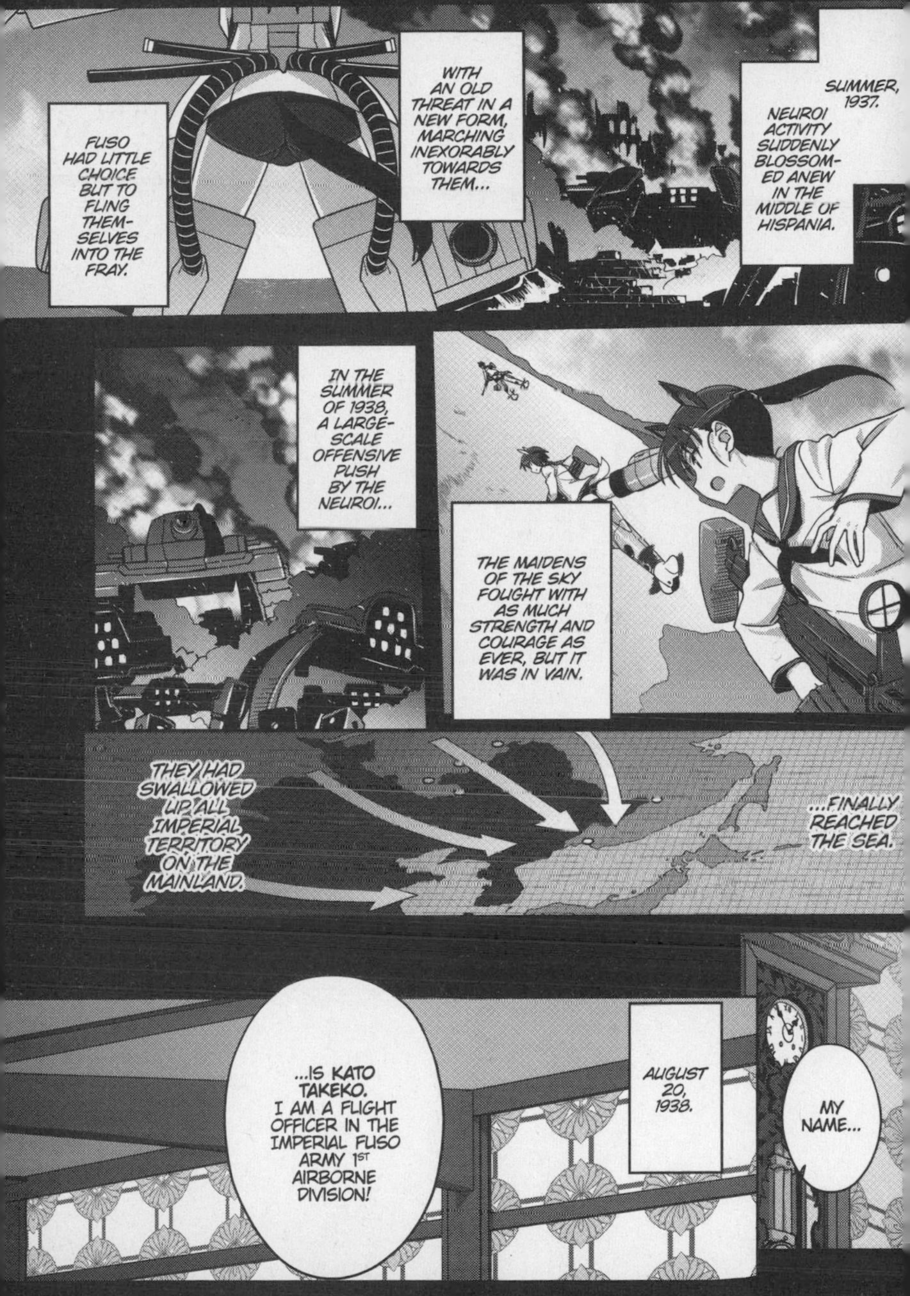

SUMMER, 1937.
NEUROI ACTIVITY SUDDENLY BLOSSOMED ANEW IN THE MIDDLE OF HISPANIA.
WITH AN OLD THREAT IN A NEW FORM, MARCHING INEXORABLY TOWARDS THEM...
FUSO HAD LITTLE CHOICE BUT TO FLING THEMSELVES INTO THE FRAY.
THE MAIDENS OF THE SKY FOUGHT WITH AS MUCH STRENGTH AND COURAGE AS EVER, BUT IT WAS IN VAIN.
IN THE SUMMER OF 1938, A LARGE-SCALE OFFENSIVE PUSH BY THE NEUROI...
...FINALLY REACHED THE SEA.
THEY HAD SWALLOWED UP ALL IMPERIAL TERRITORY ON THE MAINLAND.
MY NAME...
AUGUST 20, 1938.
...IS KATO TAKEKO. I AM A FLIGHT OFFICER IN THE IMPERIAL FUSO ARMY 1ST AIRBORNE DIVISION!

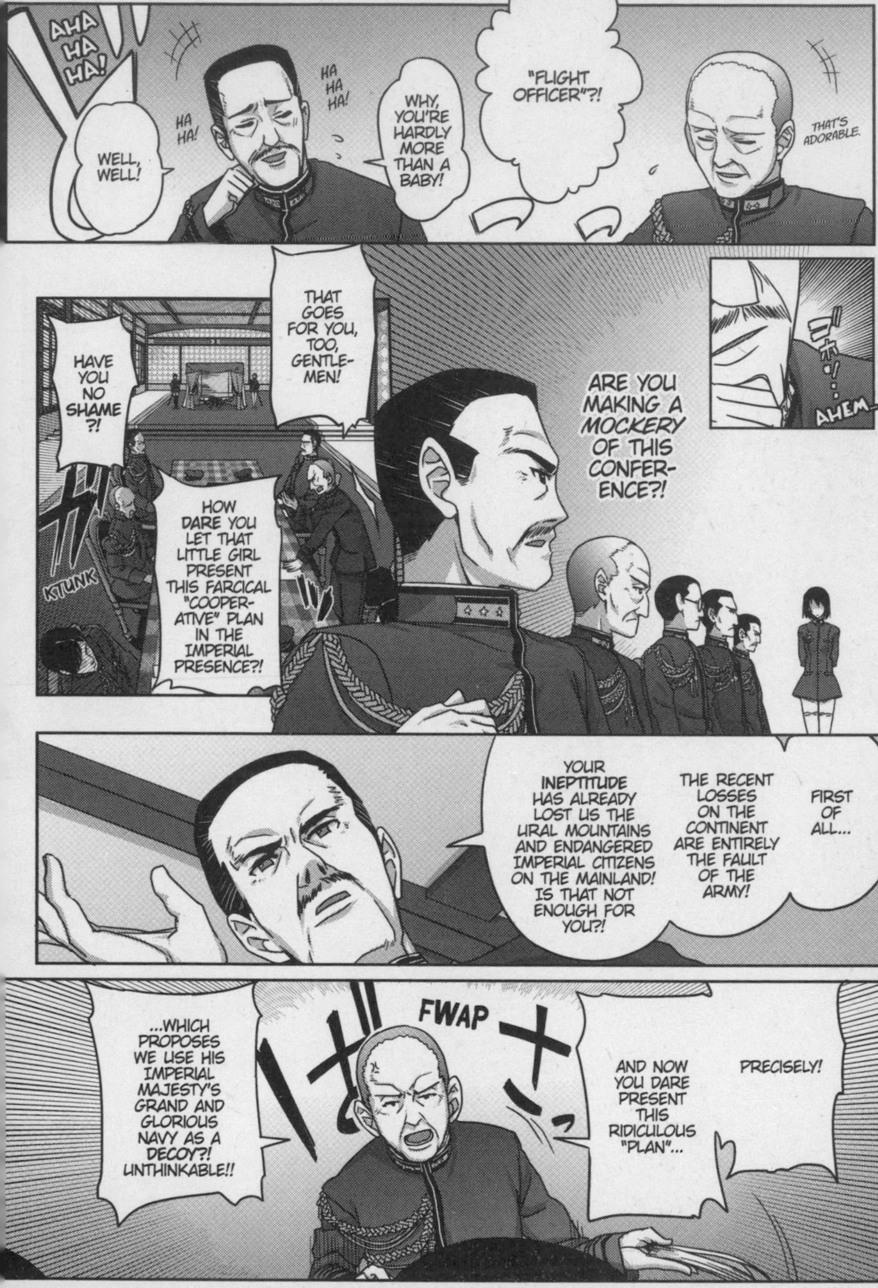
THAT'S ADORABLE.
"FLIGHT OFFICER"?!
WHY, YOU'RE HARDLY MORE THAN A BABY!
HA HA HA!
AHA HA HA!
HA HA!
WELL, WELL!
AHEM...
ARE YOU MAKING A MOCKERY OF THIS CONFERENCE?!
THAT GOES FOR YOU, TOO, GENTLEMEN!
HAVE YOU NO SHAME?!
HOW DARE YOU LET THAT LITTLE GIRL PRESENT THIS FARCICAL "COOPERATIVE" PLAN IN THE IMPERIAL PRESENCE?!
KTUNK
FIRST OF ALL...
THE RECENT LOSSES ON THE CONTINENT ARE ENTIRELY THE FAULT OF THE ARMY!
YOUR INEPTITUDE HAS ALREADY LOST US THE URAL MOUNTAINS AND ENDANGERED IMPERIAL CITIZENS ON THE MAINLAND! IS THAT NOT ENOUGH FOR YOU?!
PRECISELY!
AND NOW YOU DARE PRESENT THIS RIDICULOUS "PLAN"...
FWAP
...WHICH PROPOSES WE USE HIS IMPERIAL MAJESTY'S GRAND AND GLORIOUS NAVY AS A DECOY?! UNTHINKABLE!!

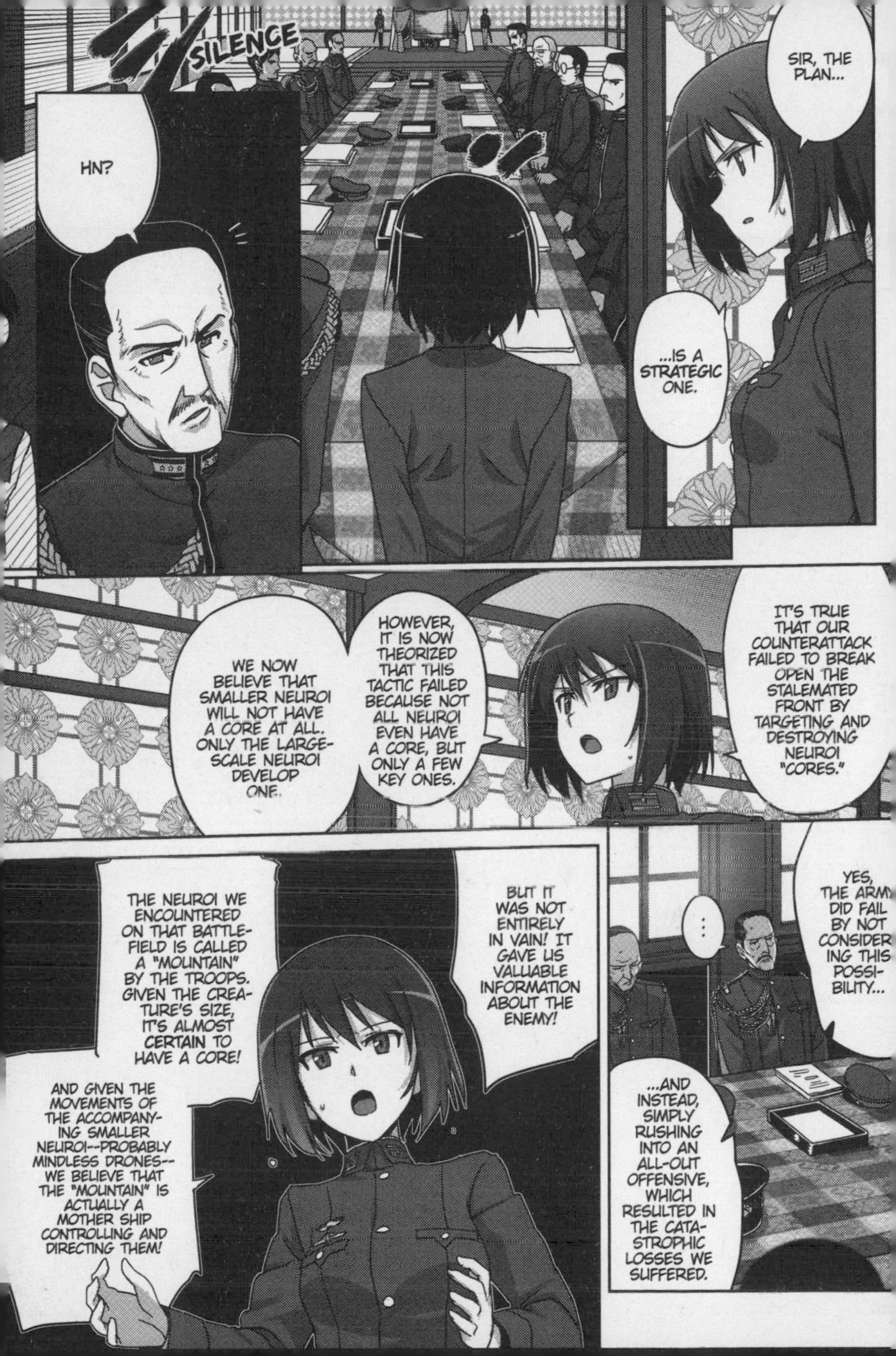

SIR, THE PLAN...
...IS A STRATEGIC ONE.
SILENCE
HN?
IT'S TRUE THAT OUR COUNTERATTACK FAILED TO BREAK OPEN THE STALEMATED FRONT BY TARGETING AND DESTROYING NEUROI "CORES."
HOWEVER, IT IS NOW THEORIZED THAT THIS TACTIC FAILED BECAUSE NOT ALL NEUROI EVEN HAVE A CORE, BUT ONLY A FEW KEY ONES.
WE NOW BELIEVE THAT SMALLER NEUROI WILL NOT HAVE A CORE AT ALL. ONLY THE LARGE-SCALE NEUROI DEVELOP ONE.
YES, THE ARMY DID FAIL BY NOT CONSIDERING THIS POSSIBILITY...
...
...AND INSTEAD, SIMPLY RUSHING INTO AN ALL-OUT OFFENSIVE, WHICH RESULTED IN THE CATASTROPHIC LOSSES WE SUFFERED.
BUT IT WAS NOT ENTIRELY IN VAIN! IT GAVE US VALUABLE INFORMATION ABOUT THE ENEMY!
THE NEUROI WE ENCOUNTERED ON THAT BATTLEFIELD IS CALLED A "MOUNTAIN" BY THE TROOPS. GIVEN THE CREATURE'S SIZE, IT'S ALMOST CERTAIN TO HAVE A CORE!
AND GIVEN THE MOVEMENTS OF THE ACCOMPANYING SMALLER NEUROI--PROBABLY MINDLESS DRONES--WE BELIEVE THAT THE "MOUNTAIN" IS ACTUALLY A MOTHER SHIP CONTROLLING AND DIRECTING THEM!

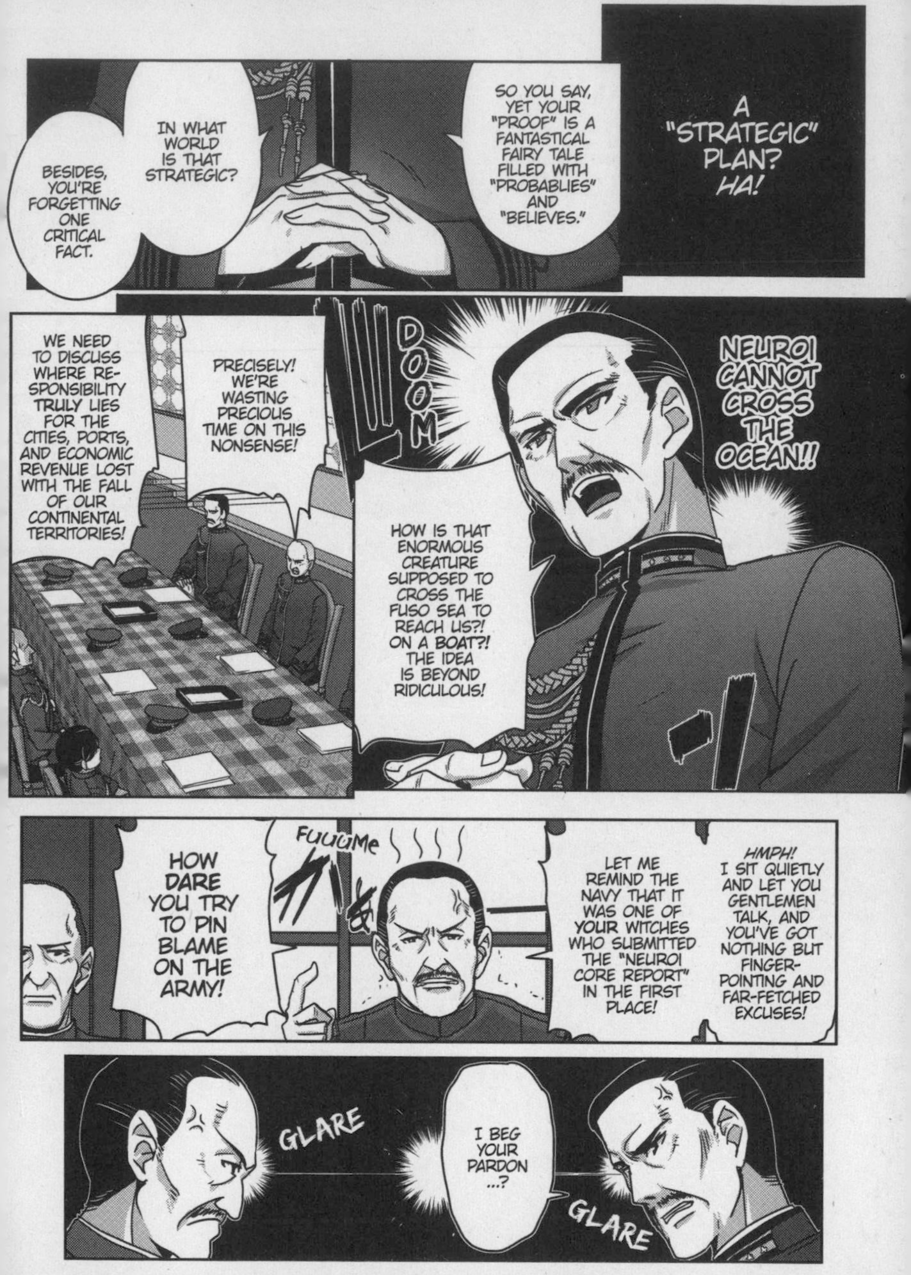
A "STRATEGIC" PLAN? HA!
SO YOU SAY, YET YOUR "PROOF" IS A FANTASTICAL FAIRY TALE FILLED WITH "PROBABLIES" AND "BELIEVES."
IN WHAT WORLD IS THAT STRATEGIC?
BESIDES, YOU'RE FORGETTING ONE CRITICAL FACT.
NEUROI CANNOT CROSS THE OCEAN!!
DOOM
HOW IS THAT ENORMOUS CREATURE SUPPOSED TO CROSS THE FUSO SEA TO REACH US?! ON A BOAT?! THE IDEA IS BEYOND RIDICULOUS!
PRECISELY! WE'RE WASTING PRECIOUS TIME ON THIS NONSENSE!
WE NEED TO DISCUSS WHERE RESPONSIBILITY TRULY LIES FOR THE CITIES, PORTS, AND ECONOMIC REVENUE LOST WITH THE FALL OF OUR CONTINENTAL TERRITORIES!
HMPH! I SIT QUIETLY AND LET YOU GENTLEMEN TALK, AND YOU'VE GOT NOTHING BUT FINGER-POINTING AND FAR-FETCHED EXCUSES!
LET ME REMIND THE NAVY THAT IT WAS ONE OF YOUR WITCHES WHO SUBMITTED THE "NEUROI CORE REPORT" IN THE FIRST PLACE!
FUUUME
HOW DARE YOU TRY TO PIN BLAME ON THE ARMY!
GLARE
I BEG YOUR PARDON ...?
GLARE

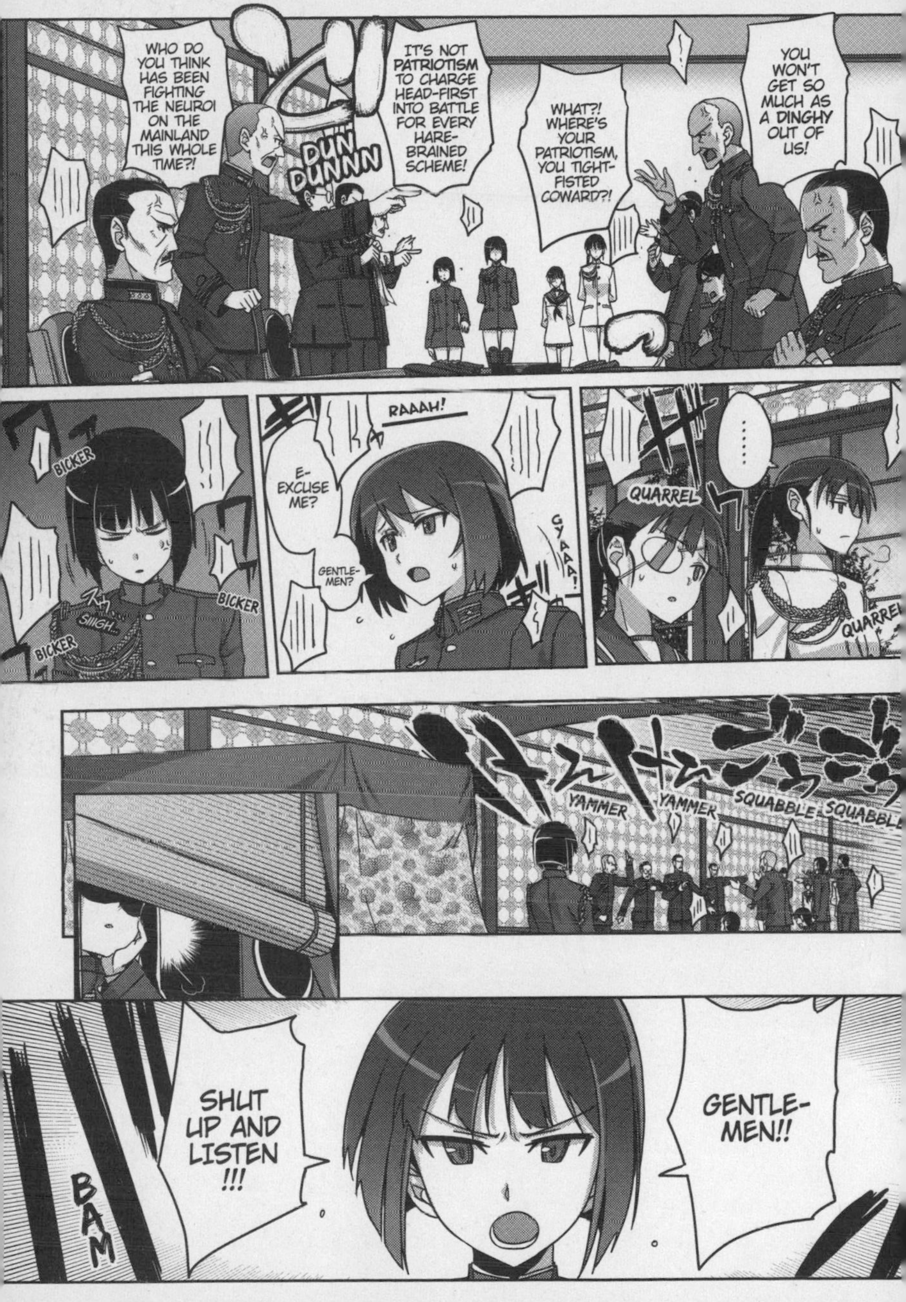
YOU WON'T GET SO MUCH AS A DINGHY OUT OF US!
WHAT?! WHERE'S YOUR PATRIOTISM, YOU TIGHT-FISTED COWARD?!
IT'S NOT PATRIOTISM TO CHARGE HEAD-FIRST INTO BATTLE FOR EVERY HARE-BRAINED SCHEME!
DUN DUNNN
WHO DO YOU THINK HAS BEEN FIGHTING THE NEUROI ON THE MAINLAND THIS WHOLE TIME?!
......
QUARREL
QUARREL
RAAAH!
E-EXCUSE ME?
GENTLE-MEN?
GYAAAA!
BICKER
SIIGH...
BICKER
BICKER
YAMMER
YAMMER
SQUABBLE
SQUABBLE
GENTLE-MEN!!
SHUT UP AND LISTEN!!!
BAM

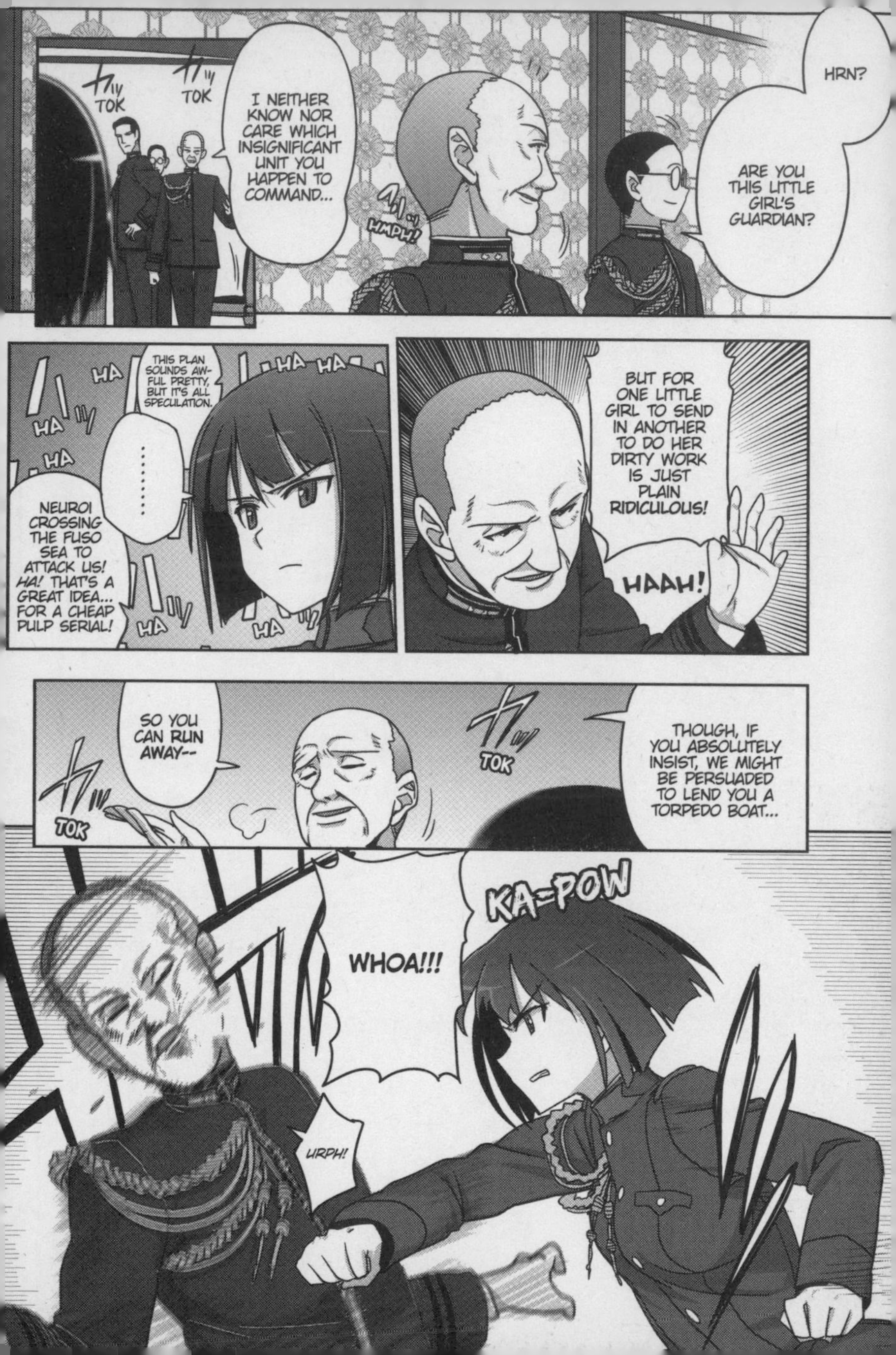
HRN?
ARE YOU THIS LITTLE GIRL'S GUARDIAN?
HMPH!
I NEITHER KNOW NOR CARE WHICH INSIGNIFICANT UNIT YOU HAPPEN TO COMMAND...
TOK
TOK
BUT FOR ONE LITTLE GIRL TO SEND IN ANOTHER TO DO HER DIRTY WORK IS JUST PLAIN RIDICULOUS!
HAAH!
HA HA HA
THIS PLAN SOUNDS AWFUL PRETTY, BUT IT'S ALL SPECULATION.
HA
HA
HA
......
NEUROI CROSSING THE FUSO SEA TO ATTACK US! HA! THAT'S A GREAT IDEA... FOR A CHEAP PULP SERIAL!
HA
HA
THOUGH, IF YOU ABSOLUTELY INSIST, WE MIGHT BE PERSUADED TO LEND YOU A TORPEDO BOAT...
TOK
SO YOU CAN RUN AWAY--
TOK
KA-POW
WHOA!!!
URPH!

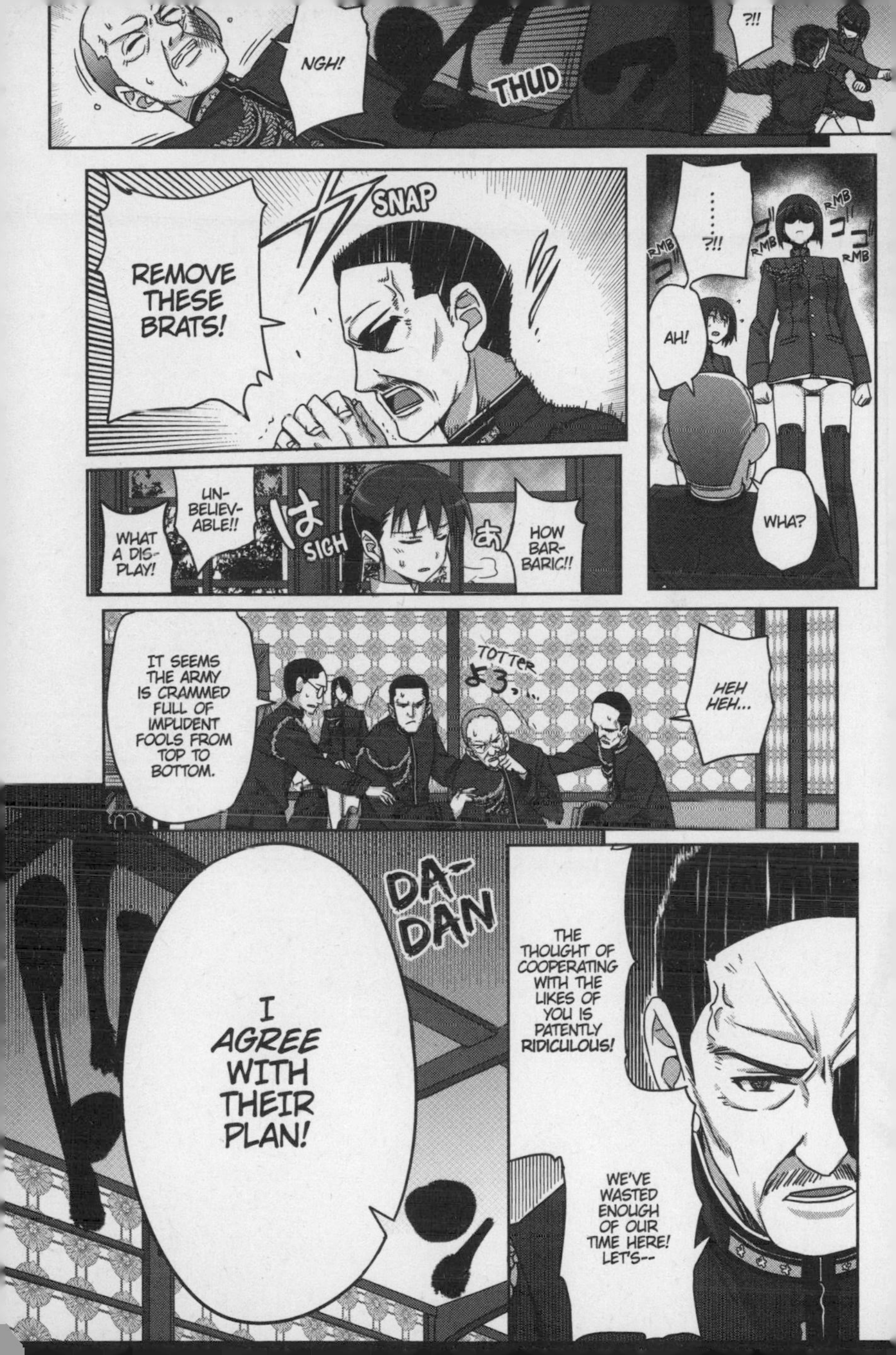
?!!
THUD
NGH!
......
?!!
RMB
RMB
RMB
RMB
AH!
WHA?
SNAP
REMOVE THESE BRATS!
HOW BAR-BARIC!!
SIGH
UN-BELIEVABLE!!
WHAT A DIS-PLAY!
HEH HEH...
TOTTER
IT SEEMS THE ARMY IS CRAMMED FULL OF IMPUDENT FOOLS FROM TOP TO BOTTOM.
THE THOUGHT OF COOPERATING WITH THE LIKES OF YOU IS PATENTLY RIDICULOUS!
WE'VE WASTED ENOUGH OF OUR TIME HERE! LET'S--
DA-DAN
I AGREE WITH THEIR PLAN!

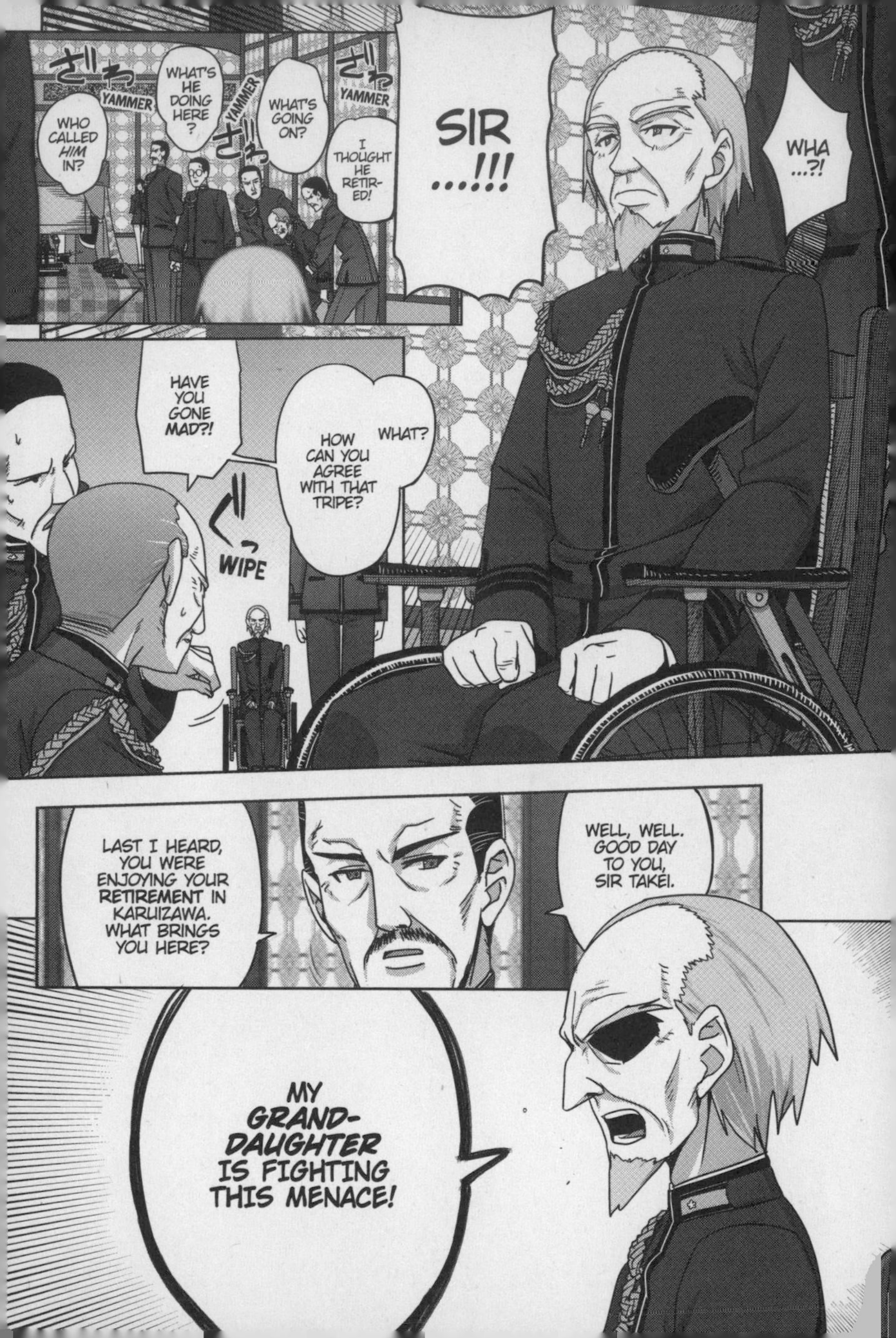
WHA ...?!
SIR ...!!!
ざわ
YAMMER
I THOUGHT HE RETIRED!
WHAT'S GOING ON?
ざわ
YAMMER
WHAT'S HE DOING HERE?
ざわ
YAMMER
WHO CALLED HIM IN?
WHAT?
HOW CAN YOU AGREE WITH THAT TRIPE?
HAVE YOU GONE MAD?!
WIPE
WELL, WELL. GOOD DAY TO YOU, SIR TAKEI.
LAST I HEARD, YOU WERE ENJOYING YOUR RETIREMENT IN KARUIZAWA. WHAT BRINGS YOU HERE?
MY GRAND-DAUGHTER IS FIGHTING THIS MENACE!

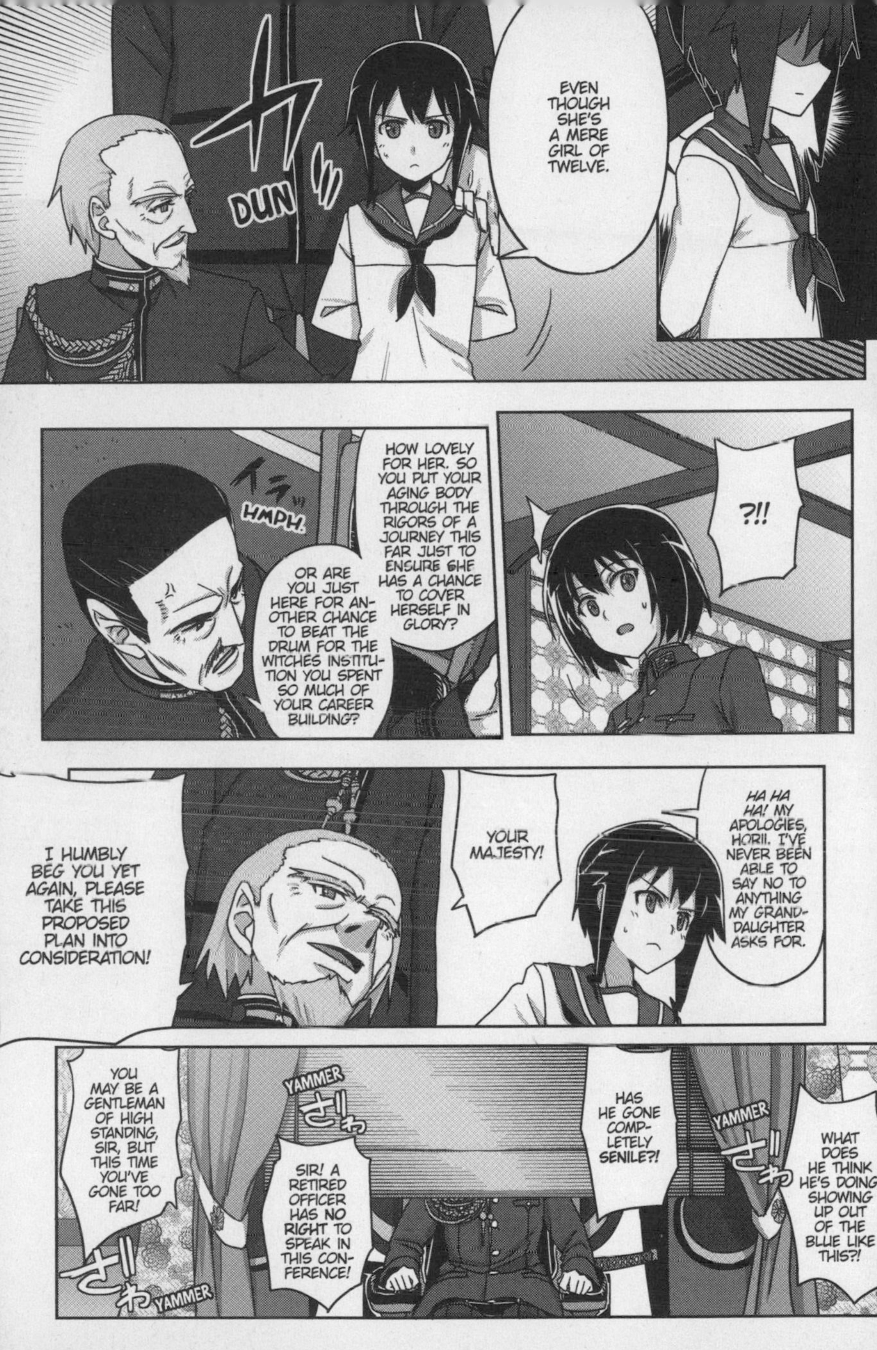
EVEN THOUGH SHE'S A MERE GIRL OF TWELVE.
DUN
?!!
HOW LOVELY FOR HER. SO YOU PUT YOUR AGING BODY THROUGH THE RIGORS OF A JOURNEY THIS FAR JUST TO ENSURE SHE HAS A CHANCE TO COVER HERSELF IN GLORY?
HMPH.
OR ARE YOU JUST HERE FOR AN-OTHER CHANCE TO BEAT THE DRUM FOR THE WITCHES INSTITU-TION YOU SPENT SO MUCH OF YOUR CAREER BUILDING?
HA HA HA! MY APOLOGIES, HORII. I'VE NEVER BEEN ABLE TO SAY NO TO ANYTHING MY GRAND-DAUGHTER ASKS FOR.
YOUR MAJESTY!
I HUMBLY BEG YOU YET AGAIN, PLEASE TAKE THIS PROPOSED PLAN INTO CONSIDERATION!
WHAT DOES HE THINK HE'S DOING, SHOWING UP OUT OF THE BLUE LIKE THIS?!
YAMMER
HAS HE GONE COMP-LETELY SENILE?!
SIR! A RETIRED OFFICER HAS NO RIGHT TO SPEAK IN THIS CON-FERENCE!
YAMMER
YOU MAY BE A GENTLEMAN OF HIGH STANDING, SIR, BUT THIS TIME YOU'VE GONE TOO FAR!
YAMMER

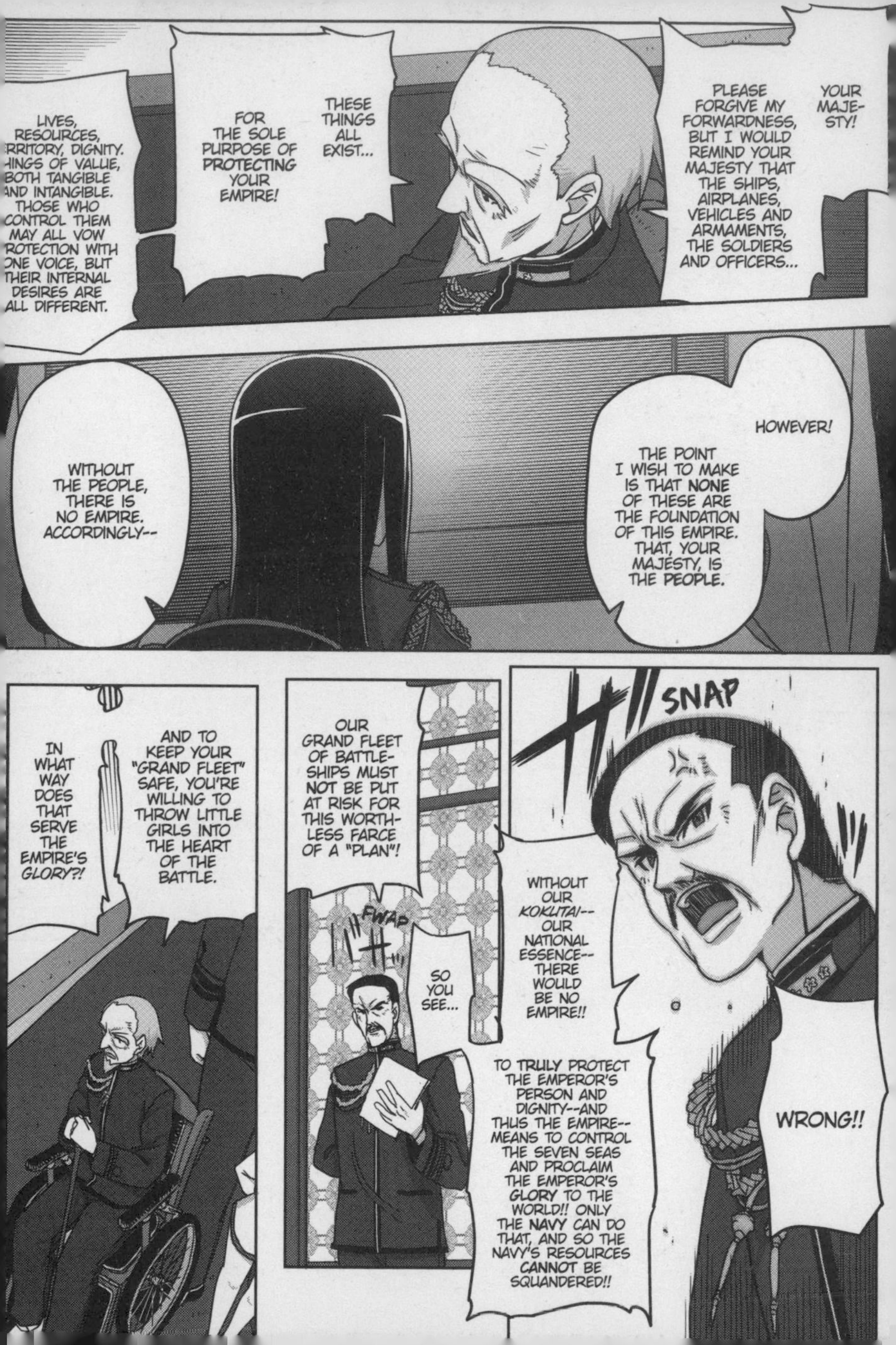
YOUR MAJE-STY!
PLEASE FORGIVE MY FORWARDNESS, BUT I WOULD REMIND YOUR MAJESTY THAT THE SHIPS, AIRPLANES, VEHICLES AND ARMAMENTS, THE SOLDIERS AND OFFICERS...
THESE THINGS ALL EXIST...
FOR THE SOLE PURPOSE OF PROTECTING YOUR EMPIRE!
LIVES, RESOURCES, RRITORY, DIGNITY. HINGS OF VALUE, BOTH TANGIBLE AND INTANGIBLE. THOSE WHO CONTROL THEM MAY ALL VOW ROTECTION WITH ONE VOICE, BUT THEIR INTERNAL DESIRES ARE ALL DIFFERENT.
HOWEVER!
THE POINT I WISH TO MAKE IS THAT NONE OF THESE ARE THE FOUNDATION OF THIS EMPIRE. THAT, YOUR MAJESTY, IS THE PEOPLE.
WITHOUT THE PEOPLE, THERE IS NO EMPIRE. ACCORDINGLY--
SNAP
WRONG!!
WITHOUT OUR *KOKUTAI*-- OUR NATIONAL ESSENCE-- THERE WOULD BE NO EMPIRE!!
TO TRULY PROTECT THE EMPEROR'S PERSON AND DIGNITY--AND THUS THE EMPIRE-- MEANS TO CONTROL THE SEVEN SEAS AND PROCLAIM THE EMPEROR'S GLORY TO THE WORLD!! ONLY THE NAVY CAN DO THAT, AND SO THE NAVY'S RESOURCES CANNOT BE SQUANDERED!!
OUR GRAND FLEET OF BATTLE-SHIPS MUST NOT BE PUT AT RISK FOR THIS WORTH-LESS FARCE OF A "PLAN"!
FWAP
SO YOU SEE...
AND TO KEEP YOUR "GRAND FLEET" SAFE, YOU'RE WILLING TO THROW LITTLE GIRLS INTO THE HEART OF THE BATTLE.
IN WHAT WAY DOES THAT SERVE THE EMPIRE'S *GLORY*?!

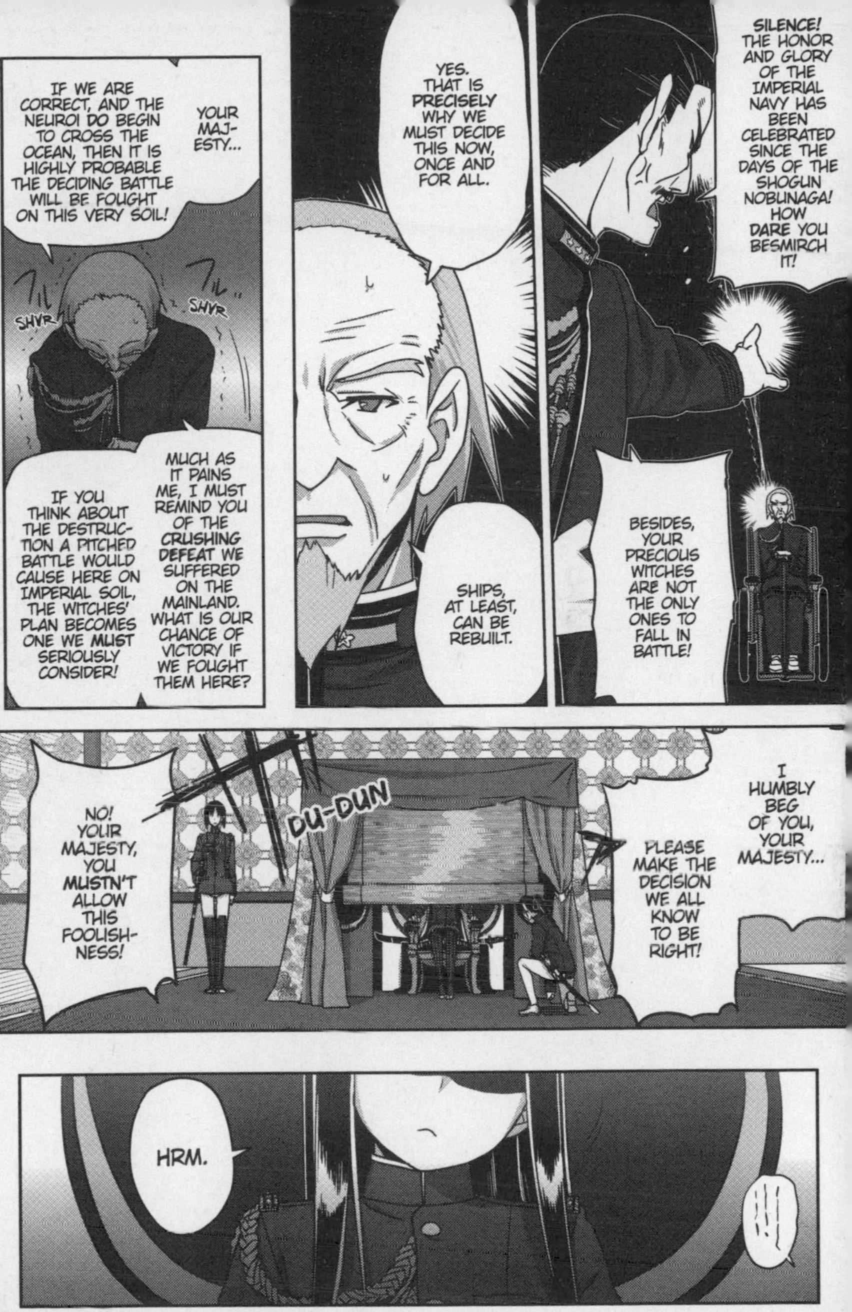
SILENCE! THE HONOR AND GLORY OF THE IMPERIAL NAVY HAS BEEN CELEBRATED SINCE THE DAYS OF THE SHOGUN NOBUNAGA! HOW DARE YOU BESMIRCH IT!
BESIDES, YOUR PRECIOUS WITCHES ARE NOT THE ONLY ONES TO FALL IN BATTLE!
YES. THAT IS PRECISELY WHY WE MUST DECIDE THIS NOW, ONCE AND FOR ALL.
SHIPS, AT LEAST, CAN BE REBUILT.
YOUR MAJ-ESTY...
IF WE ARE CORRECT, AND THE NEUROI DO BEGIN TO CROSS THE OCEAN, THEN IT IS HIGHLY PROBABLE THE DECIDING BATTLE WILL BE FOUGHT ON THIS VERY SOIL!
SHVR
SHVR
MUCH AS IT PAINS ME, I MUST REMIND YOU OF THE CRUSHING DEFEAT WE SUFFERED ON THE MAINLAND. WHAT IS OUR CHANCE OF VICTORY IF WE FOUGHT THEM HERE?
IF YOU THINK ABOUT THE DESTRUC-TION A PITCHED BATTLE WOULD CAUSE HERE ON IMPERIAL SOIL, THE WITCHES' PLAN BECOMES ONE WE MUST SERIOUSLY CONSIDER!
I HUMBLY BEG OF YOU, YOUR MAJESTY...
PLEASE MAKE THE DECISION WE ALL KNOW TO BE RIGHT!
DU-DUN
NO! YOUR MAJESTY, YOU MUSTN'T ALLOW THIS FOOLISH-NESS!
!!
HRM.

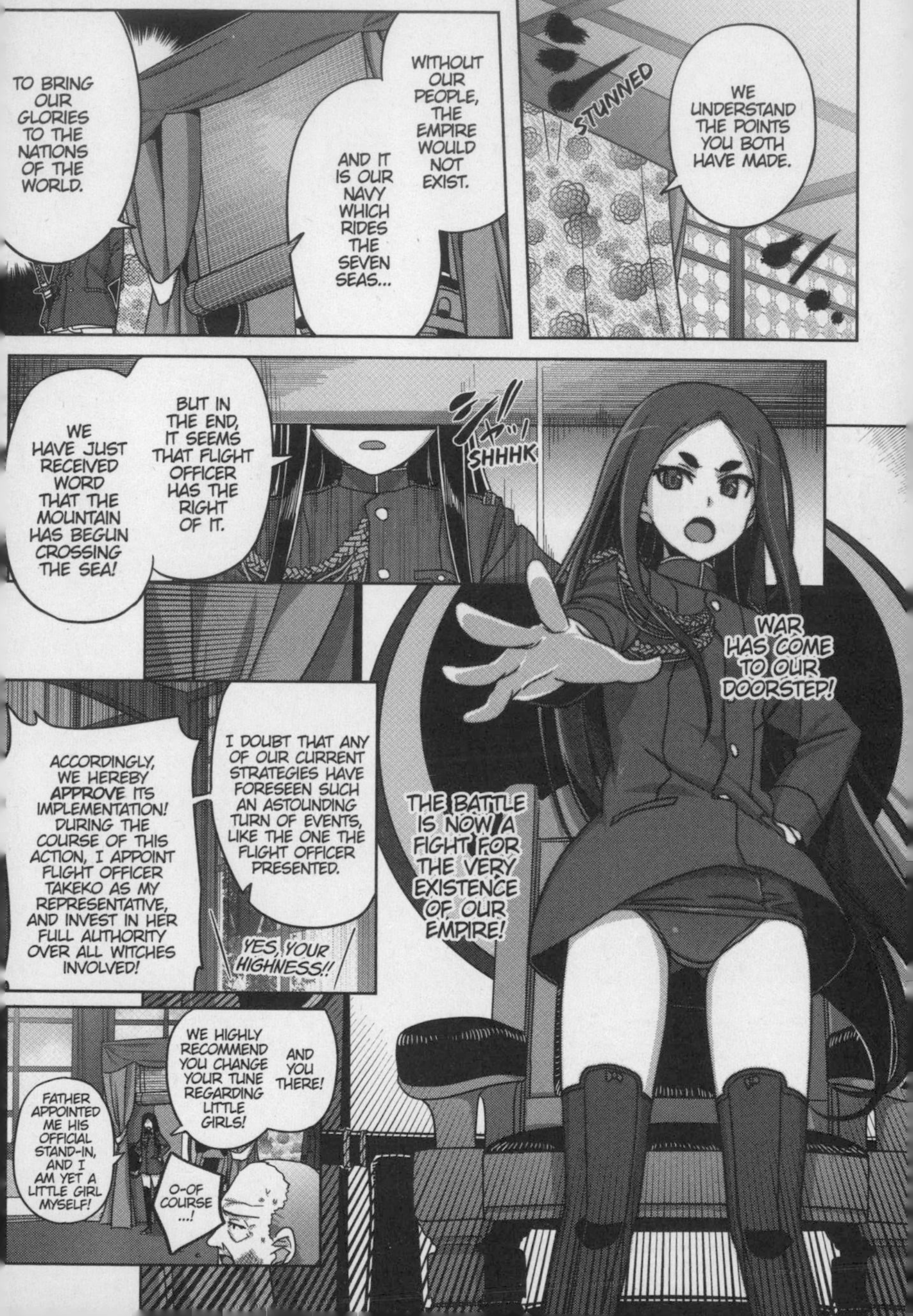
STUNNED
WE UNDERSTAND THE POINTS YOU BOTH HAVE MADE.
WITHOUT OUR PEOPLE, THE EMPIRE WOULD NOT EXIST.
AND IT IS OUR NAVY WHICH RIDES THE SEVEN SEAS...
TO BRING OUR GLORIES TO THE NATIONS OF THE WORLD.
WAR HAS COME TO OUR DOORSTEP!
THE BATTLE IS NOW A FIGHT FOR THE VERY EXISTENCE OF OUR EMPIRE!
SHHHK
BUT IN THE END, IT SEEMS THAT FLIGHT OFFICER HAS THE RIGHT OF IT.
WE HAVE JUST RECEIVED WORD THAT THE MOUNTAIN HAS BEGUN CROSSING THE SEA!
I DOUBT THAT ANY OF OUR CURRENT STRATEGIES HAVE FORESEEN SUCH AN ASTOUNDING TURN OF EVENTS, LIKE THE ONE THE FLIGHT OFFICER PRESENTED.
ACCORDINGLY, WE HEREBY **APPROVE** ITS IMPLEMENTATION! DURING THE COURSE OF THIS ACTION, I APPOINT FLIGHT OFFICER TAKEKO AS MY REPRESENTATIVE, AND INVEST IN HER FULL AUTHORITY OVER ALL WITCHES INVOLVED!
YES, YOUR HIGHNESS!!
AND YOU THERE!
WE HIGHLY RECOMMEND YOU CHANGE YOUR TUNE REGARDING LITTLE GIRLS!
FATHER APPOINTED ME HIS OFFICIAL STAND-IN, AND I AM YET A LITTLE GIRL MYSELF!
O-OF COURSE ...!

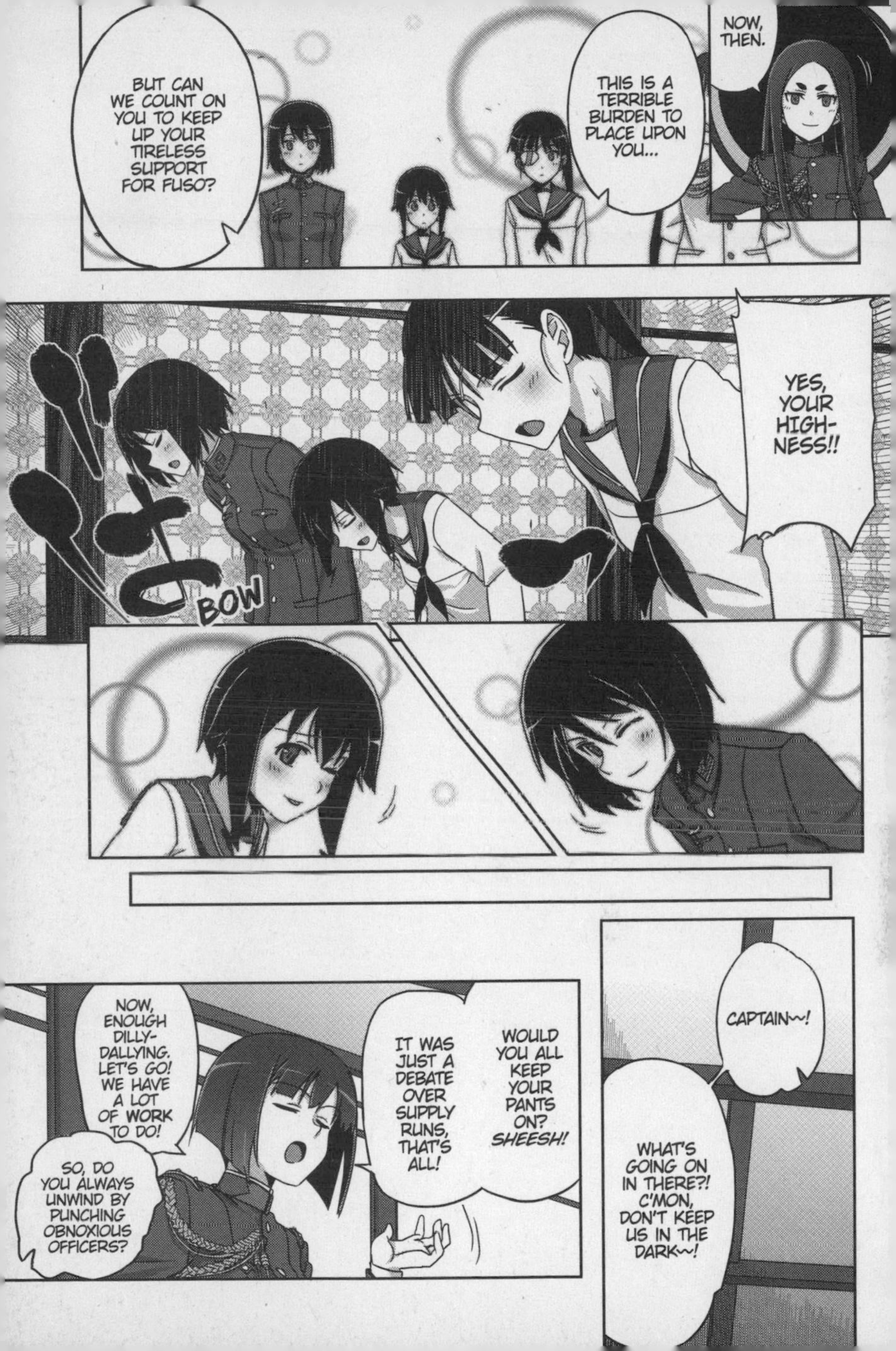
NOW, THEN.
THIS IS A TERRIBLE BURDEN TO PLACE UPON YOU...
BUT CAN WE COUNT ON YOU TO KEEP UP YOUR TIRELESS SUPPORT FOR FUSO?
YES, YOUR HIGH-NESS!!
BOW
CAPTAIN~!
WHAT'S GOING ON IN THERE?! C'MON, DON'T KEEP US IN THE DARK~!
WOULD YOU ALL KEEP YOUR PANTS ON? SHEESH!
IT WAS JUST A DEBATE OVER SUPPLY RUNS, THAT'S ALL!
NOW, ENOUGH DILLY-DALLYING. LET'S GO! WE HAVE A LOT OF WORK TO DO!
SO, DO YOU ALWAYS UNWIND BY PUNCHING OBNOXIOUS OFFICERS?

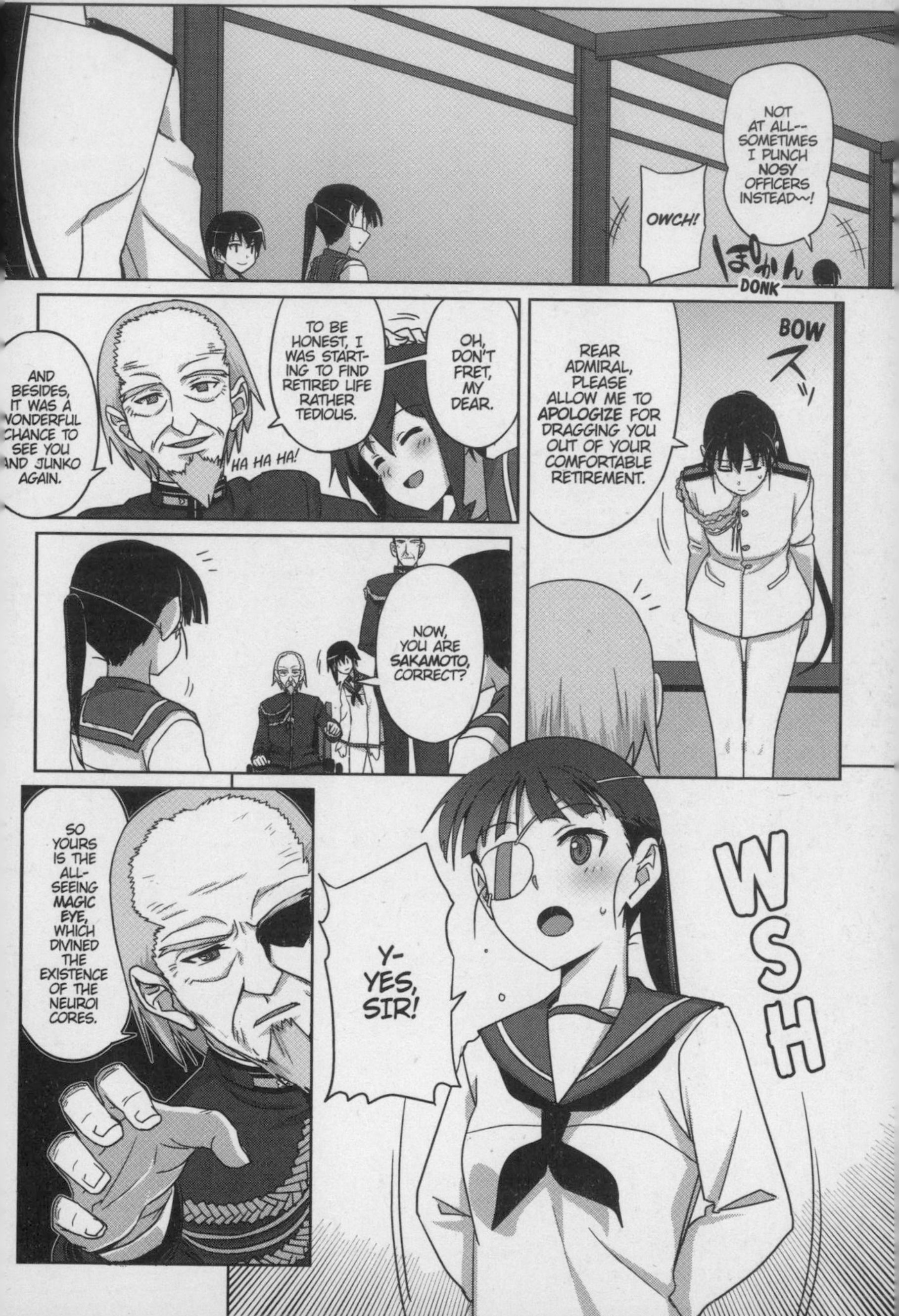
NOT AT ALL-- SOMETIMES I PUNCH NOSY OFFICERS INSTEAD~!
OWCH!
ぽかん
DONK
BOW
スッ
REAR ADMIRAL, PLEASE ALLOW ME TO APOLOGIZE FOR DRAGGING YOU OUT OF YOUR COMFORTABLE RETIREMENT.
OH, DON'T FRET, MY DEAR.
TO BE HONEST, I WAS STARTING TO FIND RETIRED LIFE RATHER TEDIOUS.
HA HA HA!
AND BESIDES, IT WAS A WONDERFUL CHANCE TO SEE YOU AND JUNKO AGAIN.
NOW, YOU ARE SAKAMOTO, CORRECT?
WSH
Y-YES, SIR!
SO YOURS IS THE ALL-SEEING MAGIC EYE, WHICH DIVINED THE EXISTENCE OF THE NEUROI CORES.

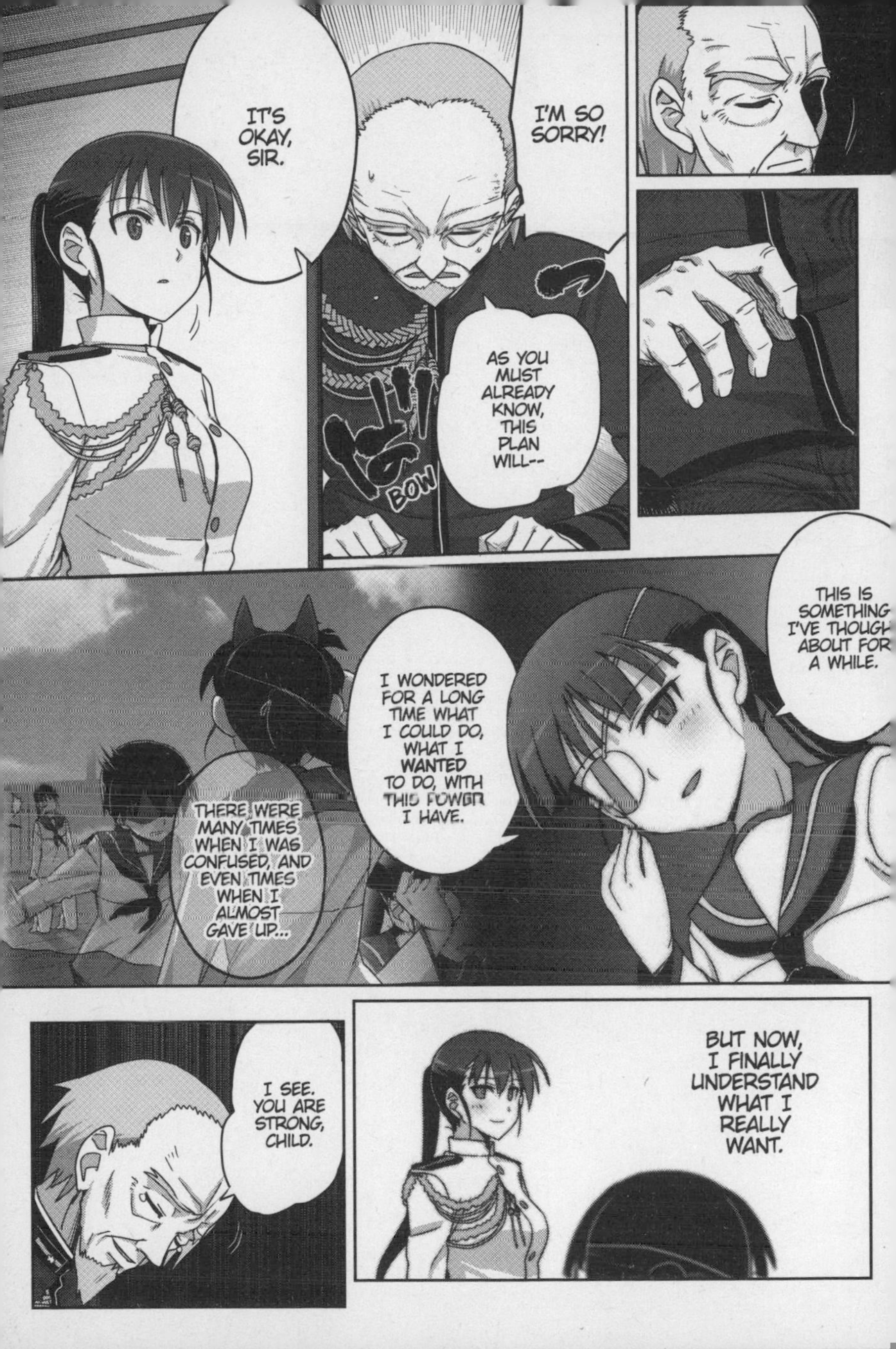
I'M SO SORRY!
AS YOU MUST ALREADY KNOW, THIS PLAN WILL--
BOW
IT'S OKAY, SIR.
THIS IS SOMETHING I'VE THOUGH ABOUT FOR A WHILE.
I WONDERED FOR A LONG TIME WHAT I COULD DO, WHAT I WANTED TO DO, WITH THIS POWER I HAVE.
THERE WERE MANY TIMES WHEN I WAS CONFUSED, AND EVEN TIMES WHEN I ALMOST GAVE UP...
BUT NOW, I FINALLY UNDERSTAND WHAT I REALLY WANT.
I SEE. YOU ARE STRONG, CHILD.

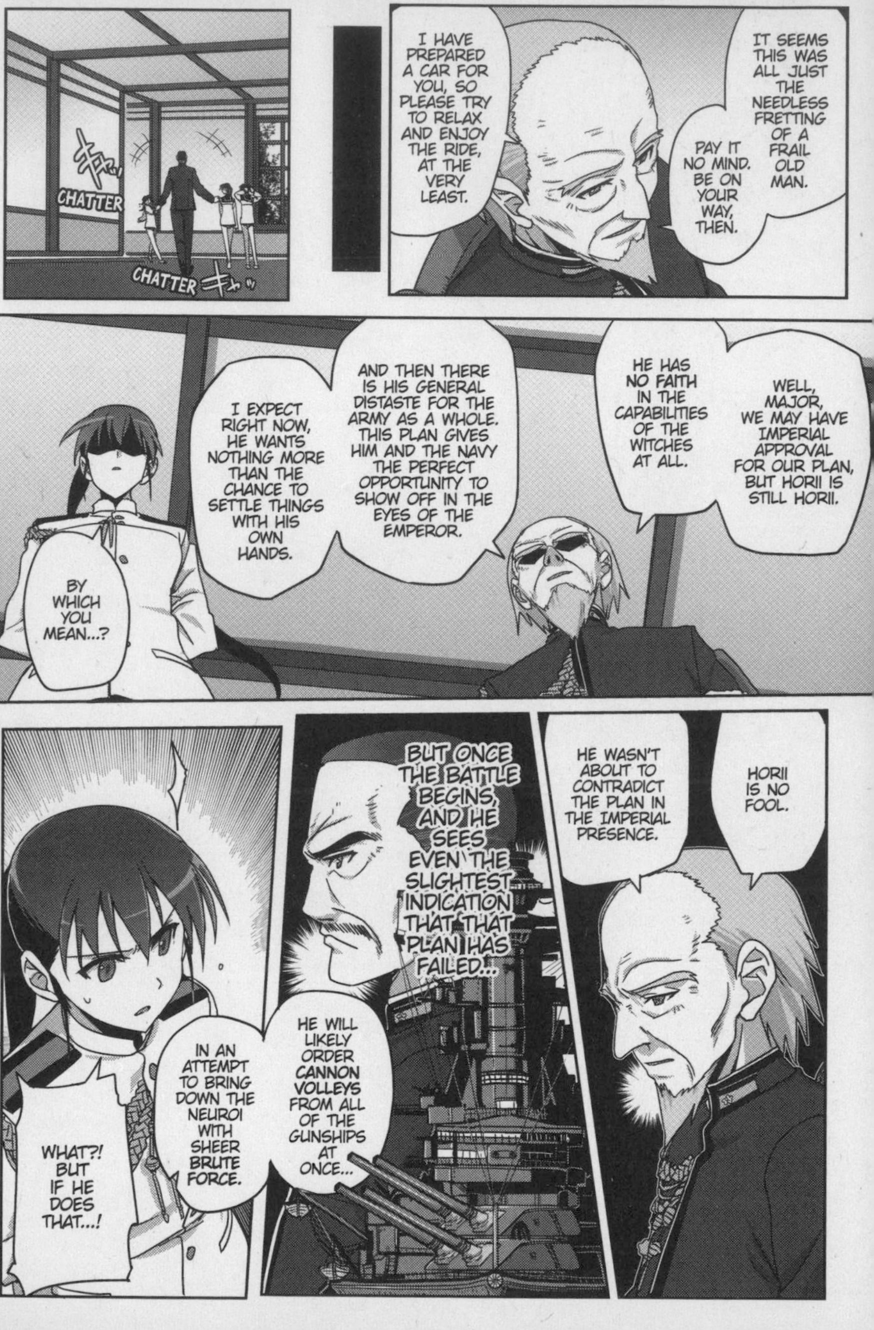

IT SEEMS THIS WAS ALL JUST THE NEEDLESS FRETTING OF A FRAIL OLD MAN.
PAY IT NO MIND. BE ON YOUR WAY, THEN.
I HAVE PREPARED A CAR FOR YOU, SO PLEASE TRY TO RELAX AND ENJOY THE RIDE, AT THE VERY LEAST.
CHATTER
CHATTER
WELL, MAJOR, WE MAY HAVE IMPERIAL APPROVAL FOR OUR PLAN, BUT HORII IS STILL HORII.
HE HAS NO FAITH IN THE CAPABILITIES OF THE WITCHES AT ALL.
AND THEN THERE IS HIS GENERAL DISTASTE FOR THE ARMY AS A WHOLE. THIS PLAN GIVES HIM AND THE NAVY THE PERFECT OPPORTUNITY TO SHOW OFF IN THE EYES OF THE EMPEROR.
I EXPECT RIGHT NOW, HE WANTS NOTHING MORE THAN THE CHANCE TO SETTLE THINGS WITH HIS OWN HANDS.
BY WHICH YOU MEAN...?
HORII IS NO FOOL.
HE WASN'T ABOUT TO CONTRADICT THE PLAN IN THE IMPERIAL PRESENCE.
BUT ONCE THE BATTLE BEGINS, AND HE SEES EVEN THE SLIGHTEST INDICATION THAT THAT PLAN HAS FAILED...
HE WILL LIKELY ORDER CANNON VOLLEYS FROM ALL OF THE GUNSHIPS AT ONCE...
IN AN ATTEMPT TO BRING DOWN THE NEUROI WITH SHEER BRUTE FORCE.
WHAT?! BUT IF HE DOES THAT...!

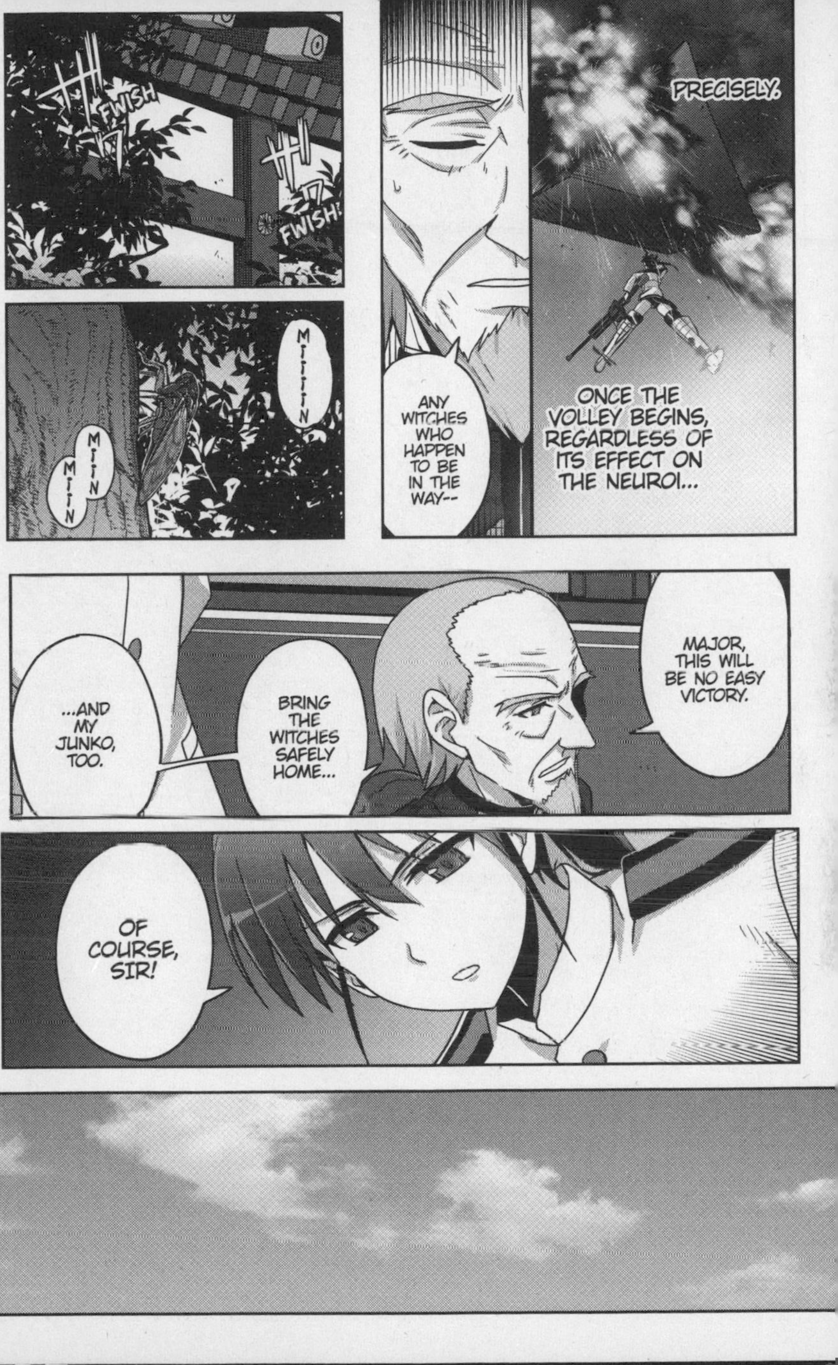
PRECISELY.
ONCE THE VOLLEY BEGINS, REGARDLESS OF ITS EFFECT ON THE NEUROI...
ANY WITCHES WHO HAPPEN TO BE IN THE WAY--
FWISH
FWISH!
MIIIIIIN
MIIN
MIIN
MAJOR, THIS WILL BE NO EASY VICTORY.
BRING THE WITCHES SAFELY HOME...
...AND MY JUNKO, TOO.
OF COURSE, SIR!

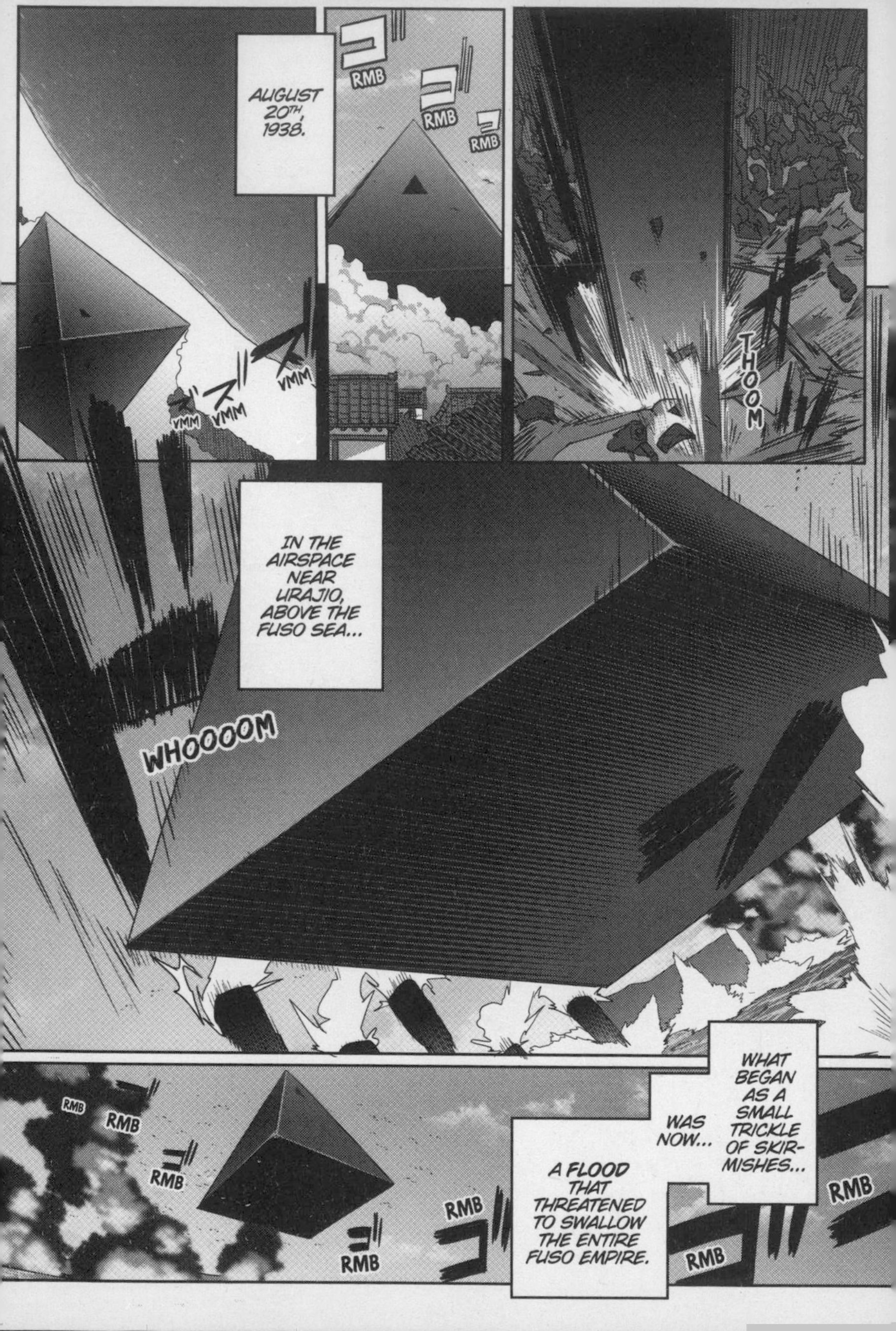

THOOM
RMB
RMB
RMB
AUGUST 20TH, 1938.
VMM
VMM
VMM
IN THE AIRSPACE NEAR URAJIO, ABOVE THE FUSO SEA...
WHOOOOM
RMB
WHAT BEGAN AS A SMALL TRICKLE OF SKIR-MISHES...
WAS NOW...
A FLOOD THAT THREATENED TO SWALLOW THE ENTIRE FUSO EMPIRE.
RMB
RMB
RMB
RMB
RMB
RMB
RMB

Chapter 9:
The Conference
[Mission Complete]

CHAPTER 10:
THE FUSO SEA INCIDENT

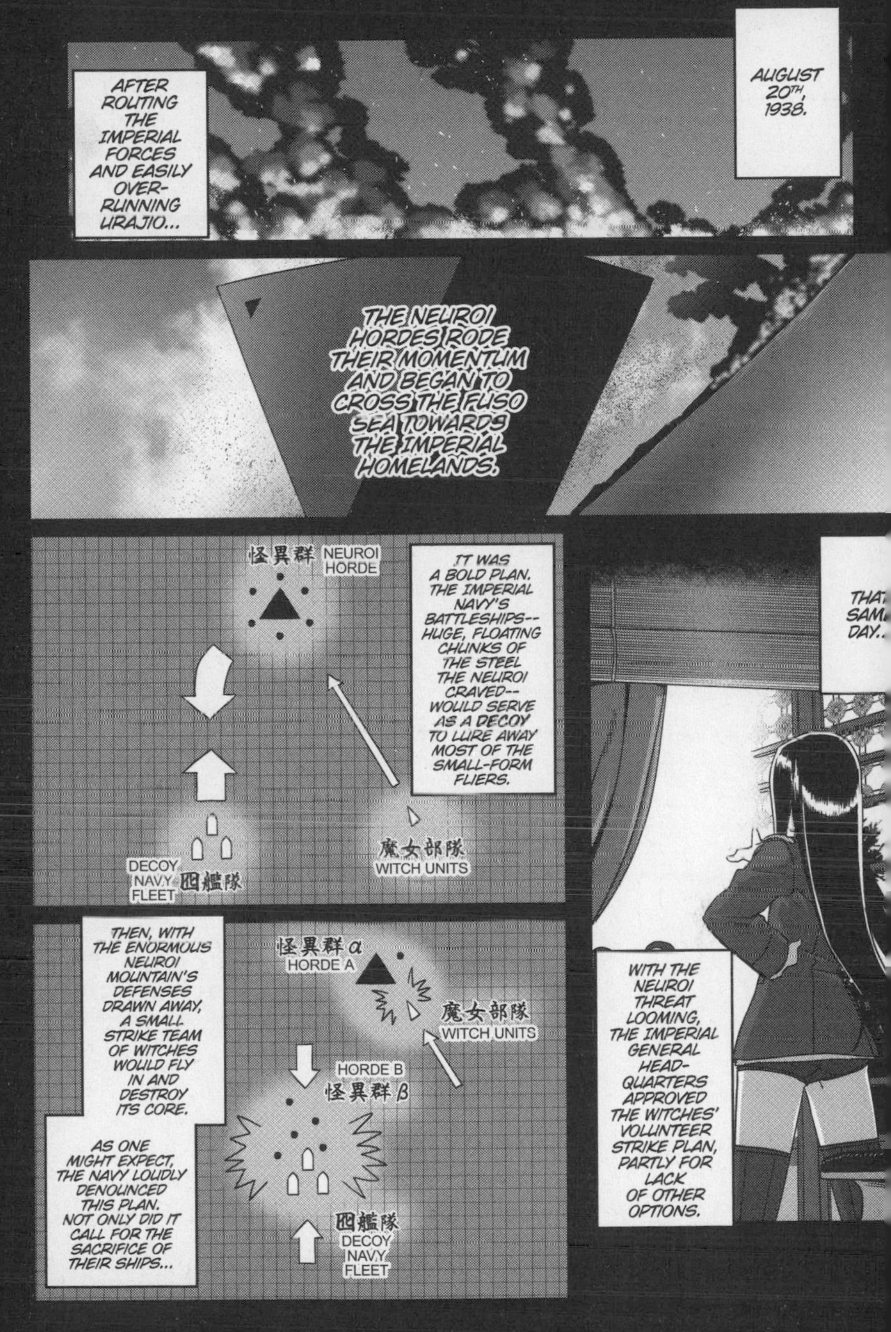
AUGUST 20TH, 1938.
AFTER ROUTING THE IMPERIAL FORCES AND EASILY OVER-RUNNING URAJIO...
THE NEUROI HORDES RODE THEIR MOMENTUM AND BEGAN TO CROSS THE FUSO SEA TOWARDS THE IMPERIAL HOMELANDS.
THAT SAME DAY...
WITH THE NEUROI THREAT LOOMING, THE IMPERIAL GENERAL HEAD-QUARTERS APPROVED THE WITCHES' VOLUNTEER STRIKE PLAN, PARTLY FOR LACK OF OTHER OPTIONS.
IT WAS A BOLD PLAN. THE IMPERIAL NAVY'S BATTLESHIPS--HUGE, FLOATING CHUNKS OF THE STEEL THE NEUROI CRAVED--WOULD SERVE AS A DECOY TO LURE AWAY MOST OF THE SMALL-FORM FLIERS.
怪異群 NEUROI HORDE
魔女部隊 WITCH UNITS
DECOY NAVY FLEET 囮艦隊
THEN, WITH THE ENORMOUS NEUROI MOUNTAIN'S DEFENSES DRAWN AWAY, A SMALL STRIKE TEAM OF WITCHES WOULD FLY IN AND DESTROY ITS CORE.
怪異群 α HORDE A
魔女部隊 WITCH UNITS
HORDE B 怪異群 β
囮艦隊 DECOY NAVY FLEET
AS ONE MIGHT EXPECT, THE NAVY LOUDLY DENOUNCED THIS PLAN. NOT ONLY DID IT CALL FOR THE SACRIFICE OF THEIR SHIPS...

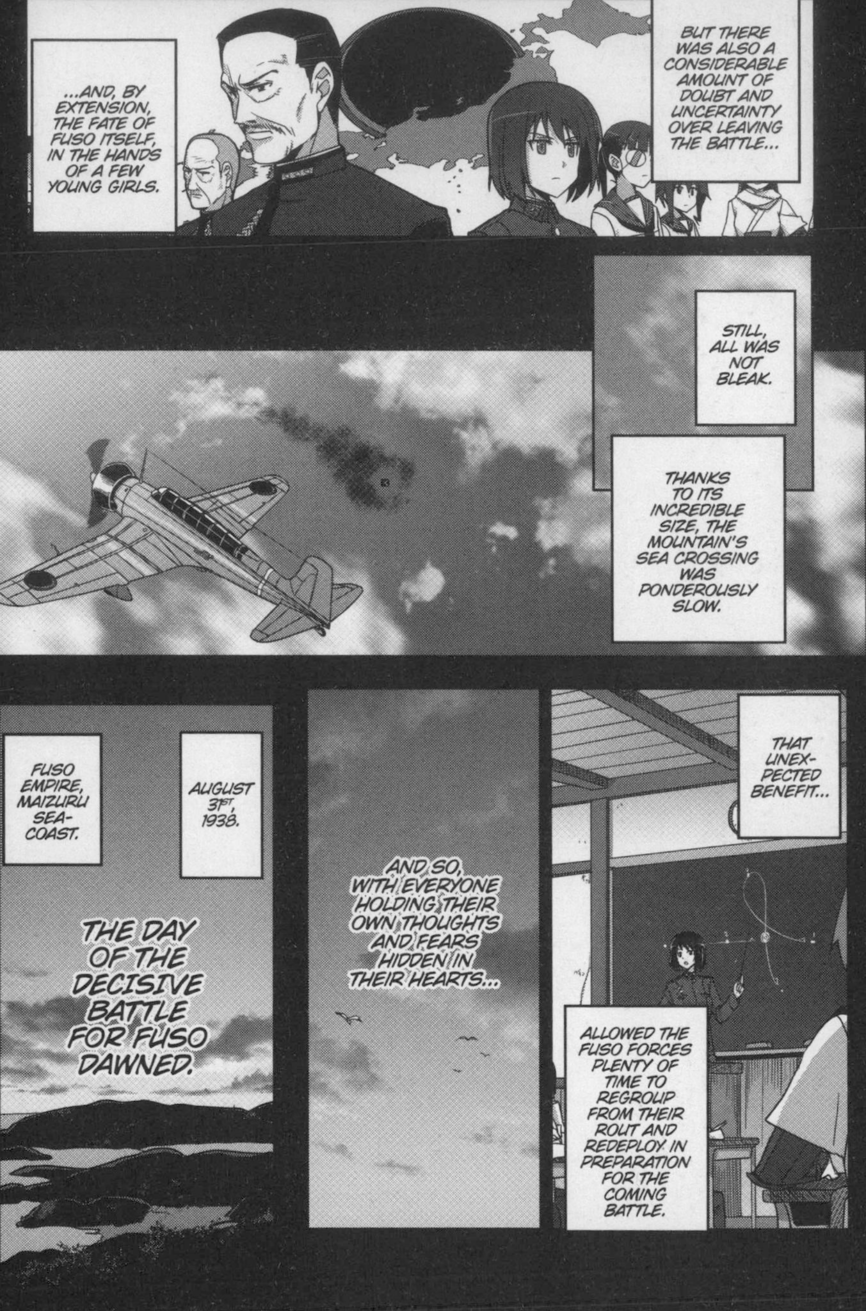
BUT THERE WAS ALSO A CONSIDERABLE AMOUNT OF DOUBT AND UNCERTAINTY OVER LEAVING THE BATTLE...
...AND, BY EXTENSION, THE FATE OF FUSO ITSELF, IN THE HANDS OF A FEW YOUNG GIRLS.
STILL, ALL WAS NOT BLEAK.
THANKS TO ITS INCREDIBLE SIZE, THE MOUNTAIN'S SEA CROSSING WAS PONDEROUSLY SLOW.
THAT UNEX-PECTED BENEFIT...
ALLOWED THE FUSO FORCES PLENTY OF TIME TO REGROUP FROM THEIR ROUT AND REDEPLOY IN PREPARATION FOR THE COMING BATTLE.
AND SO, WITH EVERYONE HOLDING THEIR OWN THOUGHTS AND FEARS HIDDEN IN THEIR HEARTS...
AUGUST 31ST, 1938.
FUSO EMPIRE, MAIZURU SEA-COAST.
THE DAY OF THE DECISIVE BATTLE FOR FUSO DAWNED.

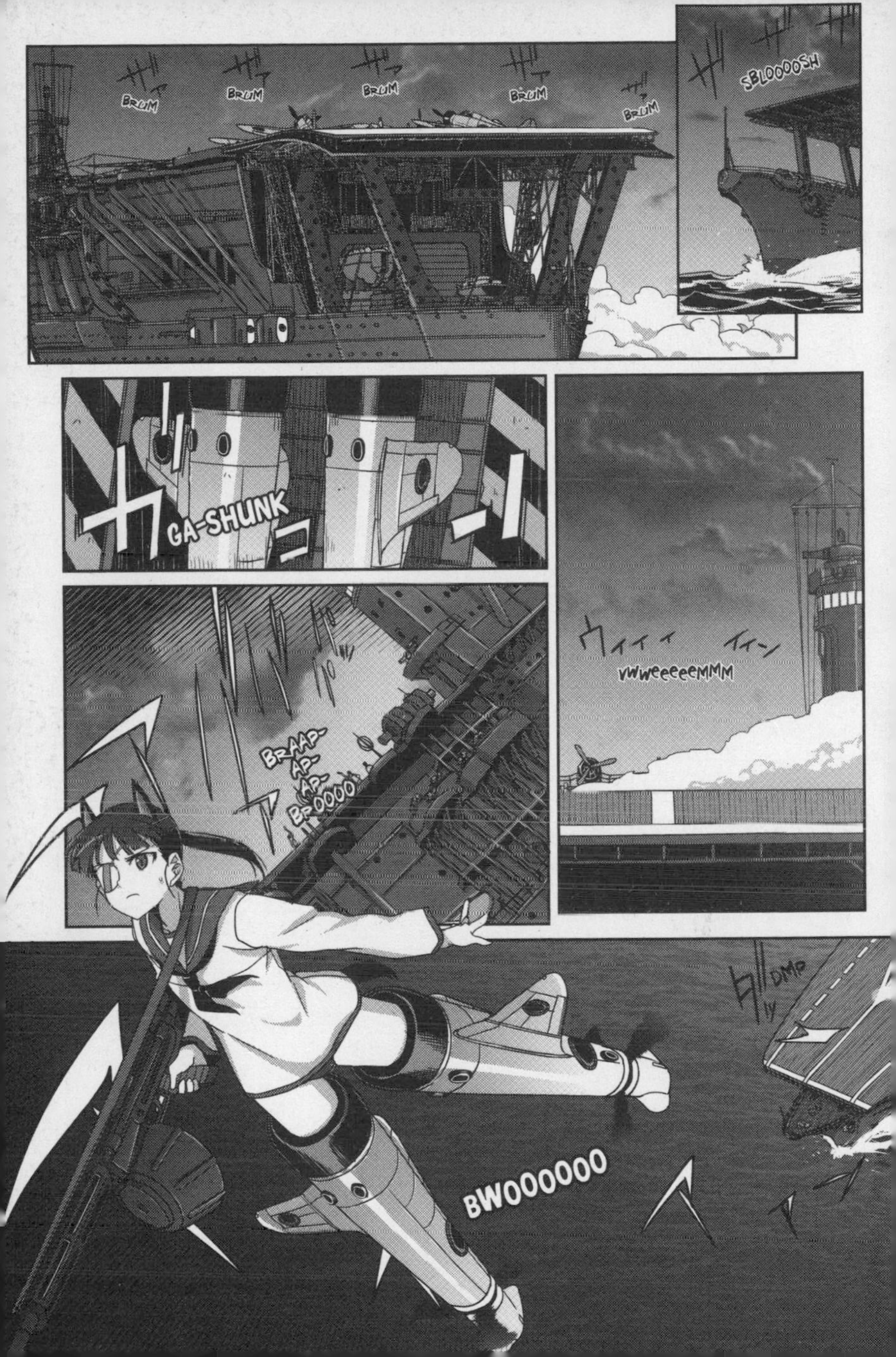
SBLOOOOSH
BRUM
BRUM
BRUM
BRUM
BRUM
vwweeeeeMMM
GA-SHUNK
BRAAP-AP-AP-BROOOO
DMP
BWOOOOOO

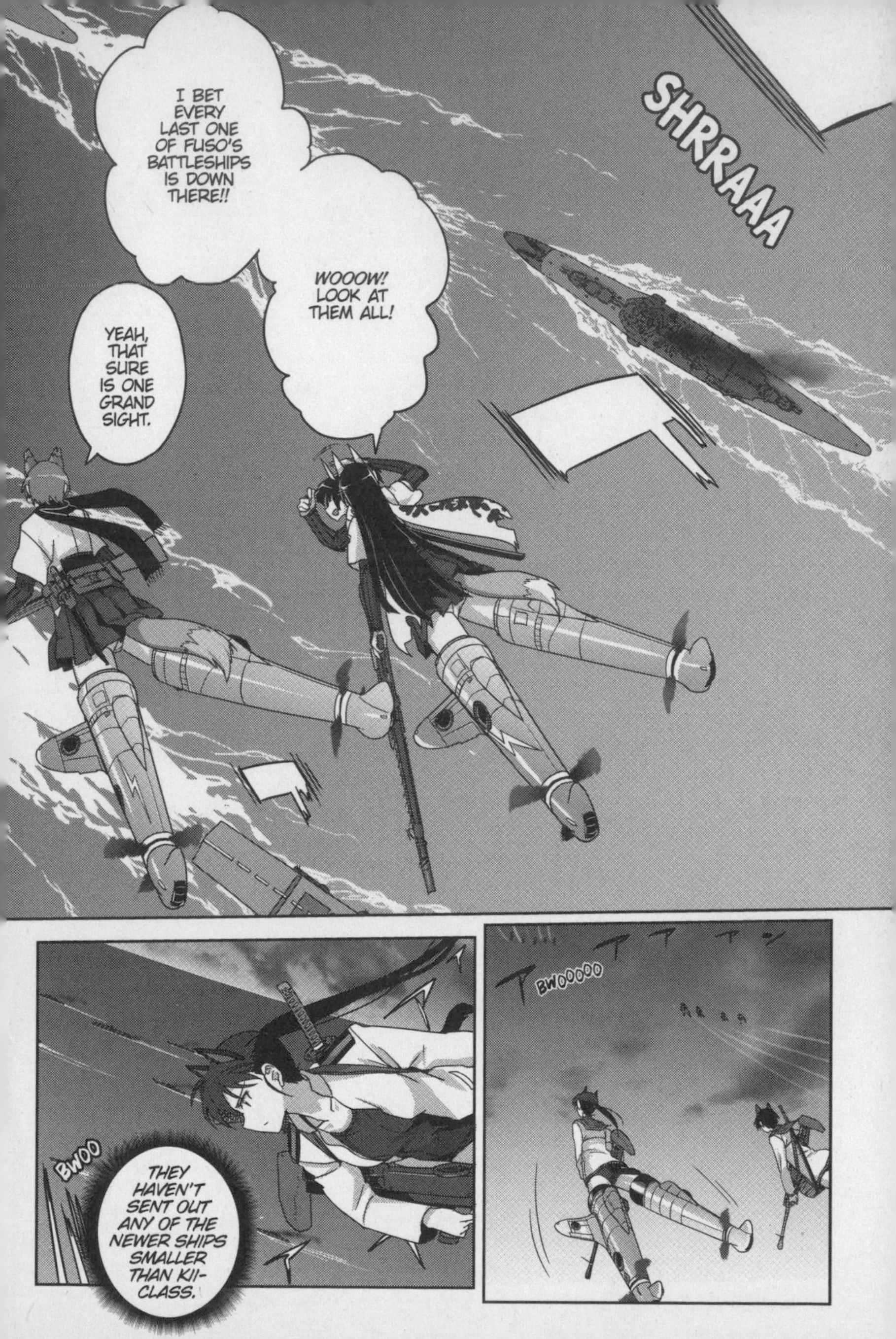
SHRRAAA
WOOOW! LOOK AT THEM ALL!
I BET EVERY LAST ONE OF FUSO'S BATTLESHIPS IS DOWN THERE!!
YEAH, THAT SURE IS ONE GRAND SIGHT.
BWOOOOO
BWOO
THEY HAVEN'T SENT OUT ANY OF THE NEWER SHIPS SMALLER THAN KII-CLASS.

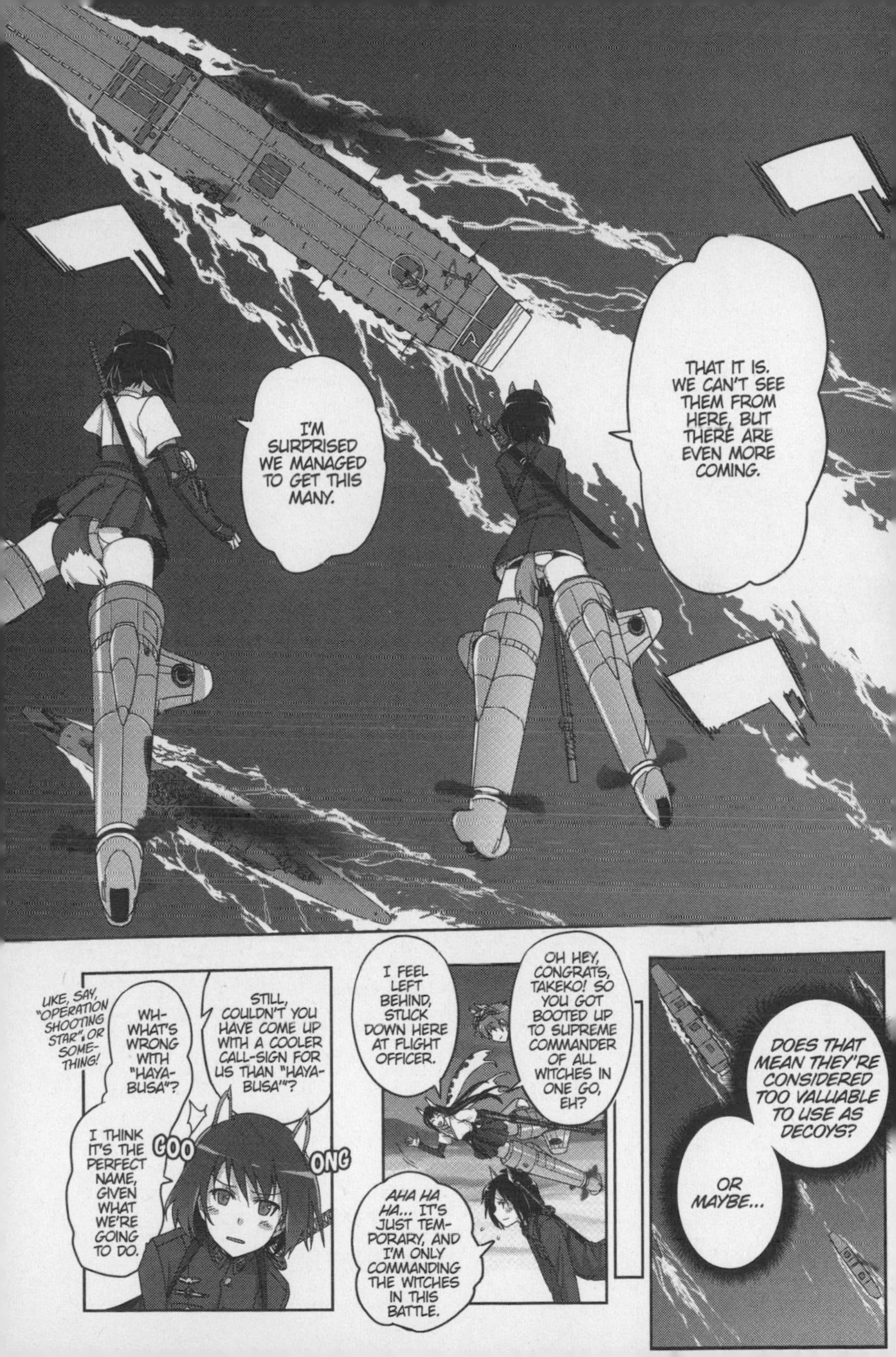
THAT IT IS. WE CAN'T SEE THEM FROM HERE, BUT THERE ARE EVEN MORE COMING.
I'M SURPRISED WE MANAGED TO GET THIS MANY.
DOES THAT MEAN THEY'RE CONSIDERED TOO VALUABLE TO USE AS DECOYS?
OR MAYBE...
OH HEY, CONGRATS, TAKEKO! SO YOU GOT BOOTED UP TO SUPREME COMMANDER OF ALL WITCHES IN ONE GO, EH?
I FEEL LEFT BEHIND, STUCK DOWN HERE AT FLIGHT OFFICER.
AHA HA HA... IT'S JUST TEMPORARY, AND I'M ONLY COMMANDING THE WITCHES IN THIS BATTLE.
STILL, COULDN'T YOU HAVE COME UP WITH A COOLER CALL-SIGN FOR US THAN "HAYABUSA"?
WH-WHAT'S WRONG WITH "HAYABUSA"?
LIKE, SAY, "OPERATION SHOOTING STAR", OR SOMETHING!
GOO
ONG
I THINK IT'S THE PERFECT NAME, GIVEN WHAT WE'RE GOING TO DO.

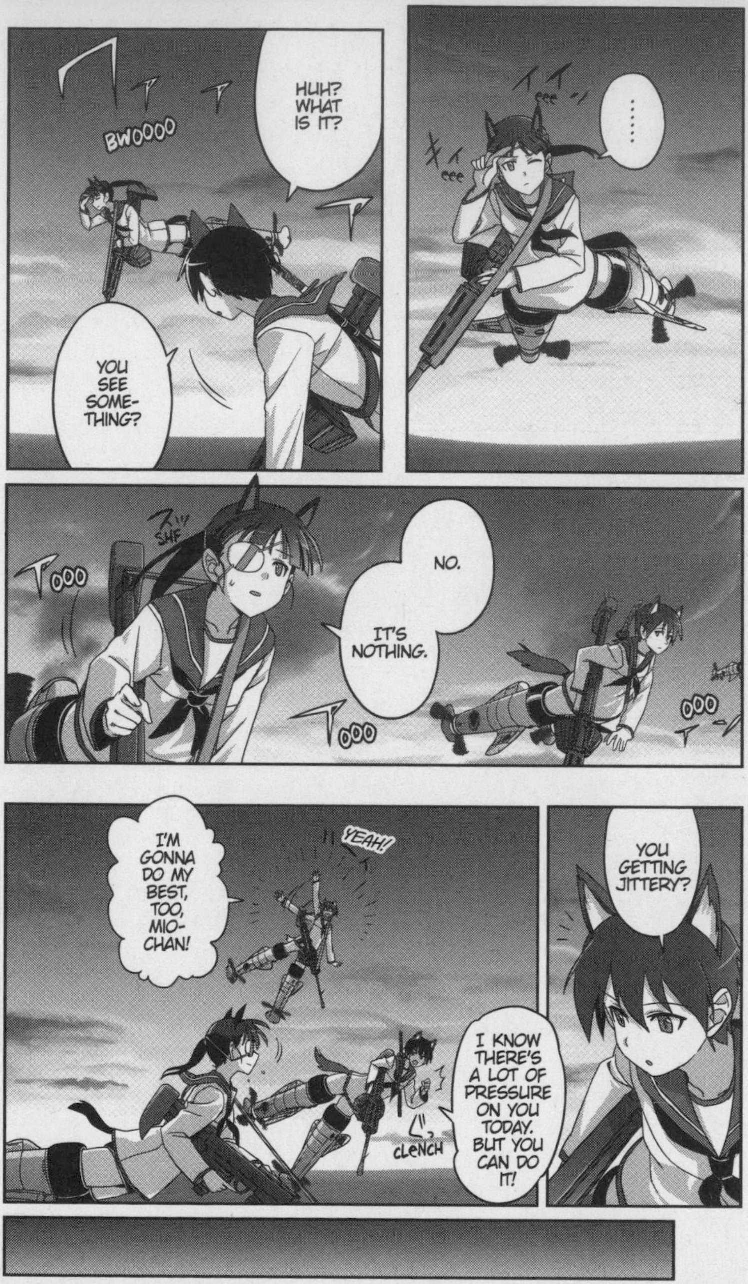
eee
......
eee
HUH? WHAT IS IT?
BWOOOO
YOU SEE SOMETHING?
OOO
NO.
IT'S NOTHING.
SHF
OOO
OOO
YOU GETTING JITTERY?
I KNOW THERE'S A LOT OF PRESSURE ON YOU TODAY. BUT YOU CAN DO IT!
YEAH!
I'M GONNA DO MY BEST, TOO, MIO-CHAN!
CLENCH

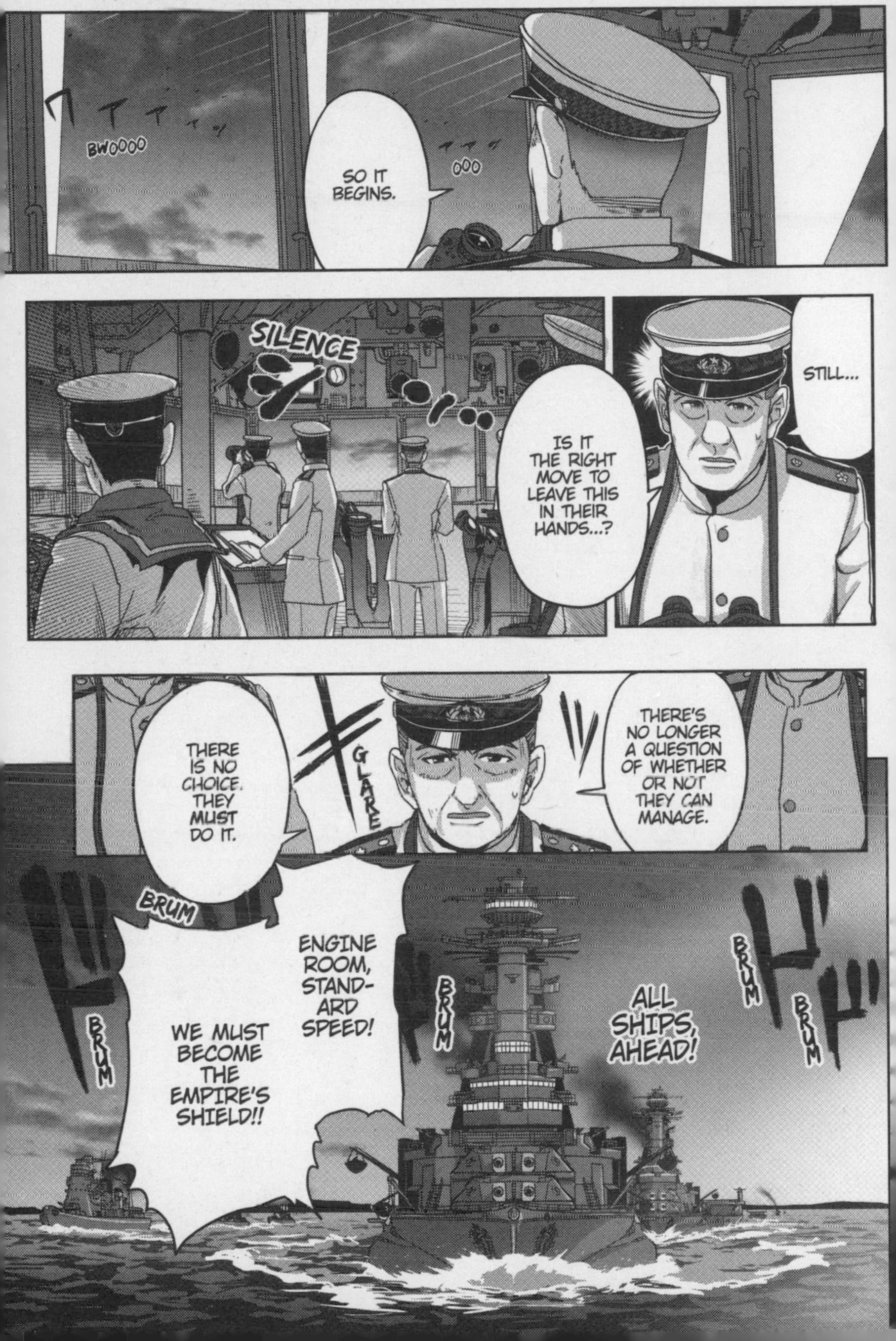
OOO
SO IT BEGINS.
BWOOOO
STILL...
IS IT THE RIGHT MOVE TO LEAVE THIS IN THEIR HANDS...?
SILENCE
THERE'S NO LONGER A QUESTION OF WHETHER OR NOT THEY CAN MANAGE.
GLARE
THERE IS NO CHOICE. THEY MUST DO IT.
BRUM
BRUM
ALL SHIPS, AHEAD!
BRUM
ENGINE ROOM, STAND-ARD SPEED!
WE MUST BECOME THE EMPIRE'S SHIELD!!
BRUM
BRUM

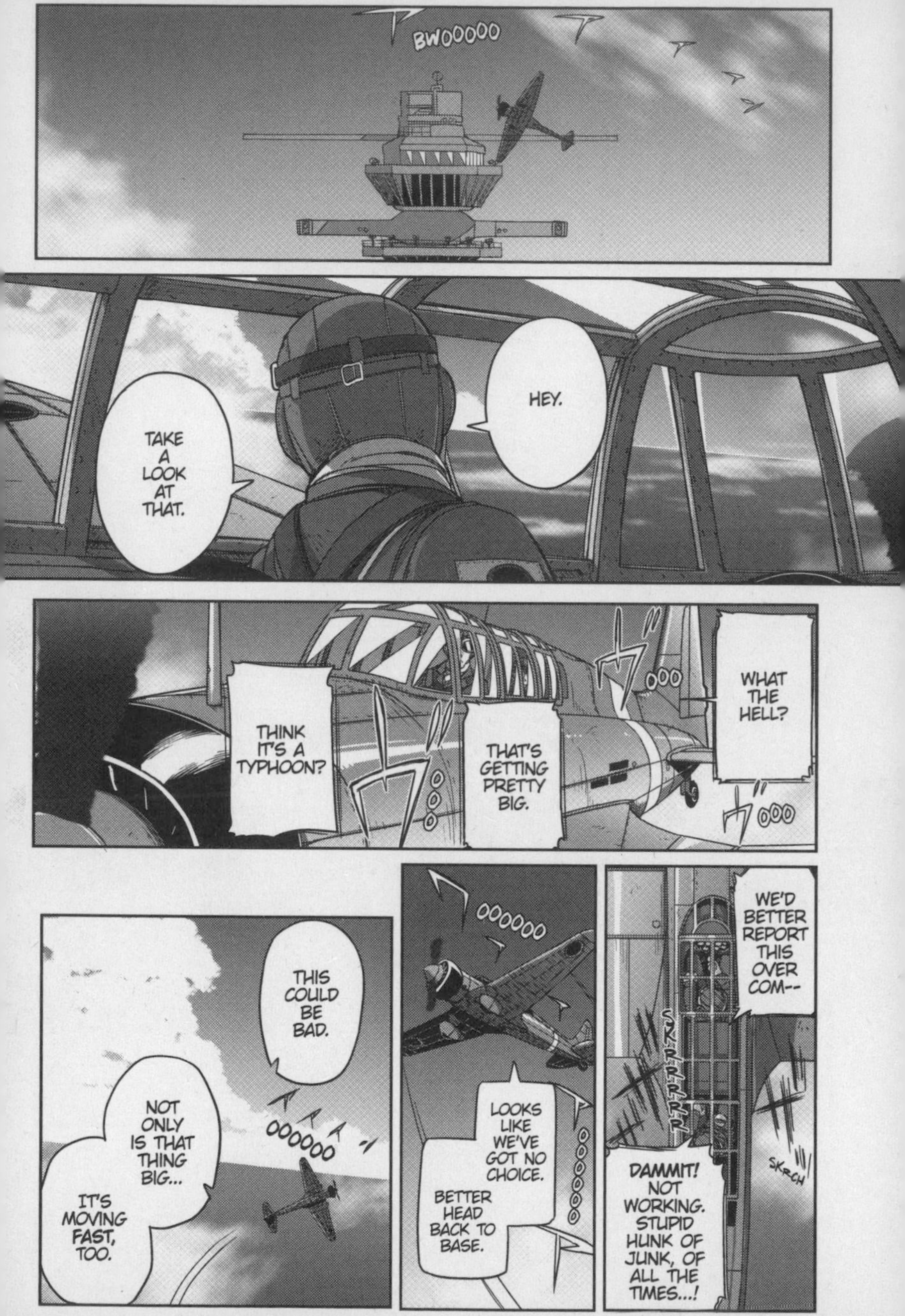
BWOOOOO
HEY.
TAKE A LOOK AT THAT.
WHAT THE HELL?
OOO
OOO
THAT'S GETTING PRETTY BIG.
THINK IT'S A TYPHOON?
OOO
WE'D BETTER REPORT THIS OVER COM--
SKRRRRRRR
SKRCH
DAMMIT! NOT WORKING. STUPID HUNK OF JUNK, OF ALL THE TIMES...!
OOOOOO
LOOKS LIKE WE'VE GOT NO CHOICE.
BETTER HEAD BACK TO BASE.
OOOOOOO
THIS COULD BE BAD.
NOT ONLY IS THAT THING BIG...
IT'S MOVING FAST, TOO.
OOOOOO

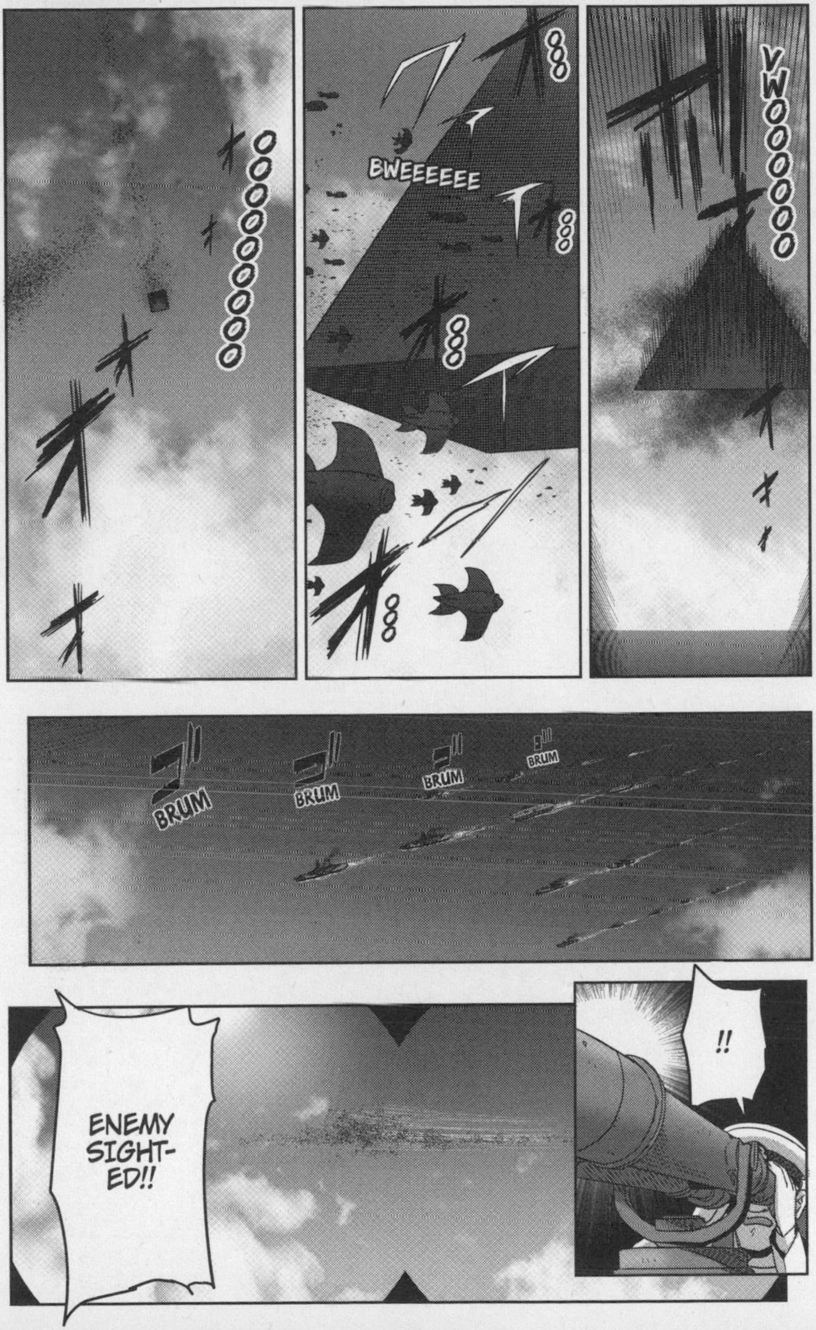
VWOOOOOO
OOO
BWEEEEEE
OOO
OOO
OOO
OOOOOOOOO
BRUM
BRUM
BRUM
BRUM
!!
ENEMY SIGHTED!!

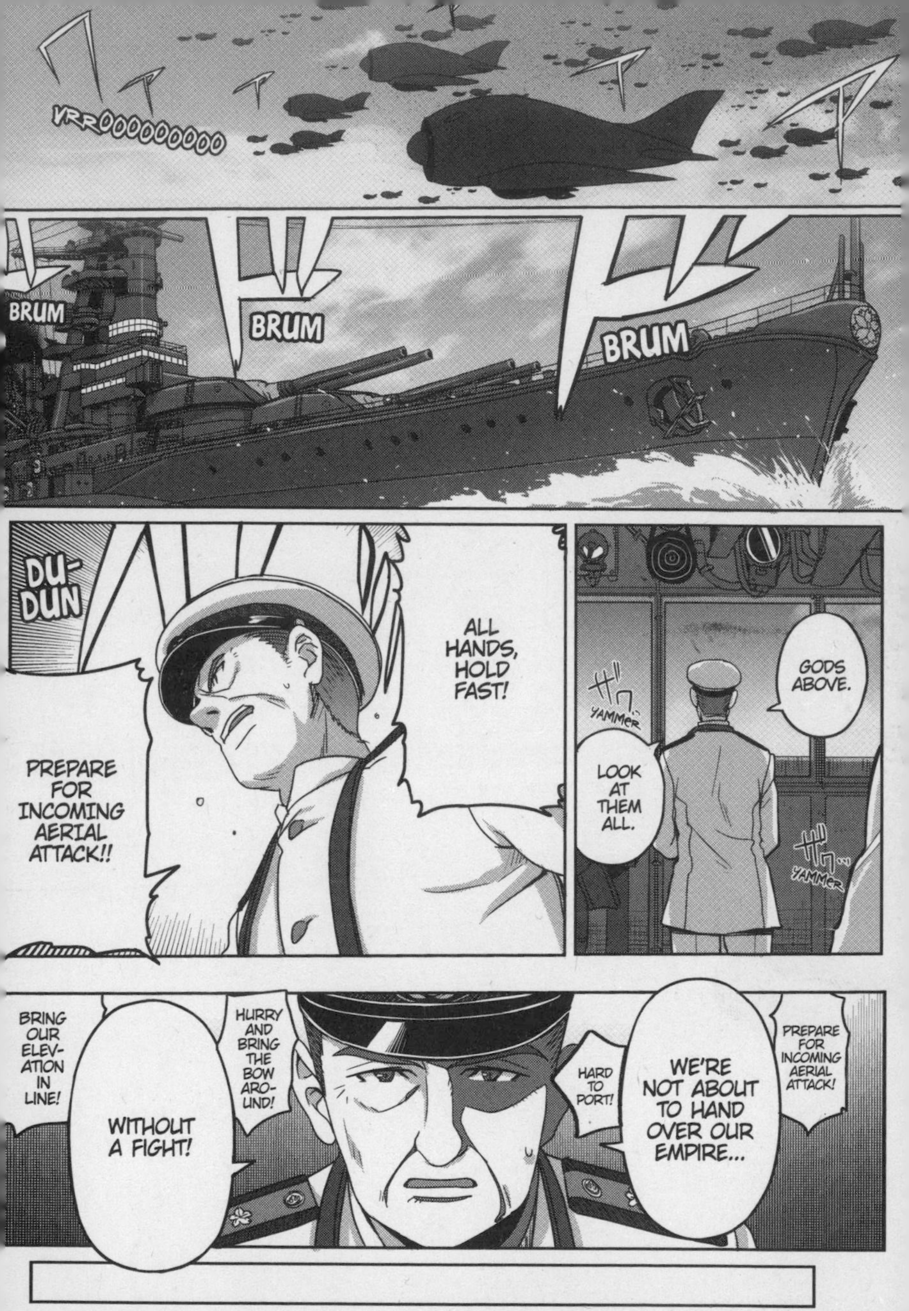

VRROOOOOOOOOO
BRUM
BRUM
BRUM
GODS ABOVE.
YAMMER
LOOK AT THEM ALL.
YAMMER
ALL HANDS, HOLD FAST!
PREPARE FOR INCOMING AERIAL ATTACK!!
DU-DUN
PREPARE FOR INCOMING AERIAL ATTACK!
WE'RE NOT ABOUT TO HAND OVER OUR EMPIRE...
HARD TO PORT!
HURRY AND BRING THE BOW ARO-UND!
WITHOUT A FIGHT!
BRING OUR ELEV-ATION IN LINE!

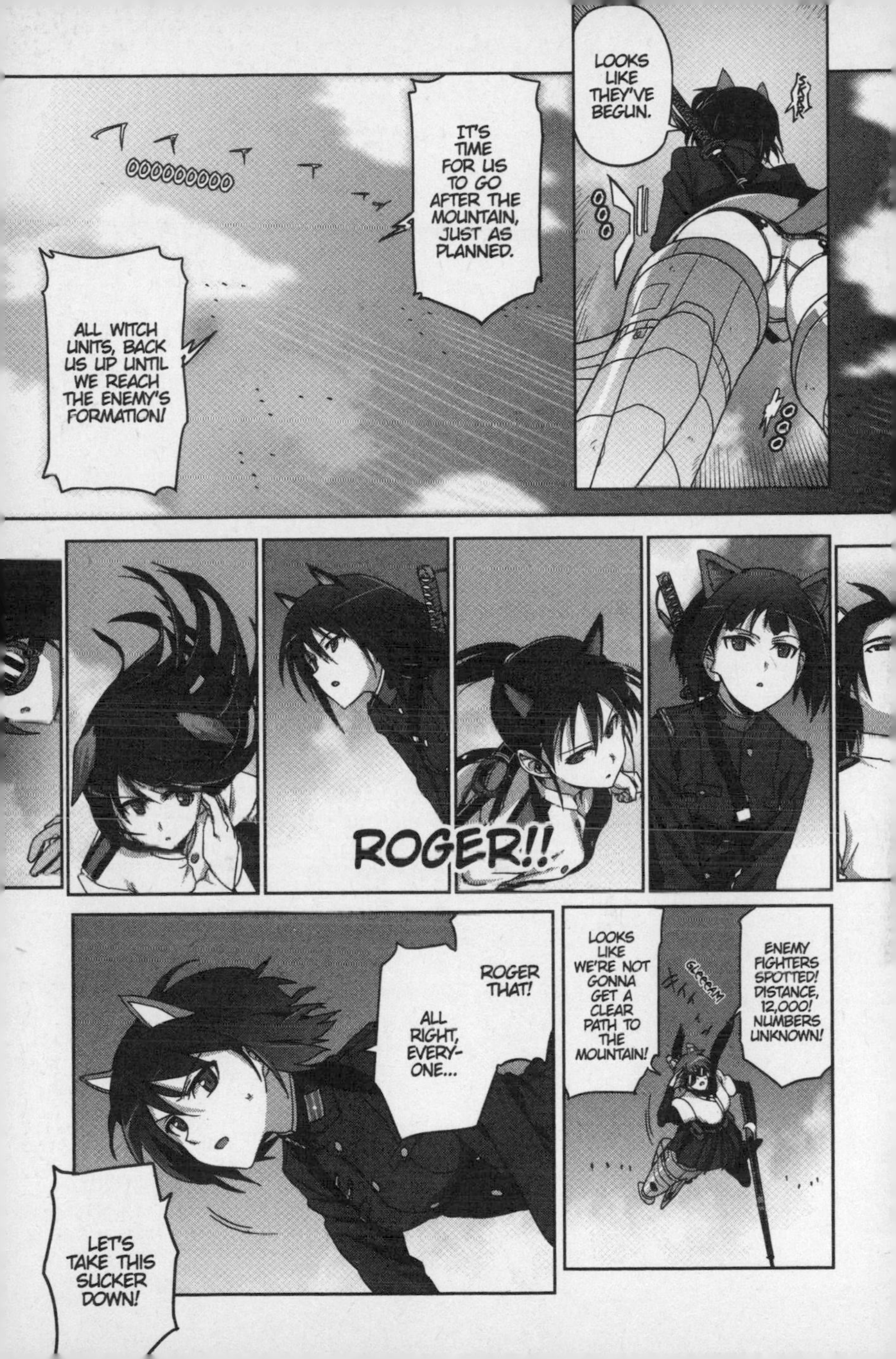
LOOKS LIKE THEY'VE BEGUN.
IT'S TIME FOR US TO GO AFTER THE MOUNTAIN, JUST AS PLANNED.
OOOOOOOOO
ALL WITCH UNITS, BACK US UP UNTIL WE REACH THE ENEMY'S FORMATION!
ROGER!!
ENEMY FIGHTERS SPOTTED! DISTANCE, 12,000! NUMBERS UNKNOWN!
LOOKS LIKE WE'RE NOT GONNA GET A CLEAR PATH TO THE MOUNTAIN!
ROGER THAT!
ALL RIGHT, EVERY-ONE...
LET'S TAKE THIS SUCKER DOWN!

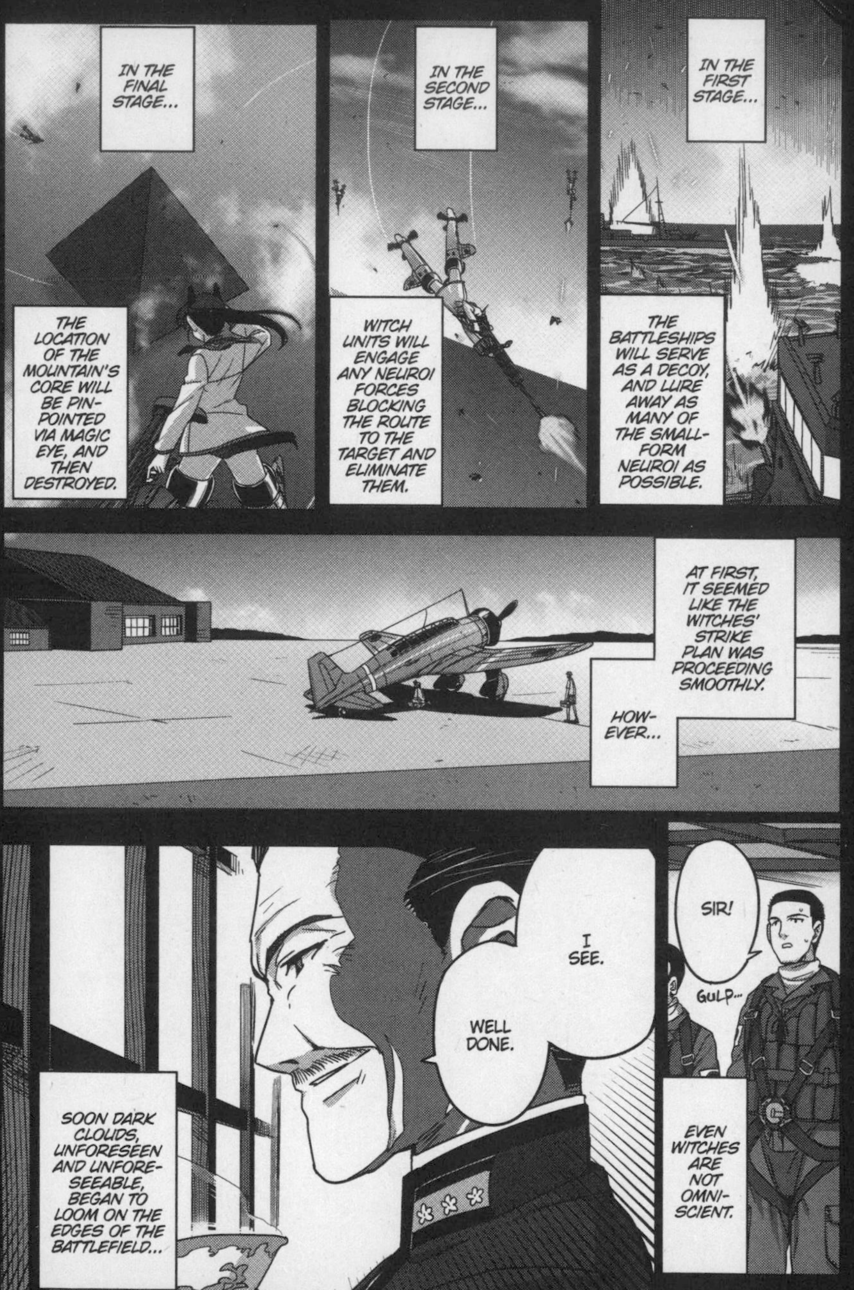
IN THE FIRST STAGE...
THE BATTLESHIPS WILL SERVE AS A DECOY, AND LURE AWAY AS MANY OF THE SMALL-FORM NEUROI AS POSSIBLE.
IN THE SECOND STAGE...
WITCH UNITS WILL ENGAGE ANY NEUROI FORCES BLOCKING THE ROUTE TO THE TARGET AND ELIMINATE THEM.
IN THE FINAL STAGE...
THE LOCATION OF THE MOUNTAIN'S CORE WILL BE PIN-POINTED VIA MAGIC EYE, AND THEN DESTROYED.
AT FIRST, IT SEEMED LIKE THE WITCHES' STRIKE PLAN WAS PROCEEDING SMOOTHLY.
HOW-EVER...
SIR!
GULP...
EVEN WITCHES ARE NOT OMNI-SCIENT.
I SEE.
WELL DONE.
SOON DARK CLOUDS, UNFORESEEN AND UNFORE-SEEABLE, BEGAN TO LOOM ON THE EDGES OF THE BATTLEFIELD...

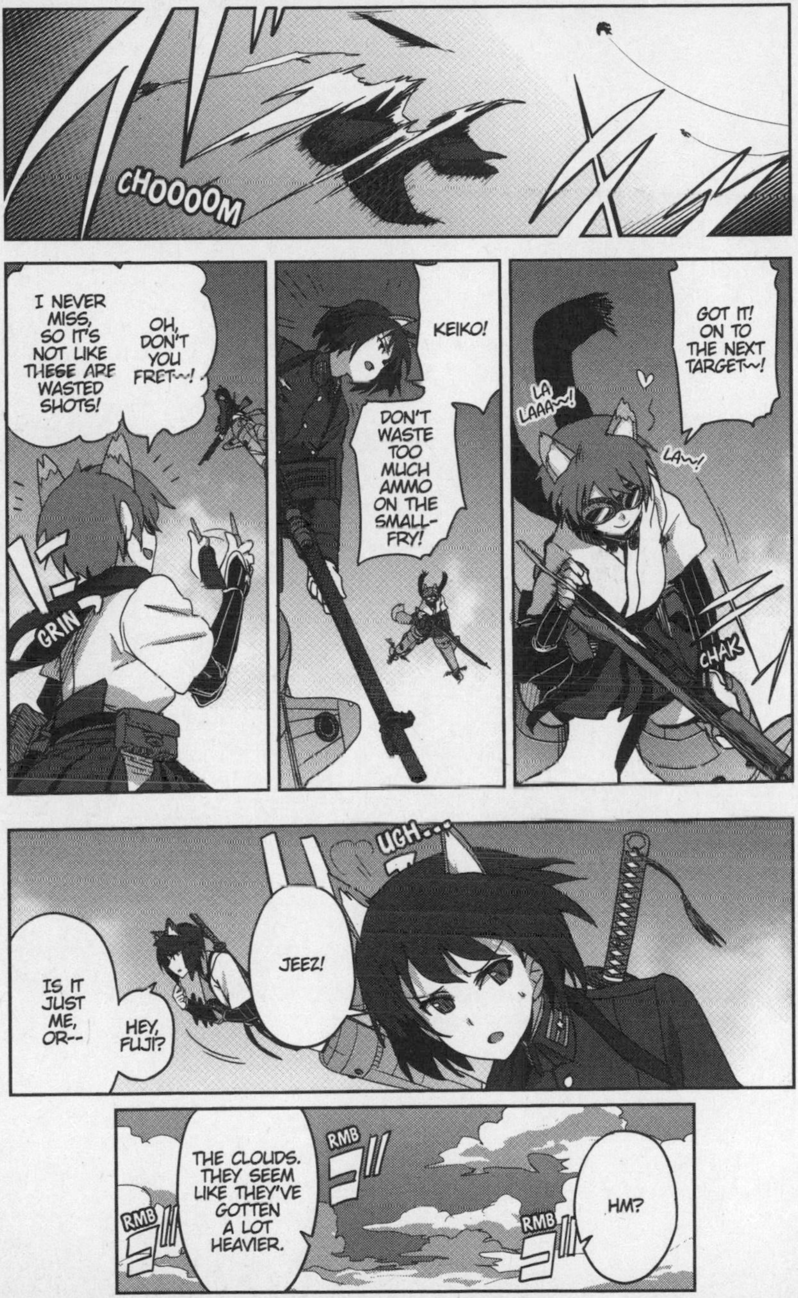
CHOOOOM
GOT IT! ON TO THE NEXT TARGET~~!
LA LAAA~~!
LA~~!
CHAK
KEIKO!
DON'T WASTE TOO MUCH AMMO ON THE SMALL-FRY!
OH, DON'T YOU FRET~~!
I NEVER MISS, SO IT'S NOT LIKE THESE ARE WASTED SHOTS!
GRIN
UGH...
JEEZ!
HEY, FUJI?
IS IT JUST ME, OR--
HM?
RMB
THE CLOUDS. THEY SEEM LIKE THEY'VE GOTTEN A LOT HEAVIER.
RMB
RMB

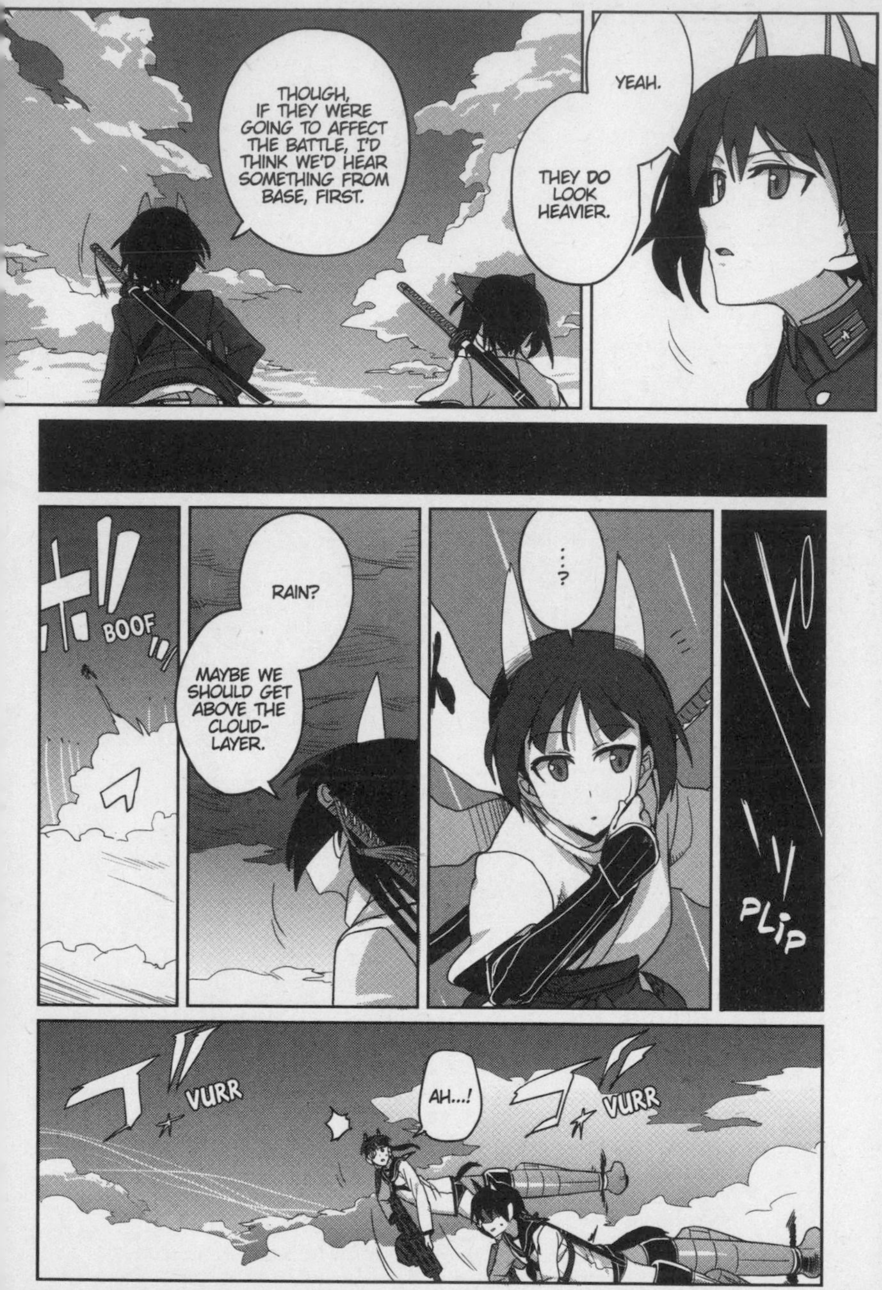
YEAH.
THEY DO LOOK HEAVIER.
THOUGH, IF THEY WERE GOING TO AFFECT THE BATTLE, I'D THINK WE'D HEAR SOMETHING FROM BASE, FIRST.
PLIP
...?
RAIN?
MAYBE WE SHOULD GET ABOVE THE CLOUD-LAYER.
BOOF
VURR
AH...!
VURR

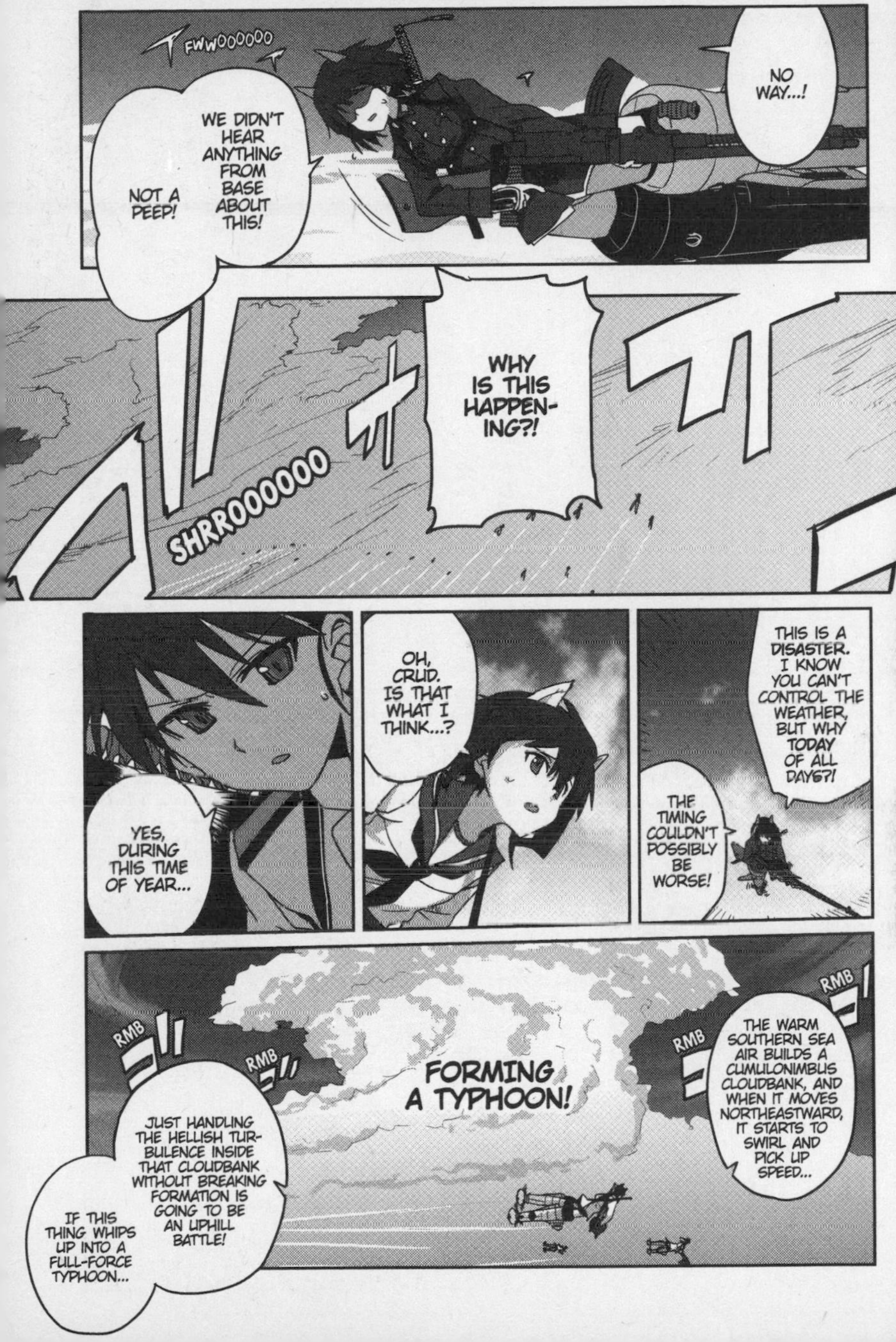

NO WAY...!
FWWOOOOOO
WE DIDN'T HEAR ANYTHING FROM BASE ABOUT THIS!
NOT A PEEP!
WHY IS THIS HAPPENING?!
SHRROOOOOOO
THIS IS A DISASTER. I KNOW YOU CAN'T CONTROL THE WEATHER, BUT WHY TODAY OF ALL DAYS?!
THE TIMING COULDN'T POSSIBLY BE WORSE!
OH, CRUD. IS THAT WHAT I THINK...?
YES, DURING THIS TIME OF YEAR...
RMB
RMB
THE WARM SOUTHERN SEA AIR BUILDS A CUMULONIMBUS CLOUDBANK, AND WHEN IT MOVES NORTHEASTWARD, IT STARTS TO SWIRL AND PICK UP SPEED...
FORMING A TYPHOON!
RMB
RMB
JUST HANDLING THE HELLISH TURBULENCE INSIDE THAT CLOUDBANK WITHOUT BREAKING FORMATION IS GOING TO BE AN UPHILL BATTLE!
IF THIS THING WHIPS UP INTO A FULL-FORCE TYPHOON...

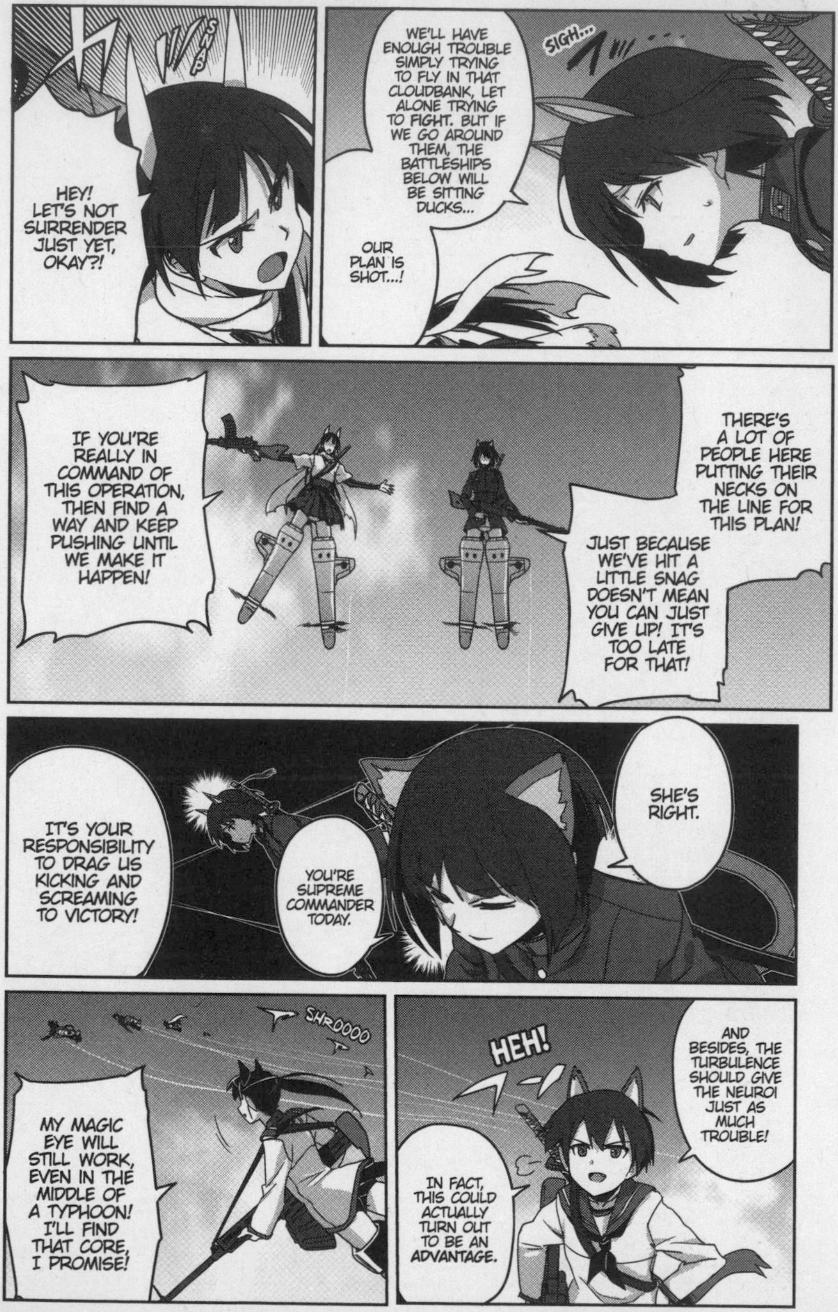
SIGH...
WE'LL HAVE ENOUGH TROUBLE SIMPLY TRYING TO FLY IN THAT CLOUDBANK, LET ALONE TRYING TO FIGHT. BUT IF WE GO AROUND THEM, THE BATTLESHIPS BELOW WILL BE SITTING DUCKS...
OUR PLAN IS SHOT...!
SNAP
HEY! LET'S NOT SURRENDER JUST YET, OKAY?!
THERE'S A LOT OF PEOPLE HERE PUTTING THEIR NECKS ON THE LINE FOR THIS PLAN!
JUST BECAUSE WE'VE HIT A LITTLE SNAG DOESN'T MEAN YOU CAN JUST GIVE UP! IT'S TOO LATE FOR THAT!
IF YOU'RE REALLY IN COMMAND OF THIS OPERATION, THEN FIND A WAY AND KEEP PUSHING UNTIL WE MAKE IT HAPPEN!
SHE'S RIGHT.
YOU'RE SUPREME COMMANDER TODAY.
IT'S YOUR RESPONSIBILITY TO DRAG US KICKING AND SCREAMING TO VICTORY!
AND BESIDES, THE TURBULENCE SHOULD GIVE THE NEUROI JUST AS MUCH TROUBLE!
HEH!
IN FACT, THIS COULD ACTUALLY TURN OUT TO BE AN ADVANTAGE.
SHROOOO
MY MAGIC EYE WILL STILL WORK, EVEN IN THE MIDDLE OF A TYPHOON! I'LL FIND THAT CORE, I PROMISE!

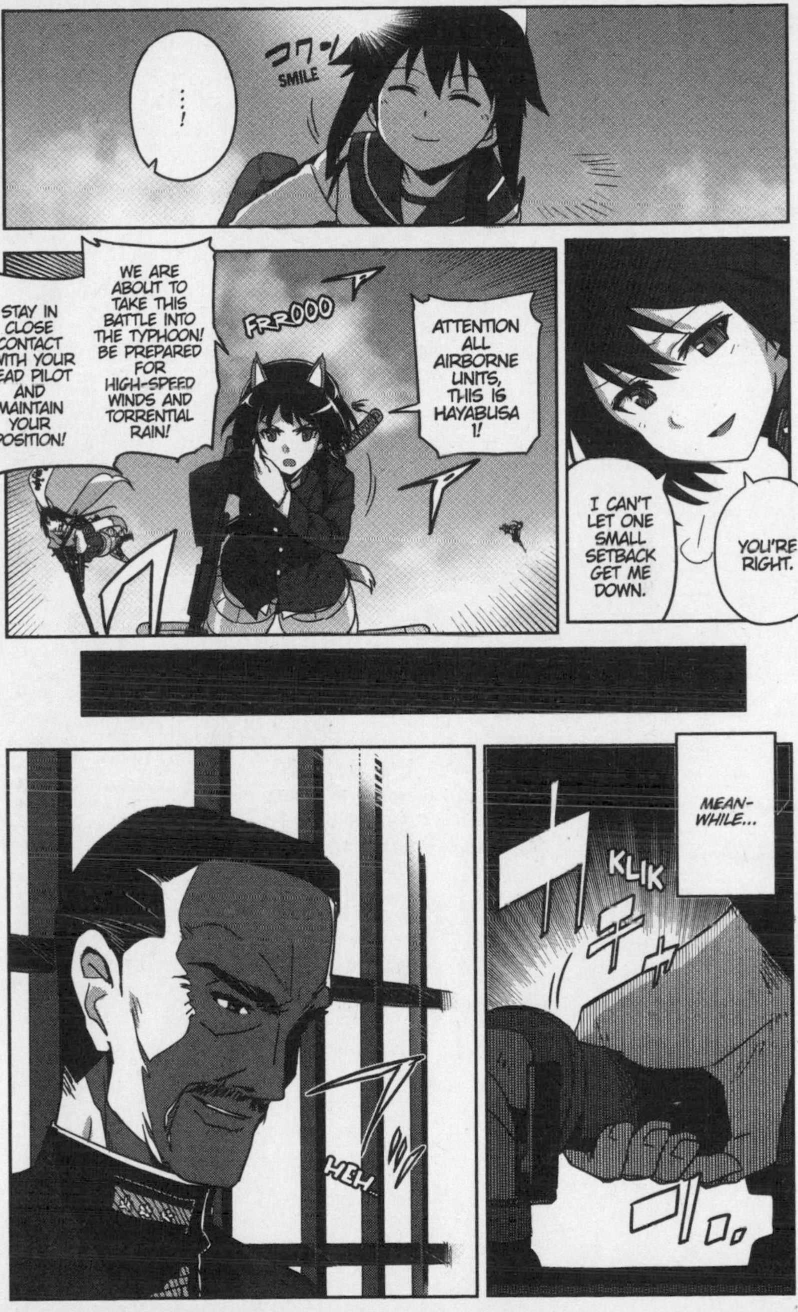
SMILE
...!
YOU'RE RIGHT.
I CAN'T LET ONE SMALL SETBACK GET ME DOWN.
ATTENTION ALL AIRBORNE UNITS, THIS IS HAYABUSA 1!
FRROOO
WE ARE ABOUT TO TAKE THIS BATTLE INTO THE TYPHOON! BE PREPARED FOR HIGH-SPEED WINDS AND TORRENTIAL RAIN!
STAY IN CLOSE CONTACT WITH YOUR LEAD PILOT AND MAINTAIN YOUR POSITION!
MEAN-WHILE...
KLIK
HEH...

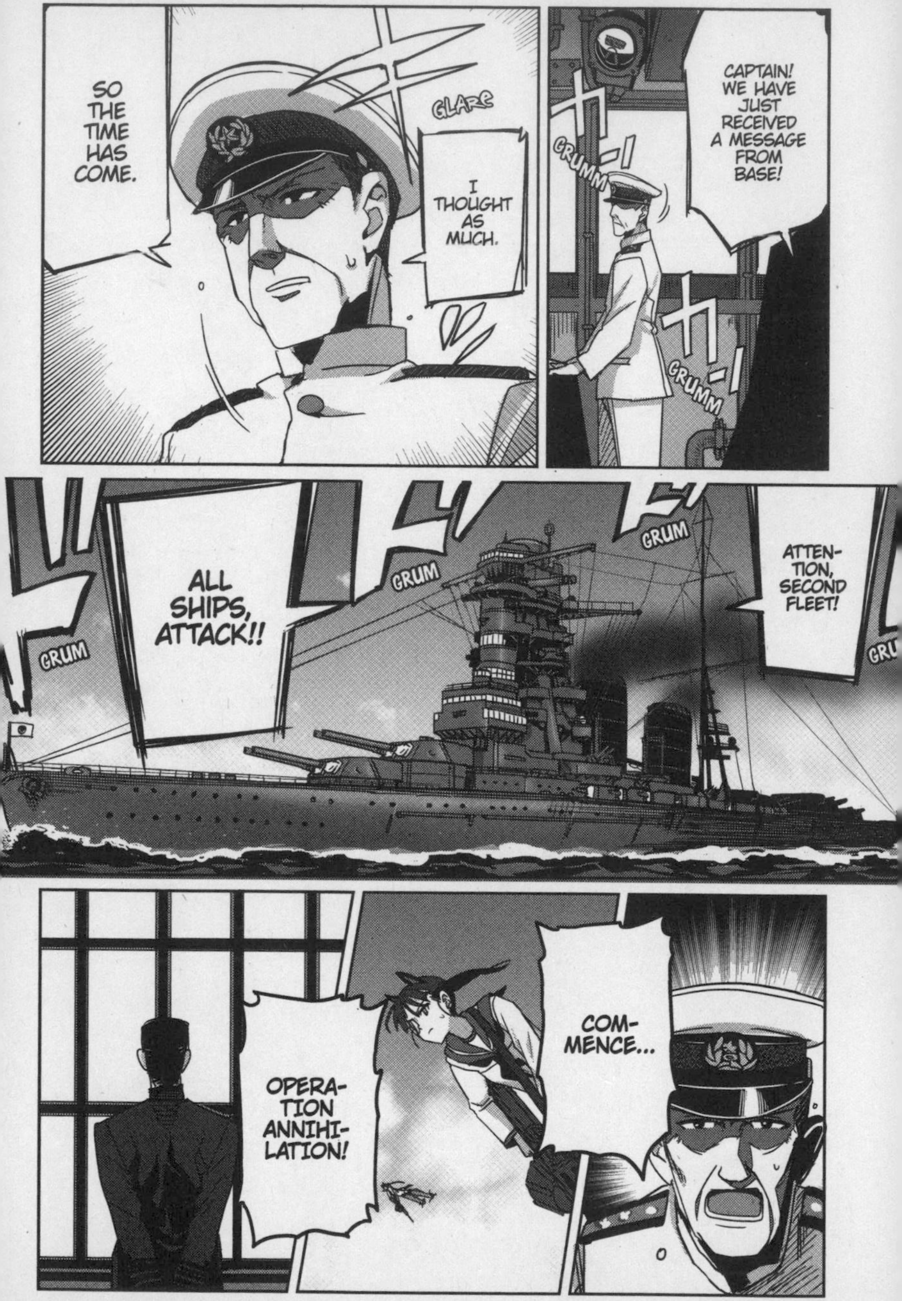
CAPTAIN! WE HAVE JUST RECEIVED A MESSAGE FROM BASE!
GRUMM
GRUMM
GLARE
I THOUGHT AS MUCH.
SO THE TIME HAS COME.
GRU
ATTEN-TION, SECOND FLEET!
GRUM
GRUM
ALL SHIPS, ATTACK!!
GRUM
COM-MENCE...
OPERA-TION ANNIHI-LATION!

Chapter 10:
The Fuso Sea Incident
[Mission Complete]

CHAPTER 11:
IF I DIE IN THE SKY

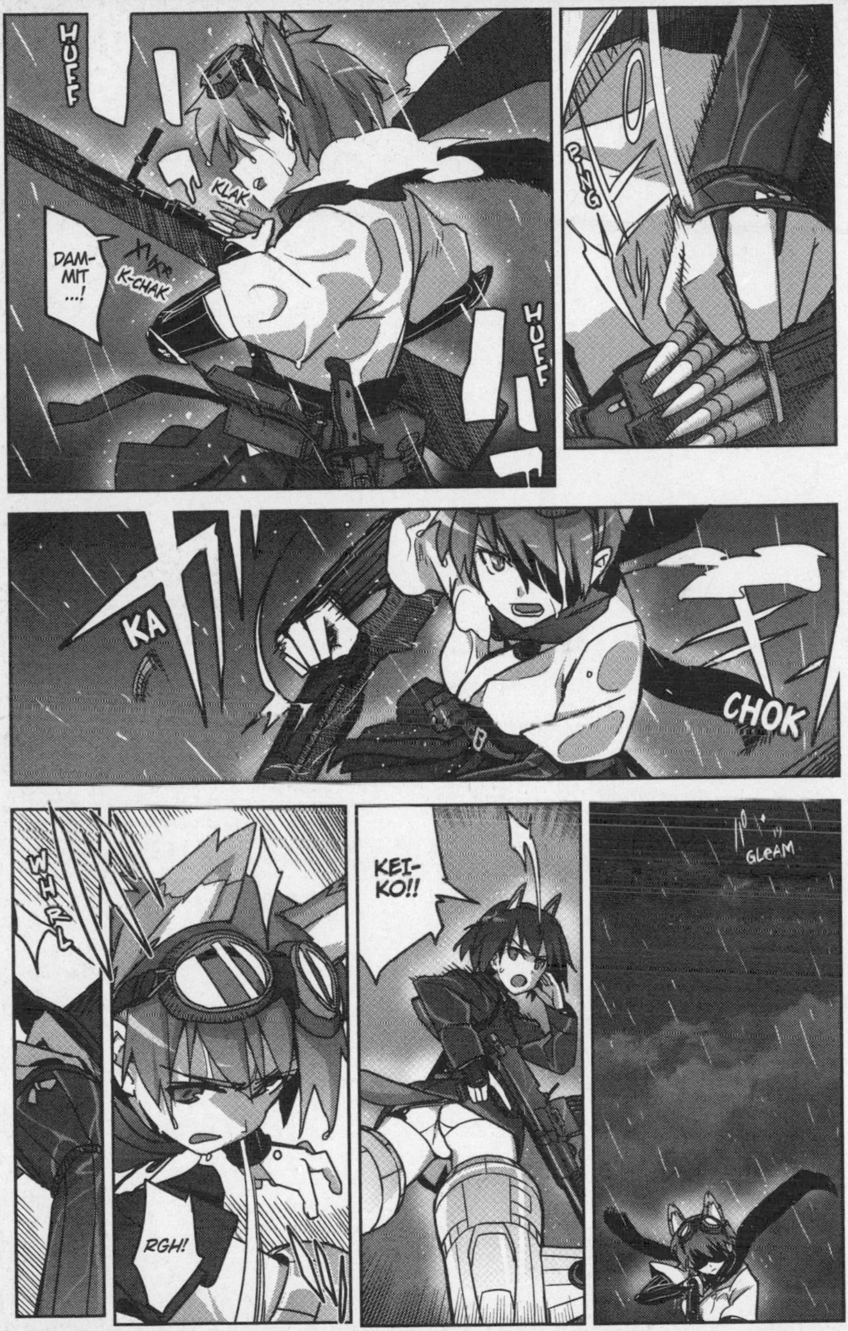
RING
HUFF
KLAK
DAM-MIT...!
K-CHAK
HUFF
CHOK
KA
GLEAM
KEI-KO!!
WHRL
RGH!

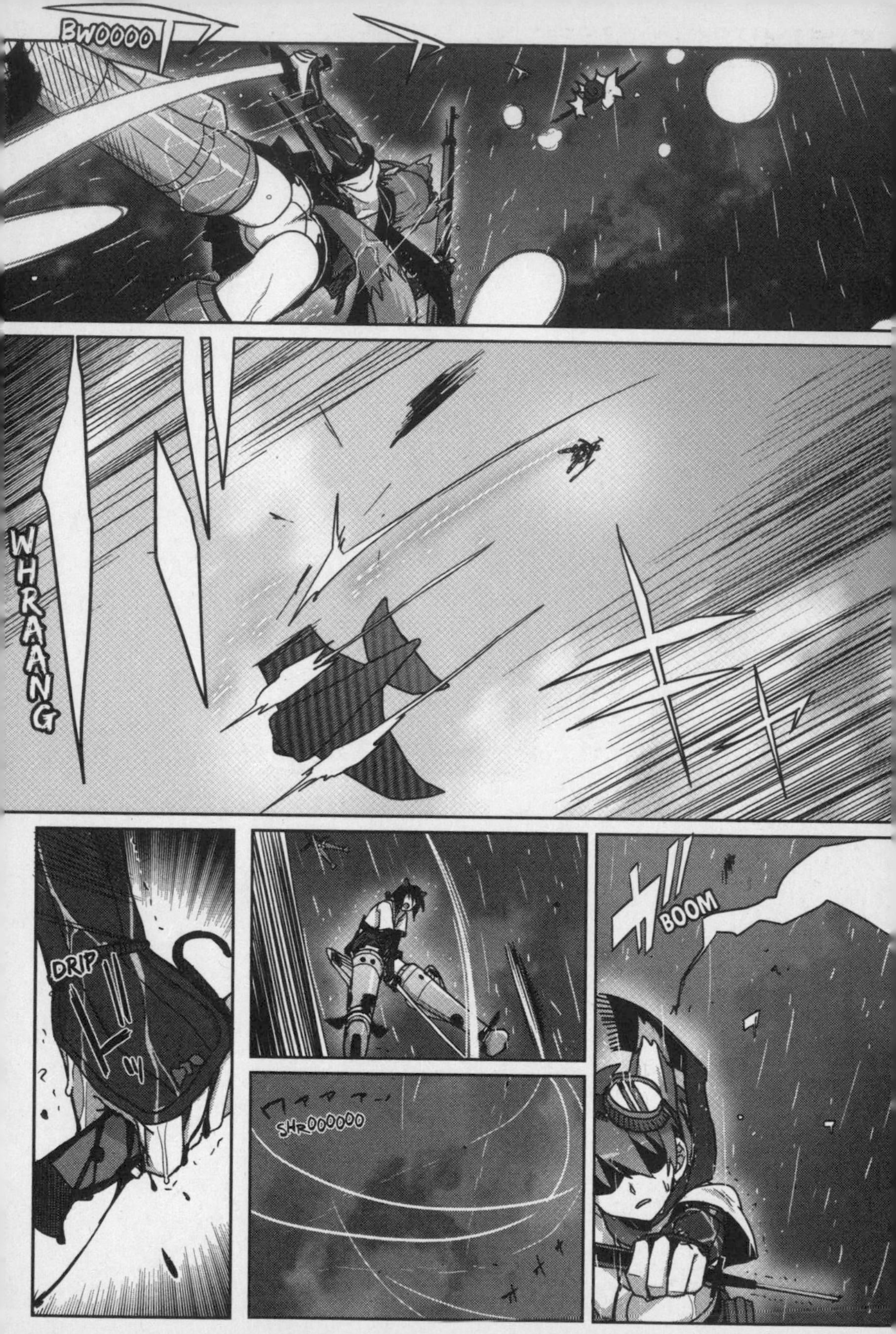
BWOOOO
WHRAAANG
BOOM
SHROOOOOO
DRIP

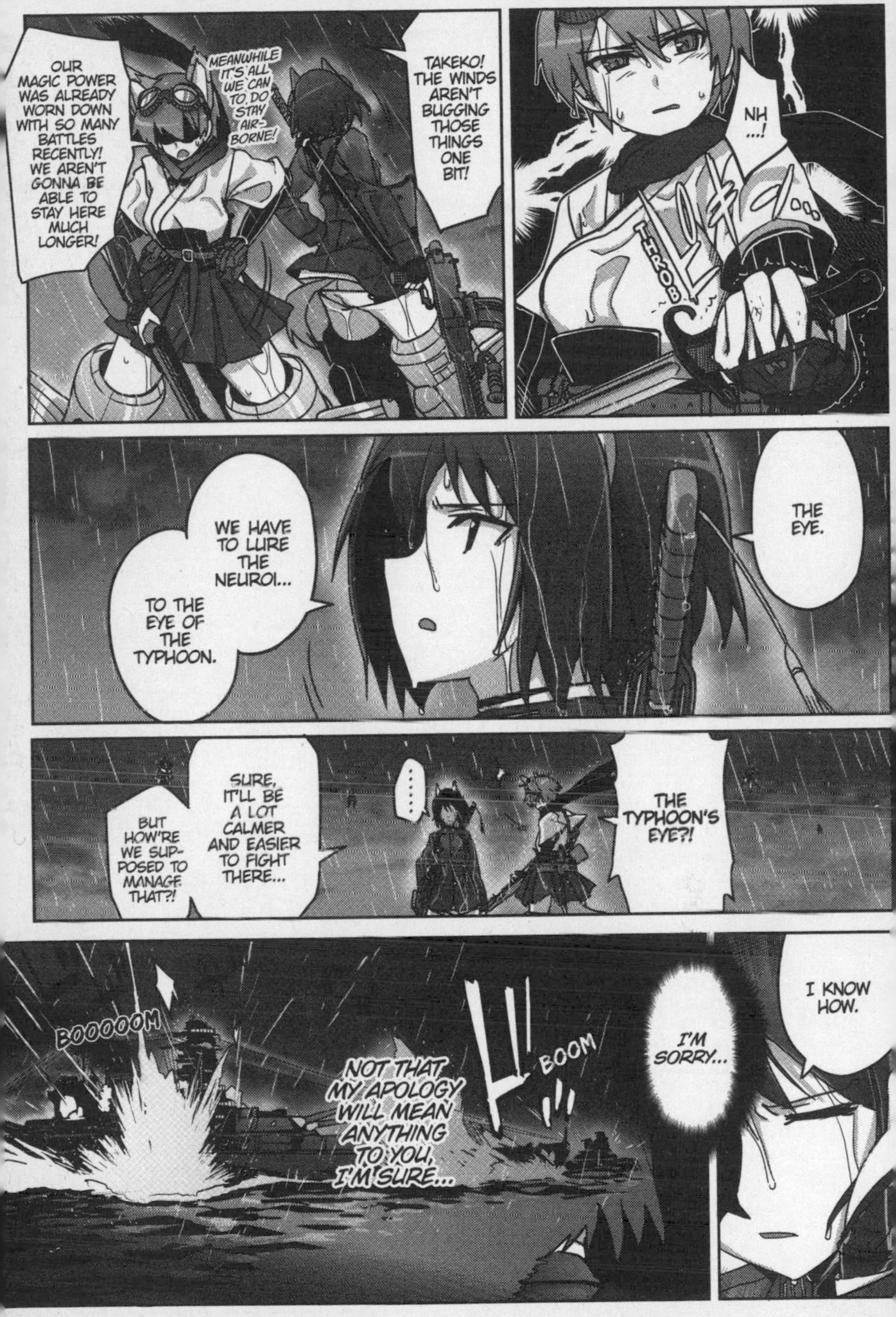
NH ...!
THROB
TAKEKO! THE WINDS AREN'T BUGGING THOSE THINGS ONE BIT!
MEANWHILE IT'S ALL WE CAN TO DO STAY AIR-BORNE!
OUR MAGIC POWER WAS ALREADY WORN DOWN WITH SO MANY BATTLES RECENTLY! WE AREN'T GONNA BE ABLE TO STAY HERE MUCH LONGER!
THE EYE.
WE HAVE TO LURE THE NEUROI...
TO THE EYE OF THE TYPHOON.
THE TYPHOON'S EYE?!
......
SURE, IT'LL BE A LOT CALMER AND EASIER TO FIGHT THERE...
BUT HOW'RE WE SUP-POSED TO MANAGE THAT?!
I KNOW HOW.
I'M SORRY...
BOOM
NOT THAT MY APOLOGY WILL MEAN ANYTHING TO YOU, I'M SURE...
BOOOOOM

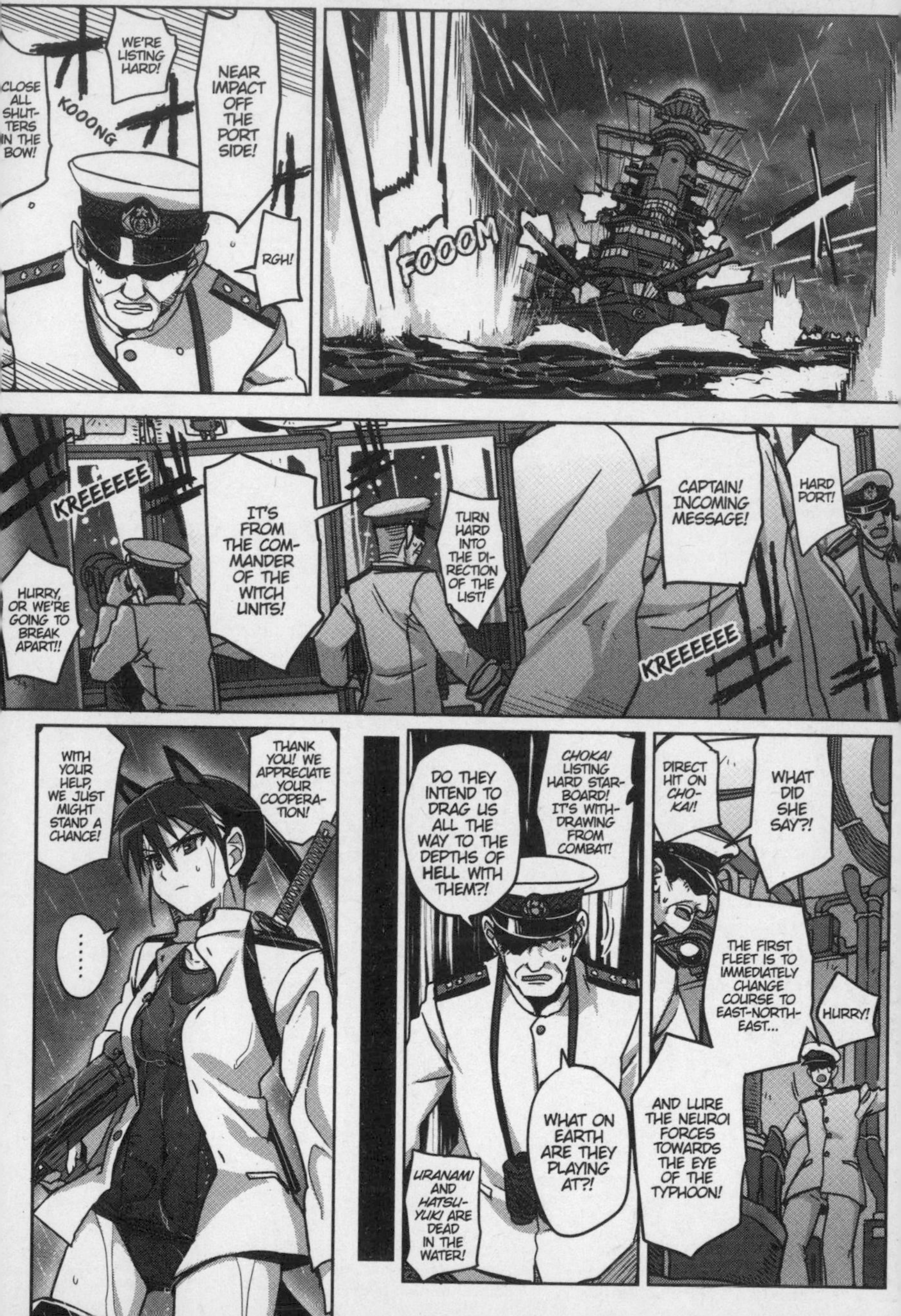
FOOOM
WE'RE LISTING HARD!
NEAR IMPACT OFF THE PORT SIDE!
CLOSE ALL SHUTTERS IN THE BOW!
KOOONG
RGH!
HARD PORT!
CAPTAIN! INCOMING MESSAGE!
KREEEEEE
TURN HARD INTO THE DIRECTION OF THE LIST!
IT'S FROM THE COMMANDER OF THE WITCH UNITS!
KREEEEEE
HURRY, OR WE'RE GOING TO BREAK APART!!
WHAT DID SHE SAY?!
DIRECT HIT ON CHOKAI!
THE FIRST FLEET IS TO IMMEDIATELY CHANGE COURSE TO EAST-NORTH-EAST...
HURRY!
AND LURE THE NEUROI FORCES TOWARDS THE EYE OF THE TYPHOON!
CHOKAI LISTING HARD STARBOARD! IT'S WITHDRAWING FROM COMBAT!
DO THEY INTEND TO DRAG US ALL THE WAY TO THE DEPTHS OF HELL WITH THEM?!
WHAT ON EARTH ARE THEY PLAYING AT?!
URANAMI AND HATSUYUKI ARE DEAD IN THE WATER!
THANK YOU! WE APPRECIATE YOUR COOPERATION!
WITH YOUR HELP, WE JUST MIGHT STAND A CHANCE!
......

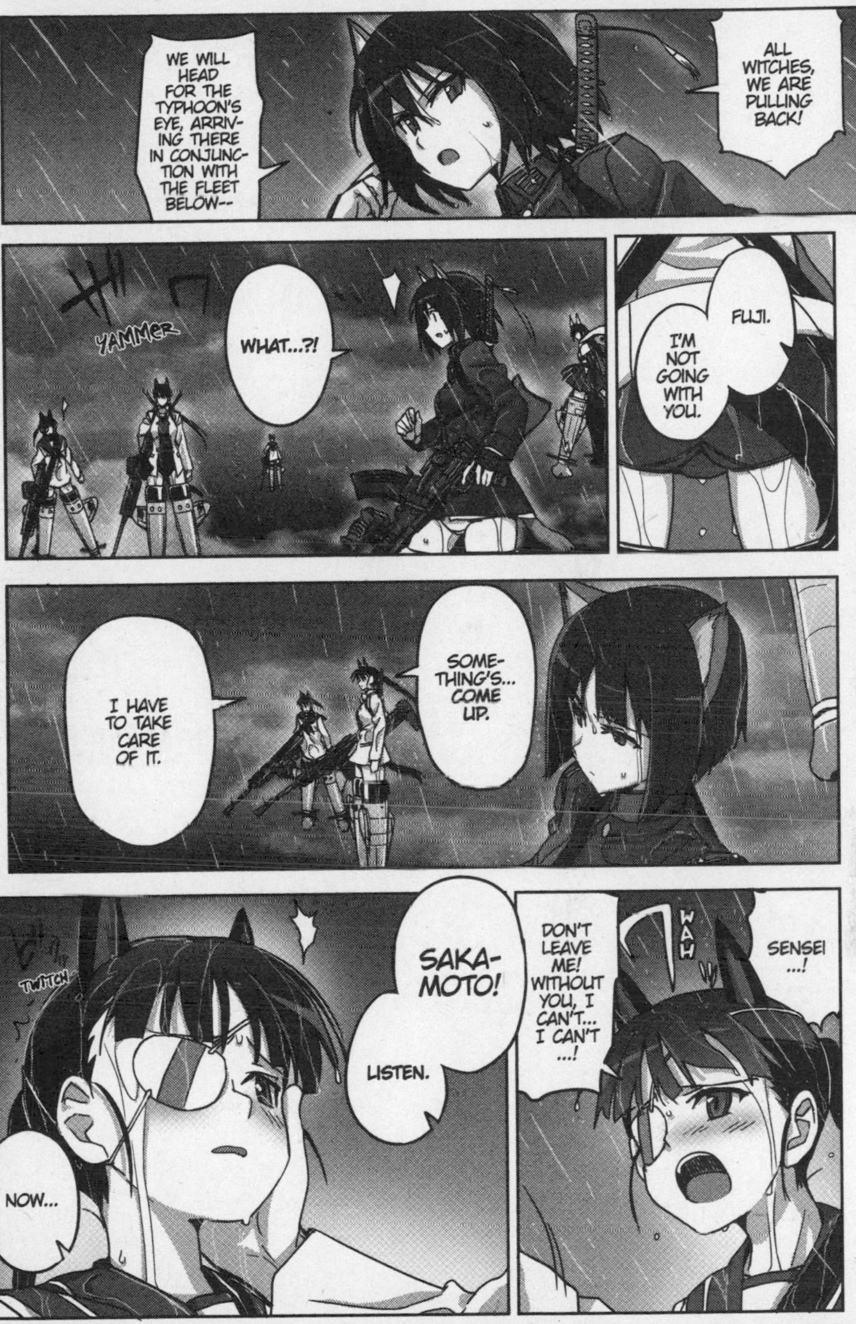
ALL WITCHES, WE ARE PULLING BACK!
WE WILL HEAD FOR THE TYPHOON'S EYE, ARRIVING THERE IN CONJUNCTION WITH THE FLEET BELOW--
FUJI.
I'M NOT GOING WITH YOU.
YAMMER
WHAT...?!
SOMETHING'S... COME UP.
I HAVE TO TAKE CARE OF IT.
SENSEI ...!
WAH
DON'T LEAVE ME! WITHOUT YOU, I CAN'T... I CAN'T ...!
SAKAMOTO!
LISTEN.
TWITCH
NOW...

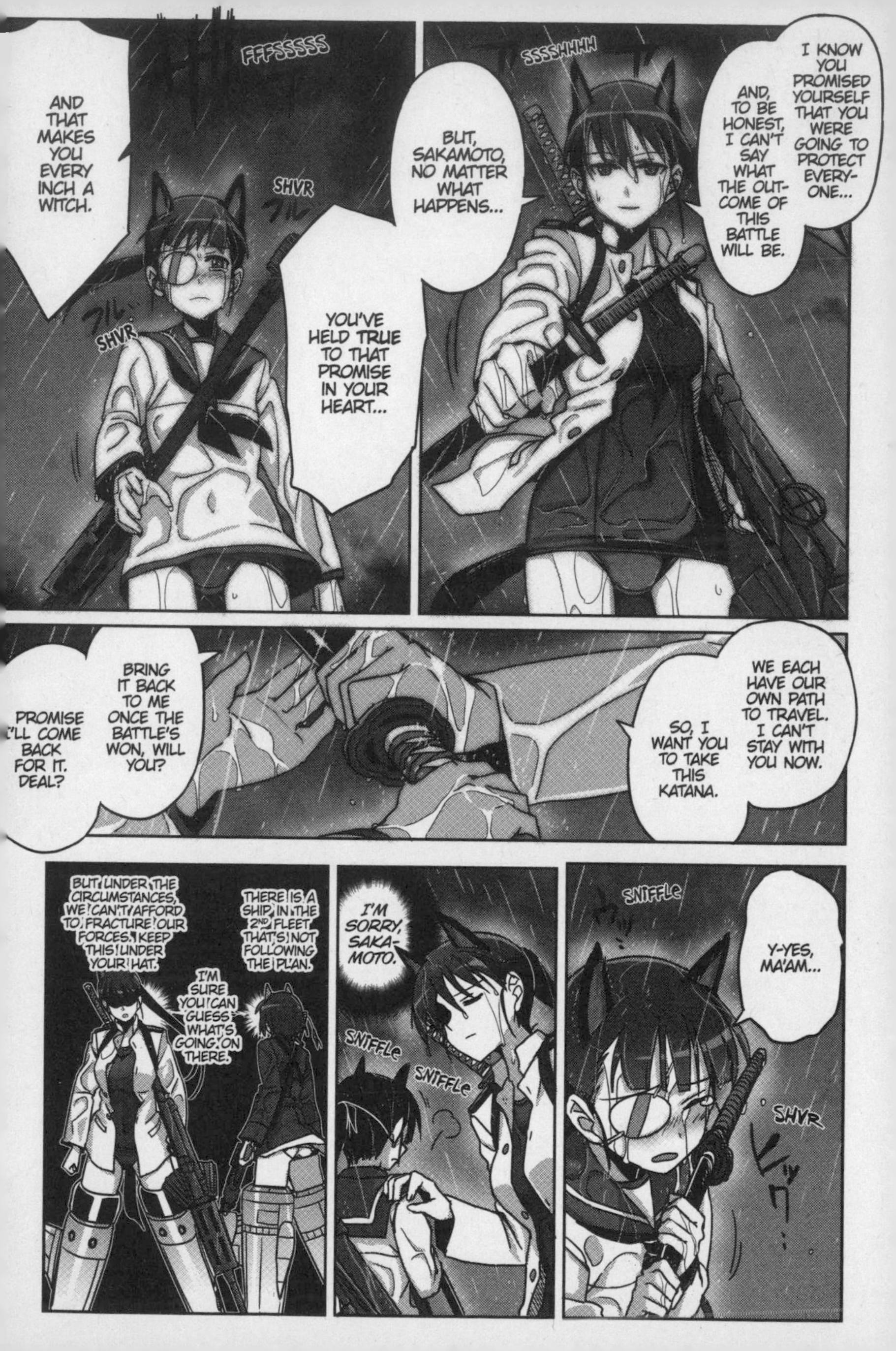
SSSSHHHH
I KNOW YOU PROMISED YOURSELF THAT YOU WERE GOING TO PROTECT EVERY-ONE...
AND, TO BE HONEST, I CAN'T SAY WHAT THE OUT-COME OF THIS BATTLE WILL BE.
BUT, SAKAMOTO, NO MATTER WHAT HAPPENS...
FFFSSSSS
YOU'VE HELD TRUE TO THAT PROMISE IN YOUR HEART...
AND THAT MAKES YOU EVERY INCH A WITCH.
SHVR
SHVR
WE EACH HAVE OUR OWN PATH TO TRAVEL. I CAN'T STAY WITH YOU NOW.
SO, I WANT YOU TO TAKE THIS KATANA.
BRING IT BACK TO ME ONCE THE BATTLE'S WON, WILL YOU?
PROMISE 'LL COME BACK FOR IT. DEAL?
SNIFFLE
Y-YES, MA'AM...
SHVR
I'M SORRY, SAKA-MOTO.
SNIFFLE
SNIFFLE
THERE IS A SHIP IN THE 2ND FLEET THAT'S NOT FOLLOWING THE PLAN.
BUT UNDER THE CIRCUMSTANCES, WE CAN'T AFFORD TO FRACTURE OUR FORCES. KEEP THIS UNDER YOUR HAT.
I'M SURE YOU CAN GUESS WHAT'S GOING ON THERE.

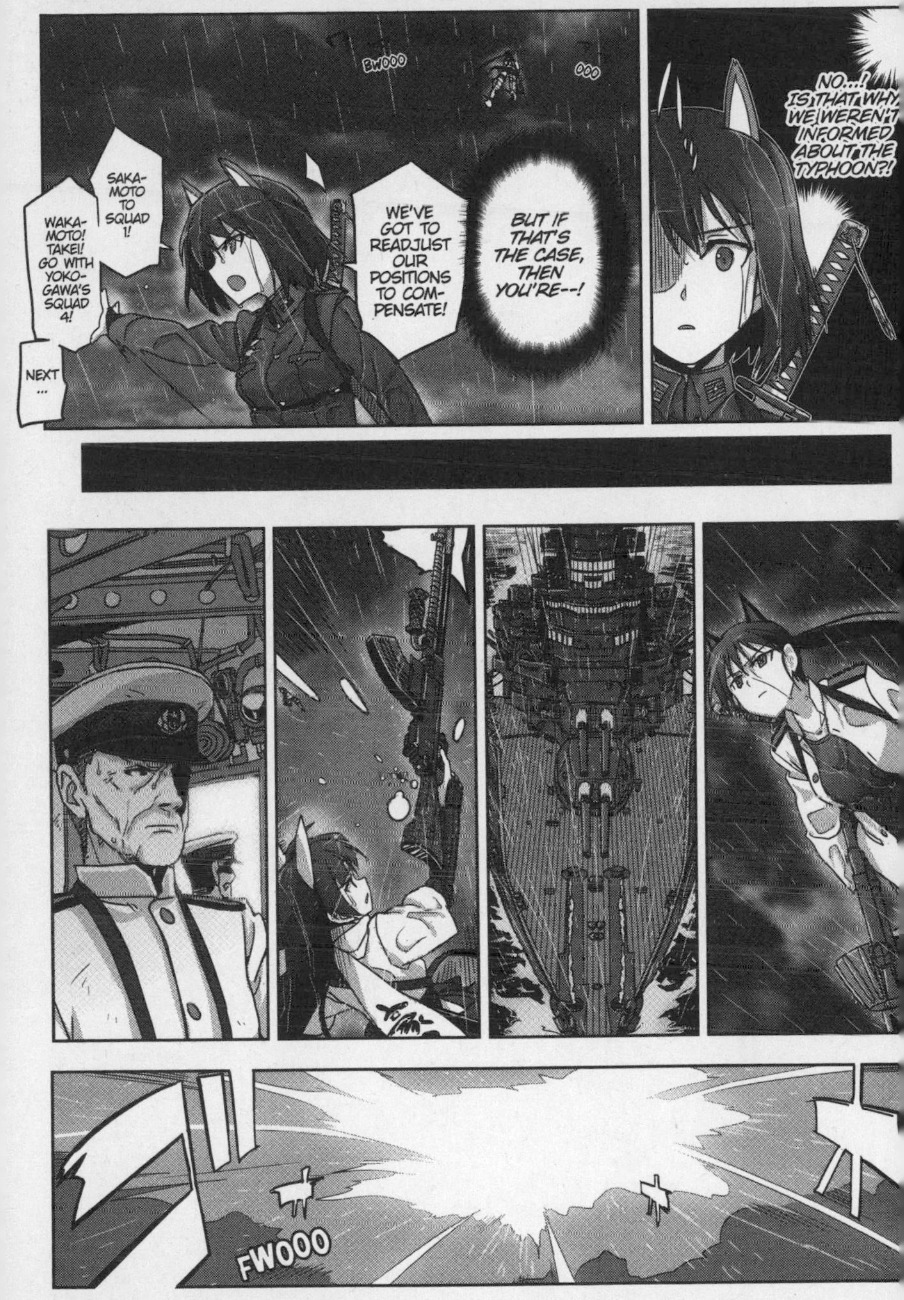
NO...! IS THAT WHY WE WEREN'T INFORMED ABOUT THE TYPHOON?!
BWOOO
OOO
BUT IF THAT'S THE CASE, THEN YOU'RE--!
WE'VE GOT TO READJUST OUR POSITIONS TO COMPENSATE!
SAKA-MOTO TO SQUAD 1!
WAKA-MOTO! TAKEI! GO WITH YOKO-GAWA'S SQUAD 4!
NEXT...
FWOOO

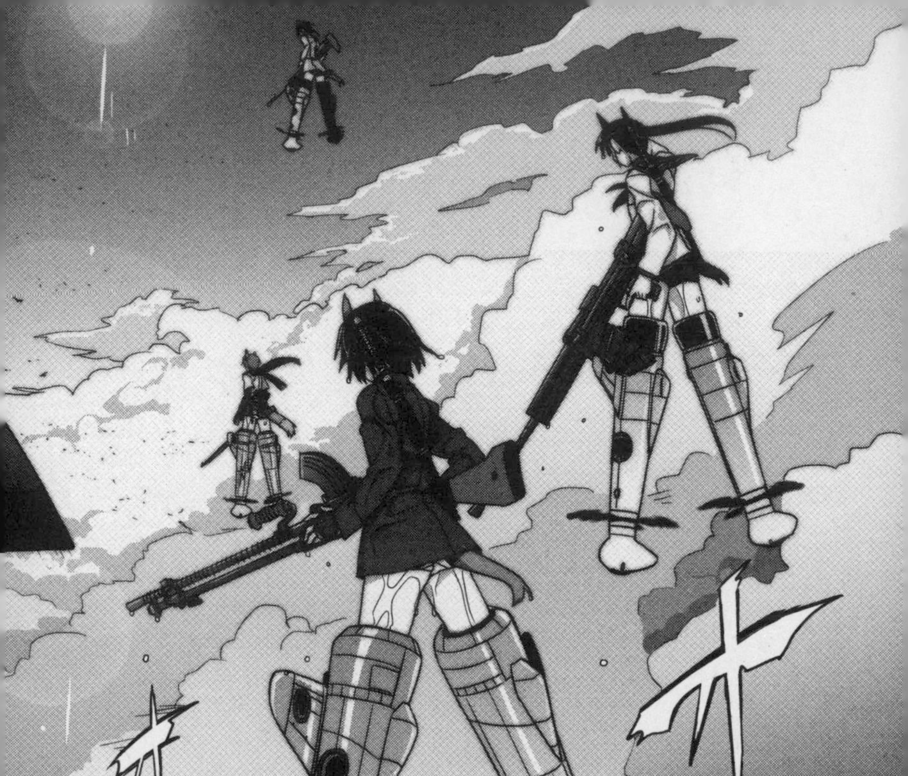

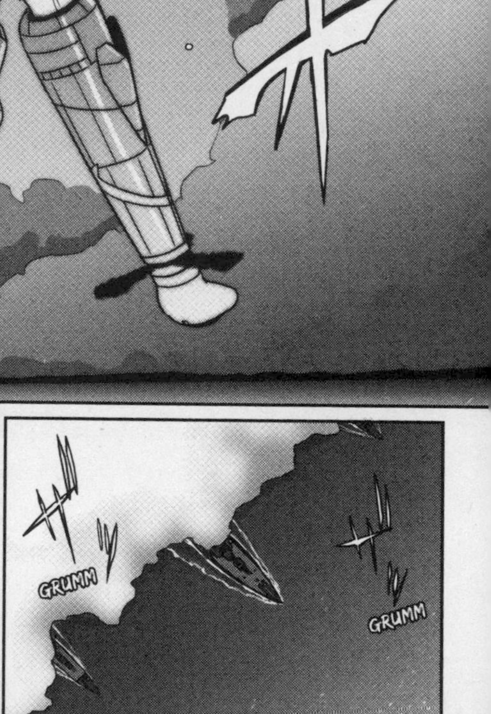
GRUMM
GRUMM

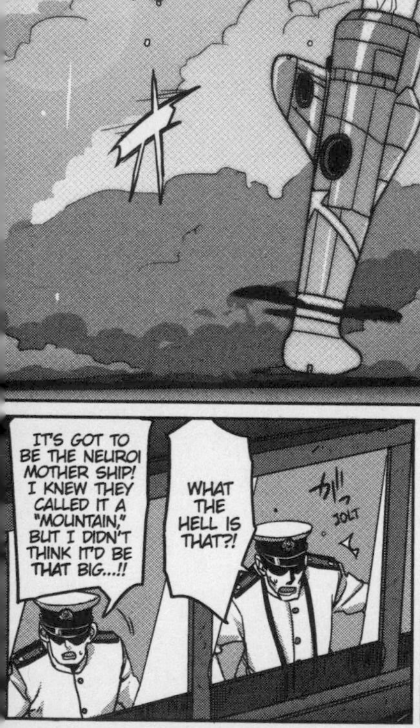
WHAT THE HELL IS THAT?!
JOLT
IT'S GOT TO BE THE NEUROI MOTHER SHIP! I KNEW THEY CALLED IT A "MOUNTAIN," BUT I DIDN'T THINK IT'D BE THAT BIG...!!

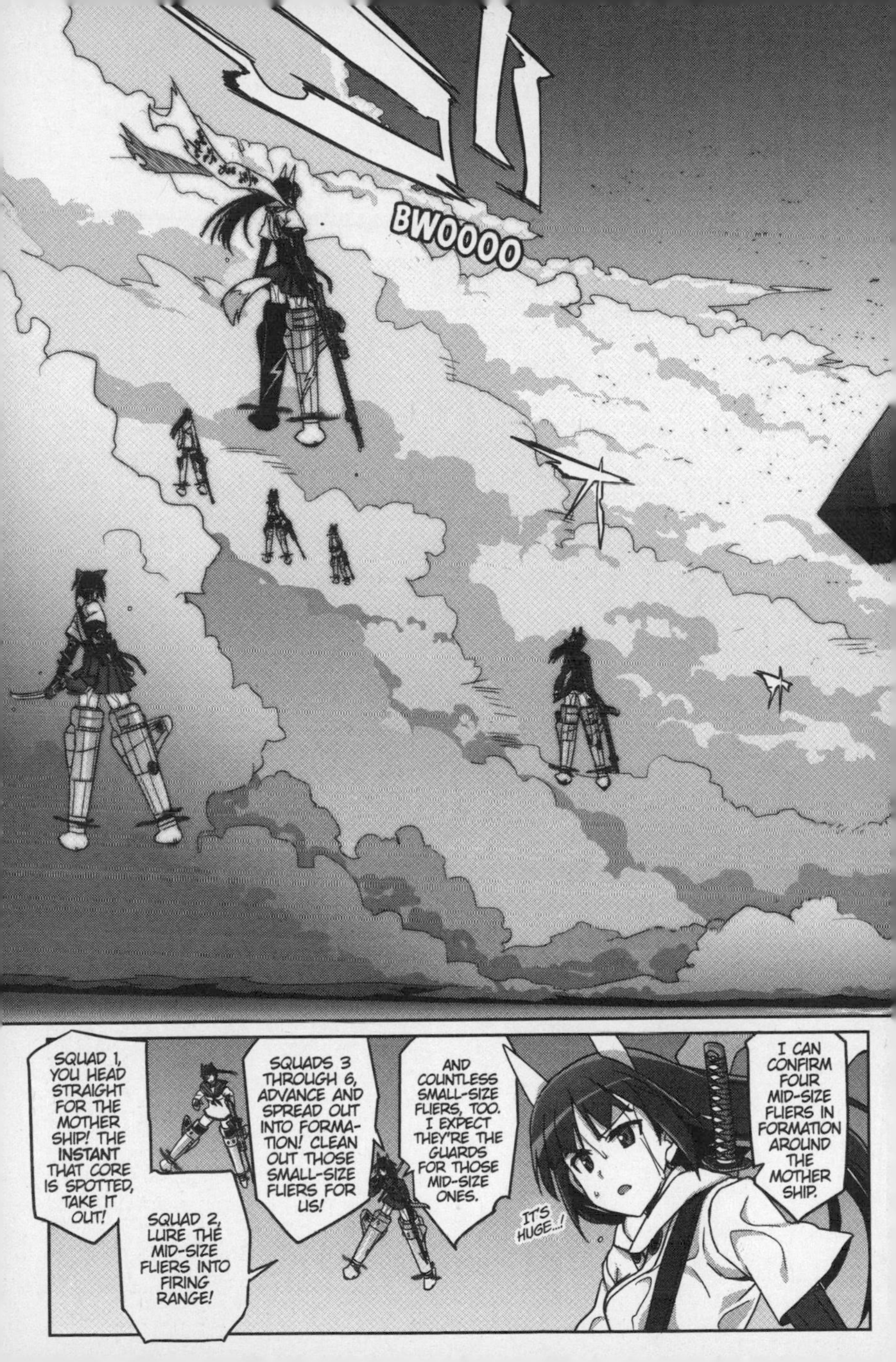
BWOOOO
I CAN CONFIRM FOUR MID-SIZE FLIERS IN FORMATION AROUND THE MOTHER SHIP.
IT'S HUGE...!
AND COUNTLESS SMALL-SIZE FLIERS, TOO. I EXPECT THEY'RE THE GUARDS FOR THOSE MID-SIZE ONES.
SQUADS 3 THROUGH 6, ADVANCE AND SPREAD OUT INTO FORMATION! CLEAN OUT THOSE SMALL-SIZE FLIERS FOR US!
SQUAD 1, YOU HEAD STRAIGHT FOR THE MOTHER SHIP! THE INSTANT THAT CORE IS SPOTTED, TAKE IT OUT!
SQUAD 2, LURE THE MID-SIZE FLIERS INTO FIRING RANGE!

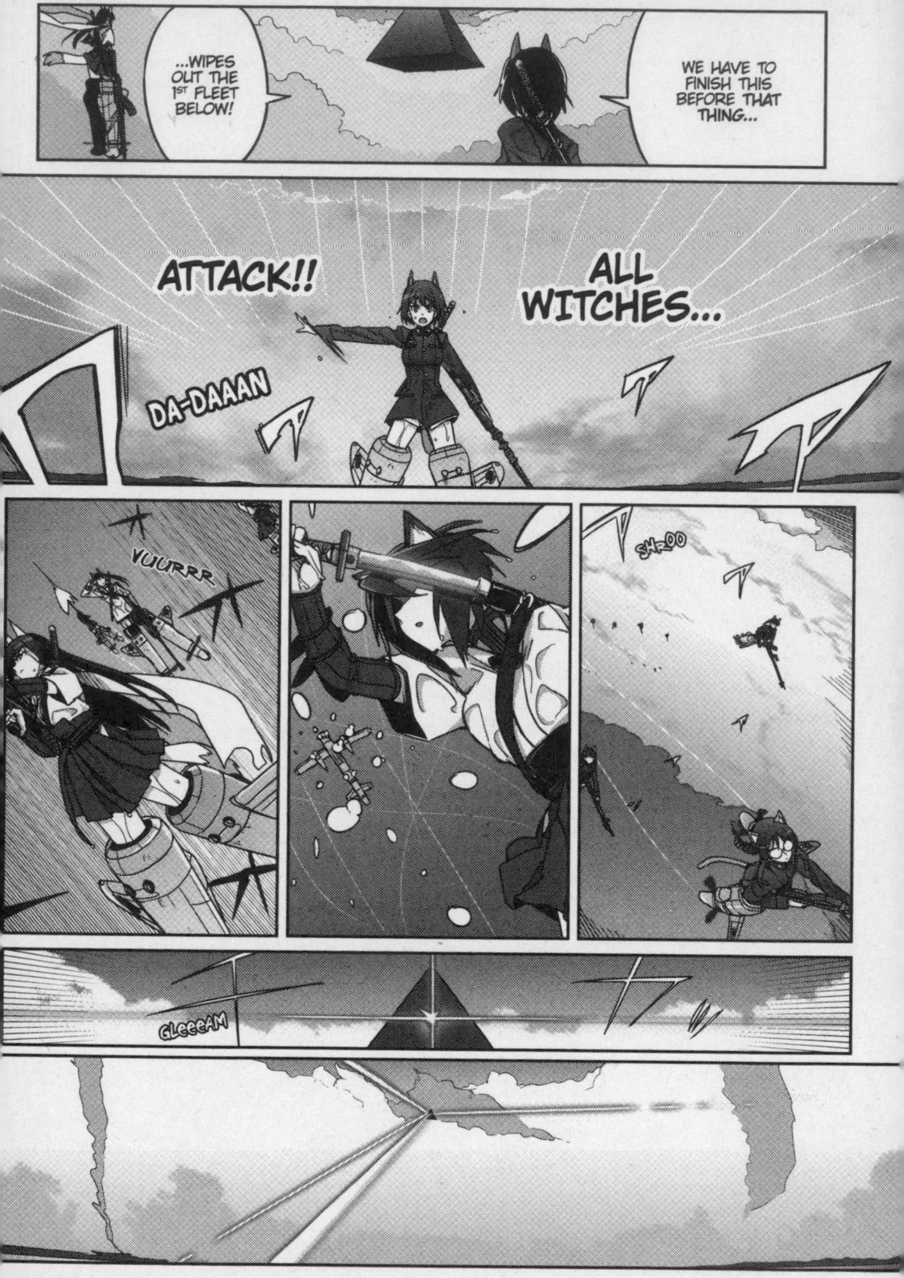
WE HAVE TO FINISH THIS BEFORE THAT THING...
...WIPES OUT THE 1ST FLEET BELOW!
ALL WITCHES...
ATTACK!!
DA-DAAAN
SHROO
VUURRR
GLEEEAM

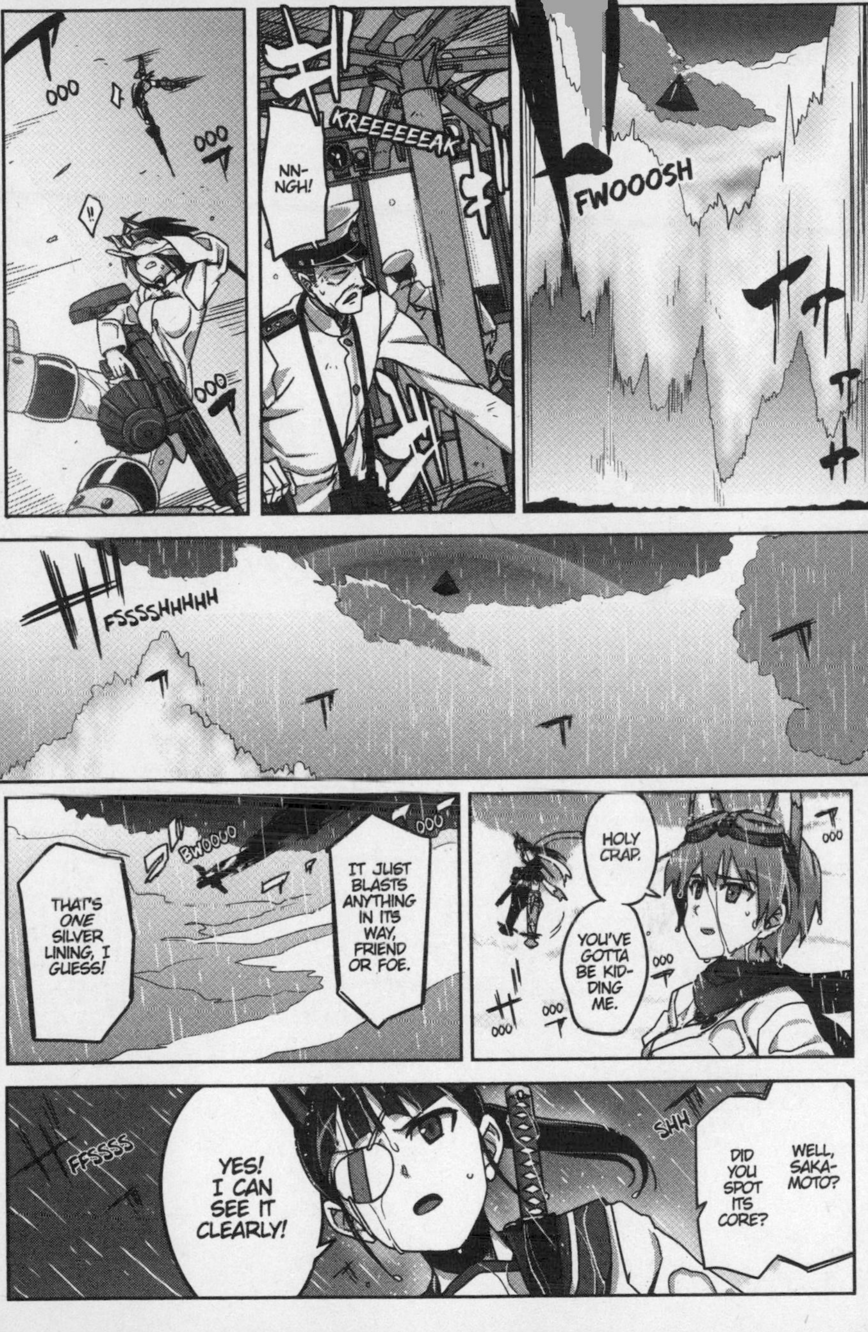
FWOOOSH
KREEEEEEAK
NN-NGH!
OOO
OOO
OOO
FSSSSHHHHH
HOLY CRAP.
YOU'VE GOTTA BE KIDDING ME.
OOO
OOO
OOO
OOO
BWOOOO
IT JUST BLASTS ANYTHING IN ITS WAY, FRIEND OR FOE.
THAT'S *ONE* SILVER LINING, I GUESS!
SHH
WELL, SAKAMOTO?
DID YOU SPOT ITS CORE?
YES! I CAN SEE IT CLEARLY!
FFSSSS

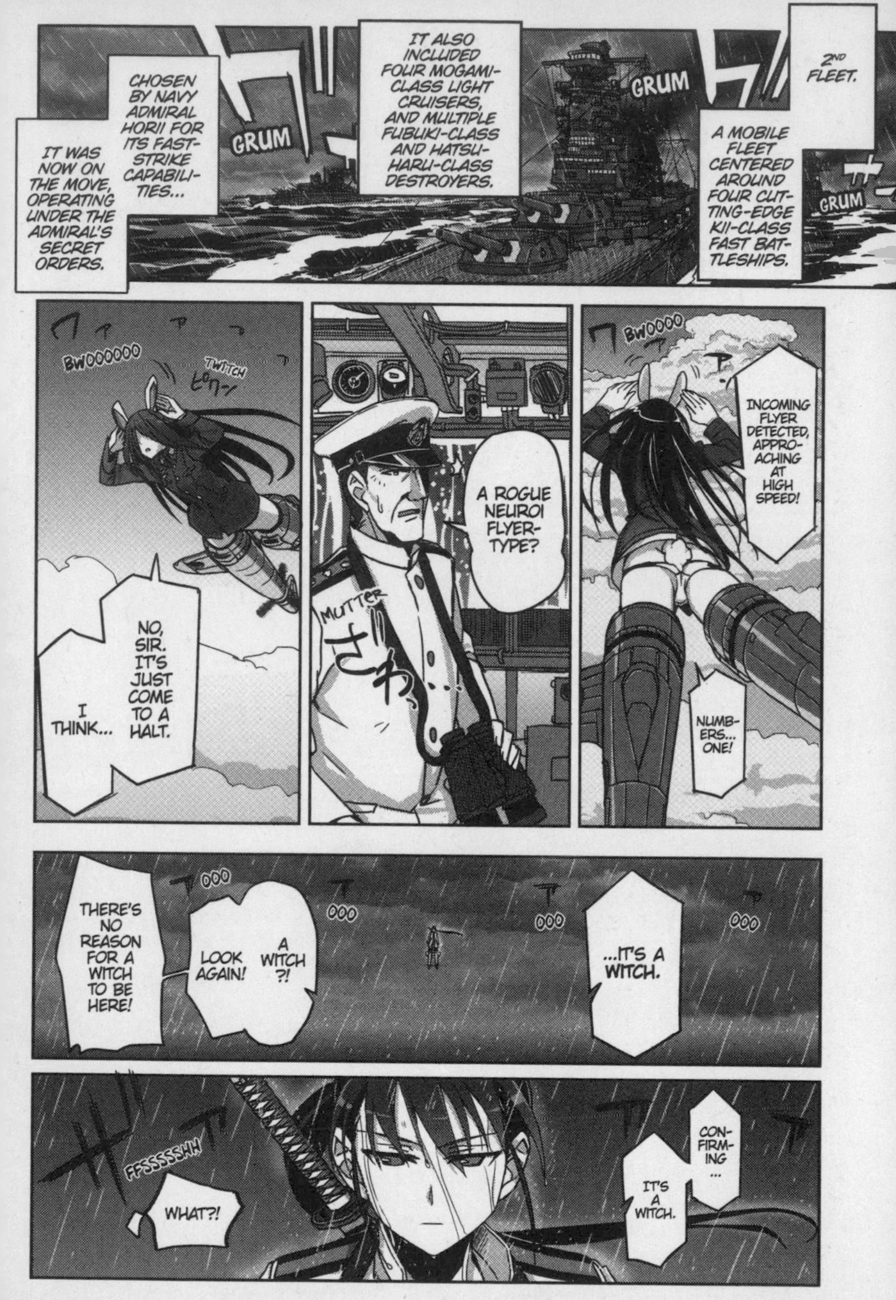
2nd FLEET.
A MOBILE FLEET CENTERED AROUND FOUR CUTTING-EDGE KII-CLASS FAST BATTLESHIPS.
GRUM
GRUM
IT ALSO INCLUDED FOUR MOGAMI-CLASS LIGHT CRUISERS, AND MULTIPLE FUBUKI-CLASS AND HATSU-HARU-CLASS DESTROYERS.
GRUM
CHOSEN BY NAVY ADMIRAL HORII FOR ITS FAST-STRIKE CAPABILI-TIES...
IT WAS NOW ON THE MOVE, OPERATING UNDER THE ADMIRAL'S SECRET ORDERS.
BWOOOO
INCOMING FLYER DETECTED, APPROA-CHING AT HIGH SPEED!
NUMB-ERS... ONE!
A ROGUE NEUROI FLYER-TYPE?
MUTTER
BWOOOOOOO
TWITCH
NO, SIR. IT'S JUST COME TO A HALT.
I THINK...
OOO
...IT'S A WITCH.
OOO
OOO
A WITCH?!
LOOK AGAIN!
OOO
THERE'S NO REASON FOR A WITCH TO BE HERE!
CON-FIRM-ING...
IT'S A WITCH.
FFSSSSSHH
WHAT?!

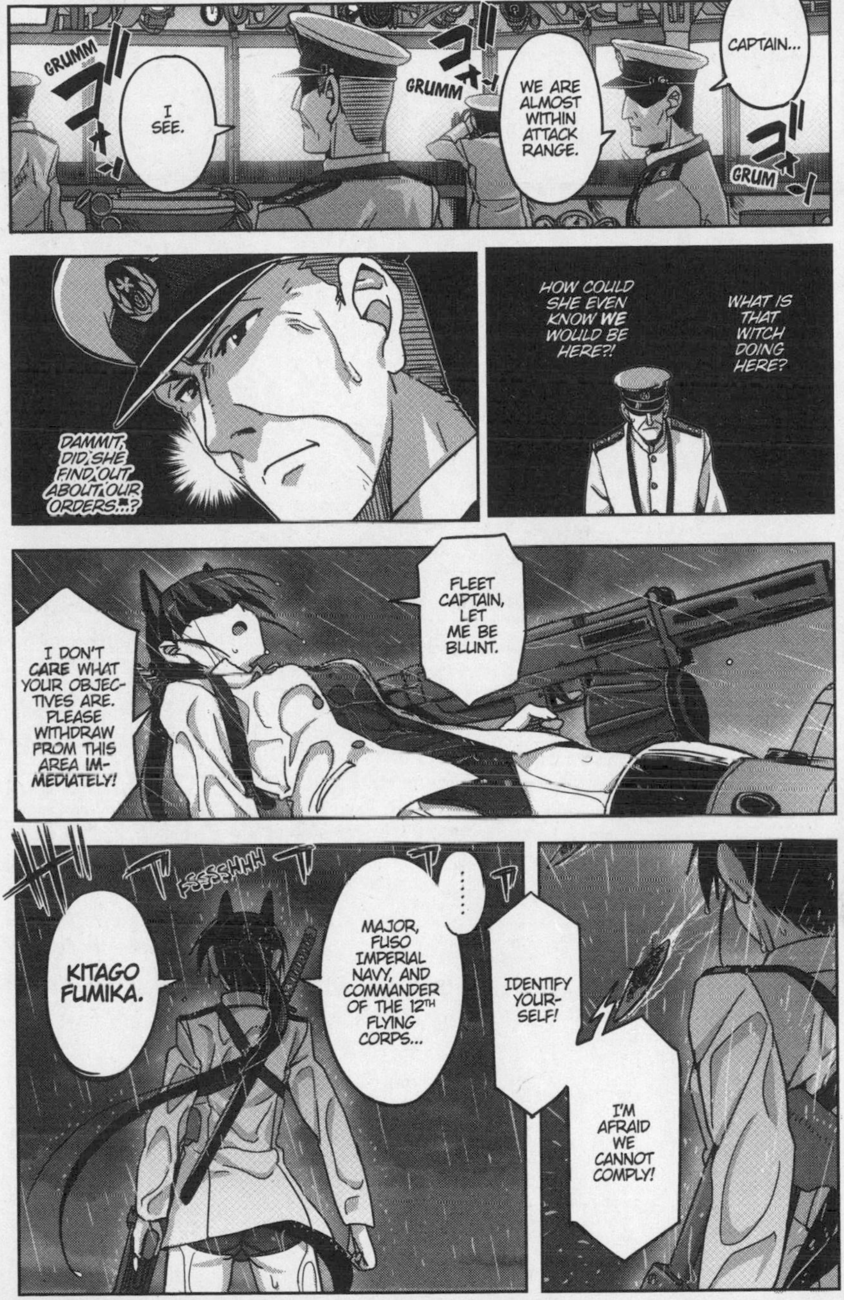
CAPTAIN...
GRUM
WE ARE ALMOST WITHIN ATTACK RANGE.
GRUMM
I SEE.
GRUMM
WHAT IS THAT WITCH DOING HERE?
HOW COULD SHE EVEN KNOW WE WOULD BE HERE?!
DAMMIT, DID SHE FIND OUT ABOUT OUR ORDERS...?
FLEET CAPTAIN, LET ME BE BLUNT.
I DON'T CARE WHAT YOUR OBJECTIVES ARE. PLEASE WITHDRAW FROM THIS AREA IMMEDIATELY!
IDENTIFY YOURSELF!
I'M AFRAID WE CANNOT COMPLY!
......
MAJOR, FUSO IMPERIAL NAVY, AND COMMANDER OF THE 12TH FLYING CORPS...
KITAGO FUMIKA.
FSSSSHHH

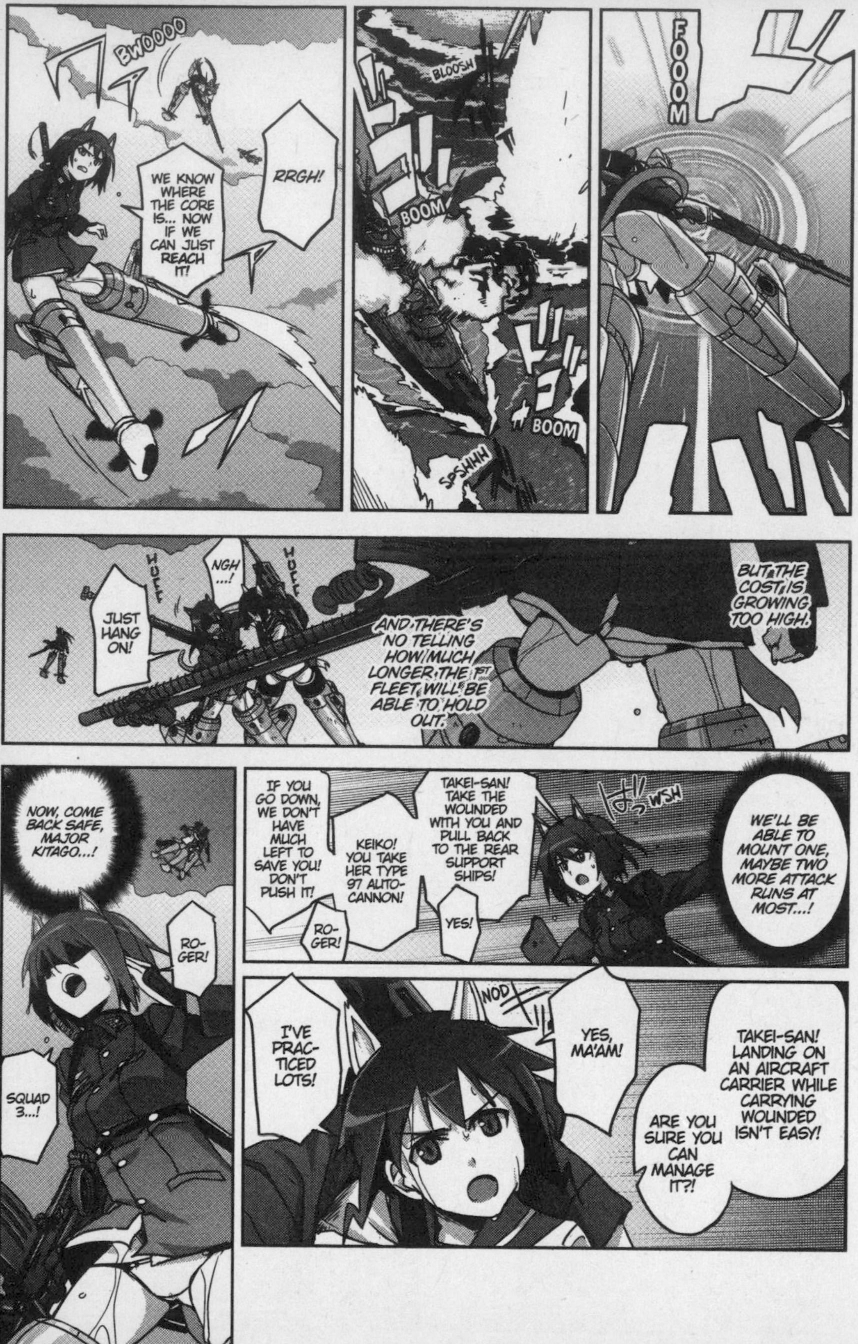
FOOOM
BLOOSH
BOOM
BOOM
SPSHHH
BWOOOO
RRGH!
WE KNOW WHERE THE CORE IS... NOW IF WE CAN JUST REACH IT!
BUT THE COST IS GROWING TOO HIGH.
AND THERE'S NO TELLING HOW MUCH LONGER THE 1ST FLEET WILL BE ABLE TO HOLD OUT.
HUFF
NGH...!
HUFF
JUST HANG ON!
WSH
WE'LL BE ABLE TO MOUNT ONE, MAYBE TWO MORE ATTACK RUNS AT MOST...!
TAKEI-SAN! TAKE THE WOUNDED WITH YOU AND PULL BACK TO THE REAR SUPPORT SHIPS!
YES!
KEIKO! YOU TAKE HER TYPE 97 AUTO-CANNON!
RO-GER!
IF YOU GO DOWN, WE DON'T HAVE MUCH LEFT TO SAVE YOU! DON'T PUSH IT!
TAKEI-SAN! LANDING ON AN AIRCRAFT CARRIER WHILE CARRYING WOUNDED ISN'T EASY!
ARE YOU SURE YOU CAN MANAGE IT?!
YES, MA'AM!
NOD
I'VE PRACTICED LOTS!
NOW, COME BACK SAFE, MAJOR KITAGO...!
RO-GER!
SQUAD 3...!

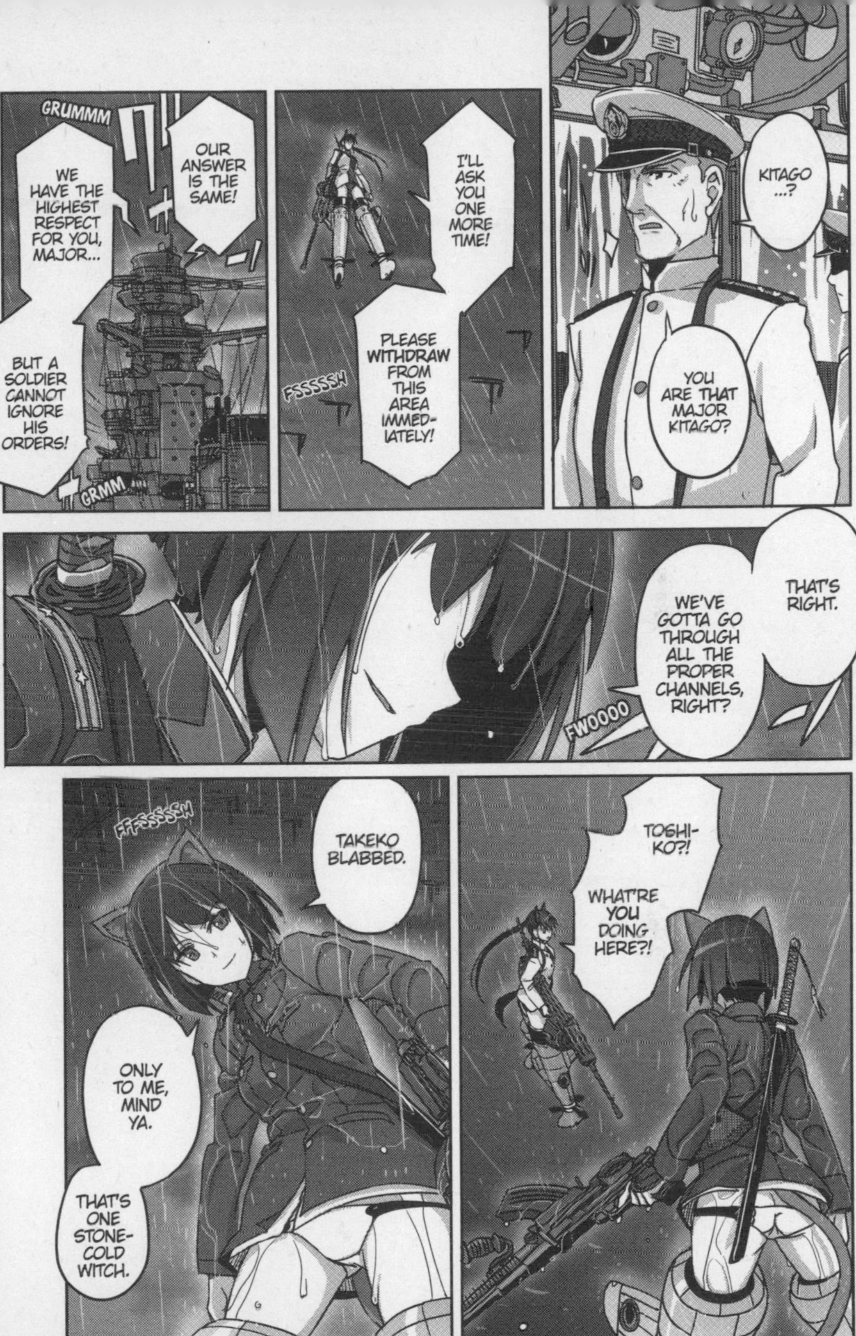
KITAGO ...?
YOU ARE THAT MAJOR KITAGO?
I'LL ASK YOU ONE MORE TIME!
PLEASE WITHDRAW FROM THIS AREA IMMED-IATELY!
FSSSSSH
GRUMMM
OUR ANSWER IS THE SAME!
WE HAVE THE HIGHEST RESPECT FOR YOU, MAJOR...
BUT A SOLDIER CANNOT IGNORE HIS ORDERS!
GRMM
THAT'S RIGHT.
WE'VE GOTTA GO THROUGH ALL THE PROPER CHANNELS, RIGHT?
FWOOOO
TOSHI-KO?!
WHAT'RE YOU DOING HERE?!
FFFSSSSSH
TAKEKO BLABBED.
ONLY TO ME, MIND YA.
THAT'S ONE STONE-COLD WITCH.

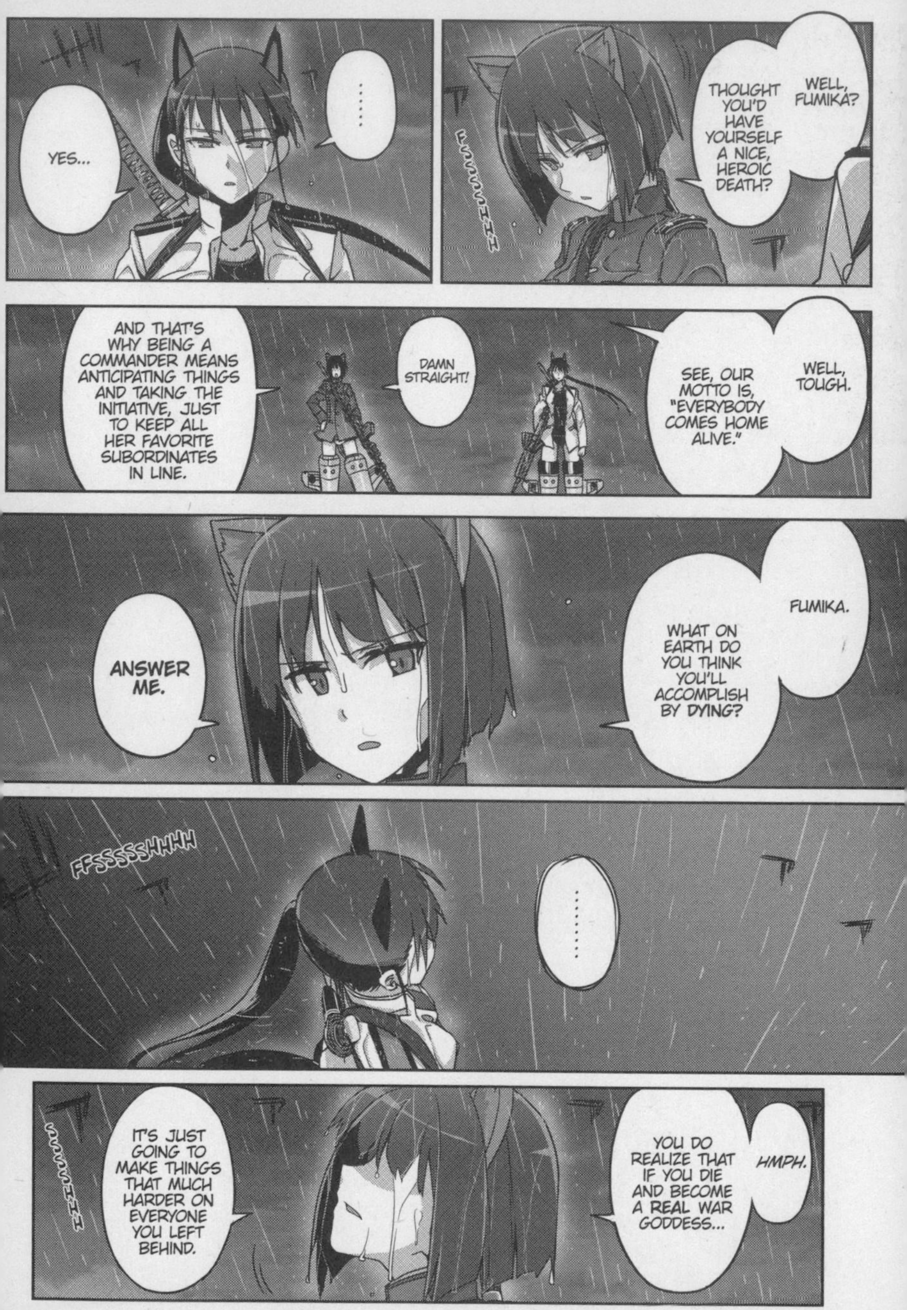
WELL, FUMIKA?
THOUGHT YOU'D HAVE YOURSELF A NICE, HEROIC DEATH?
......
YES...
WELL, TOUGH.
SEE, OUR MOTTO IS, "EVERYBODY COMES HOME ALIVE."
DAMN STRAIGHT!
AND THAT'S WHY BEING A COMMANDER MEANS ANTICIPATING THINGS AND TAKING THE INITIATIVE, JUST TO KEEP ALL HER FAVORITE SUBORDINATES IN LINE.
FUMIKA.
WHAT ON EARTH DO YOU THINK YOU'LL ACCOMPLISH BY DYING?
ANSWER ME.
......
FFSSSSSHHHH
HMPH.
YOU DO REALIZE THAT IF YOU DIE AND BECOME A REAL WAR GODDESS...
IT'S JUST GOING TO MAKE THINGS THAT MUCH HARDER ON EVERYONE YOU LEFT BEHIND.

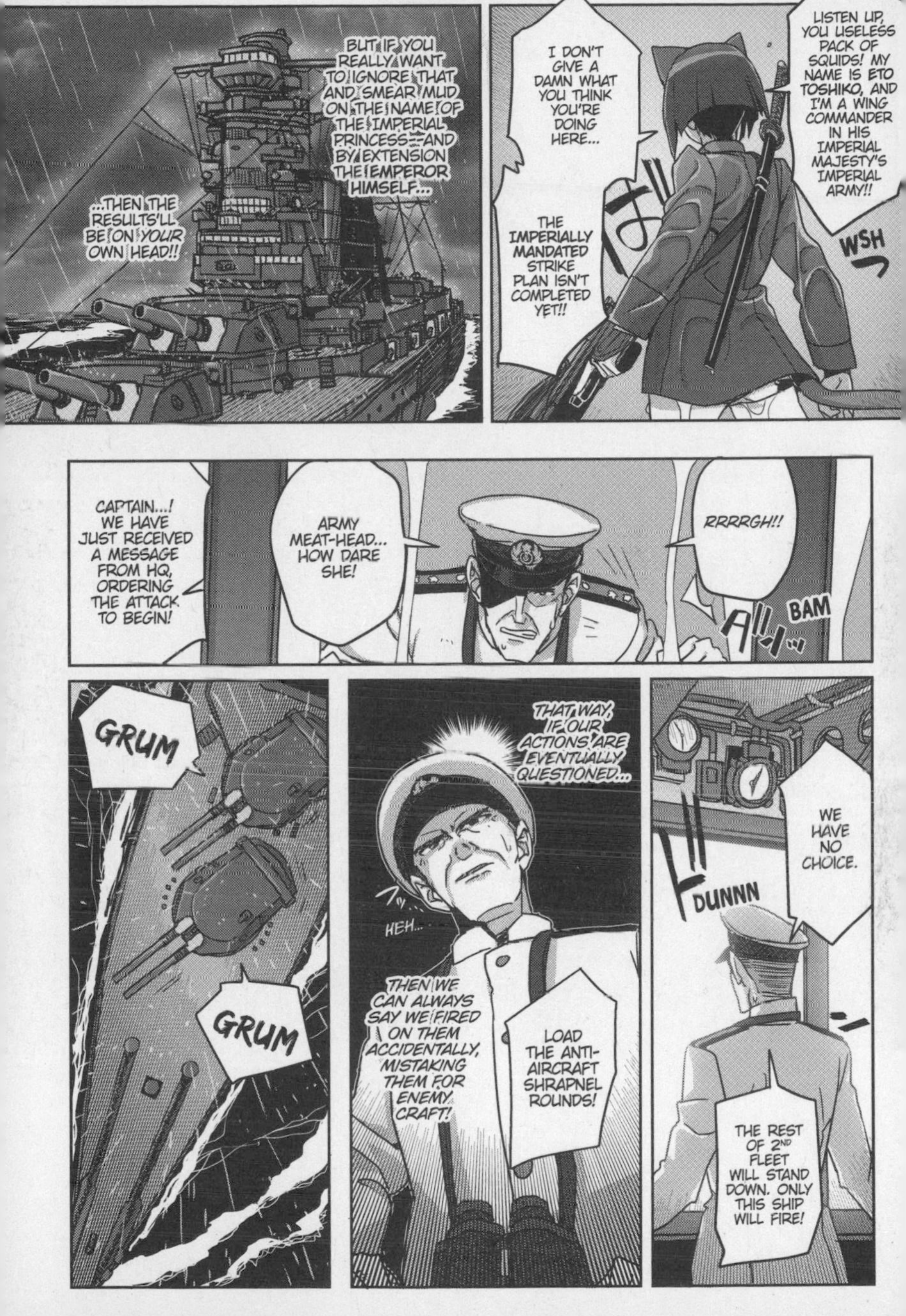
LISTEN UP, YOU USELESS PACK OF SQUIDS! MY NAME IS ETO TOSHIKO, AND I'M A WING COMMANDER IN HIS IMPERIAL MAJESTY'S IMPERIAL ARMY!!
I DON'T GIVE A DAMN WHAT YOU THINK YOU'RE DOING HERE...
THE IMPERIALLY MANDATED STRIKE PLAN ISN'T COMPLETED YET!!
WSH
BUT IF YOU REALLY WANT TO IGNORE THAT AND SMEAR MUD ON THE NAME OF THE IMPERIAL PRINCESS—AND BY EXTENSION THE EMPEROR HIMSELF...
...THEN THE RESULTS'LL BE ON *YOUR* OWN HEAD!!
RRRRGH!!
BAM
ARMY MEAT-HEAD... HOW DARE SHE!
CAPTAIN...! WE HAVE JUST RECEIVED A MESSAGE FROM HQ, ORDERING THE ATTACK TO BEGIN!
WE HAVE NO CHOICE.
DUNNN
THE REST OF 2ND FLEET WILL STAND DOWN. ONLY THIS SHIP WILL FIRE!
THAT WAY, IF OUR ACTIONS ARE EVENTUALLY QUESTIONED...
HEH...
THEN WE CAN ALWAYS SAY WE FIRED ON THEM ACCIDENTALLY, MISTAKING THEM FOR ENEMY CRAFT!
LOAD THE ANTI-AIRCRAFT SHRAPNEL ROUNDS!
GRUM
GRUM

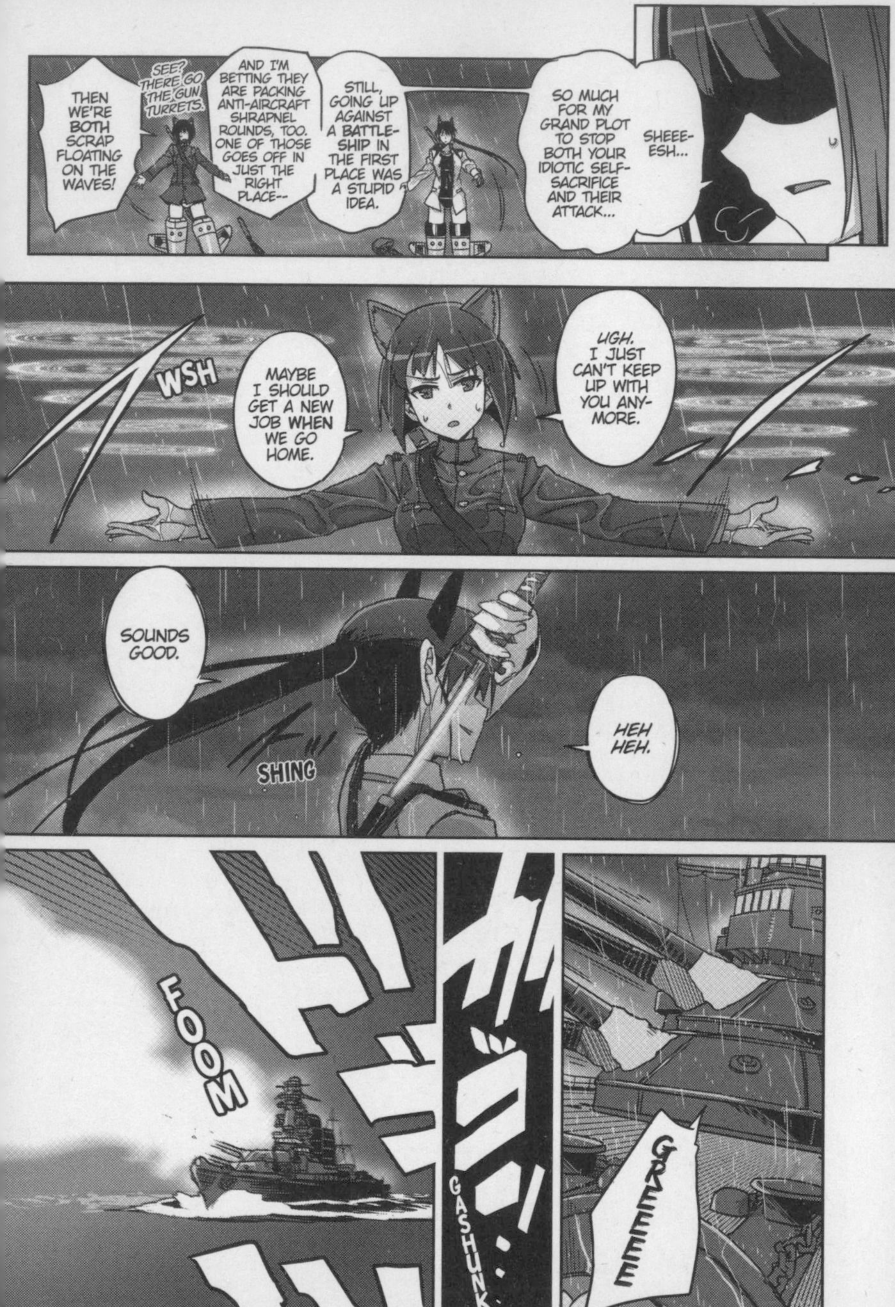
SHEEE-ESH...
SO MUCH FOR MY GRAND PLOT TO STOP BOTH YOUR IDIOTIC SELF-SACRIFICE AND THEIR ATTACK...
STILL, GOING UP AGAINST A BATTLESHIP IN THE FIRST PLACE WAS A STUPID IDEA.
AND I'M BETTING THEY ARE PACKING ANTI-AIRCRAFT SHRAPNEL ROUNDS, TOO. ONE OF THOSE GOES OFF IN JUST THE RIGHT PLACE--
SEE? THERE GO THE GUN TURRETS.
THEN WE'RE BOTH SCRAP FLOATING ON THE WAVES!
UGH. I JUST CAN'T KEEP UP WITH YOU ANYMORE.
MAYBE I SHOULD GET A NEW JOB WHEN WE GO HOME.
WSH
HEH HEH.
SOUNDS GOOD.
SHING
GREEEE
GASHUNK
FOOM

Chapter 11:
If I Die in the Sky
[Mission Complete]

CHAPTER 12:
WHAT WITCHES ARE MADE OF

THAT WAS A STORY REPEATED
COUNTLESS TIMES IN COUNTLESS WAYS...

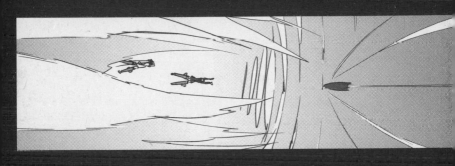

ON BATTLEFIELDS
ACROSS THE AGES--

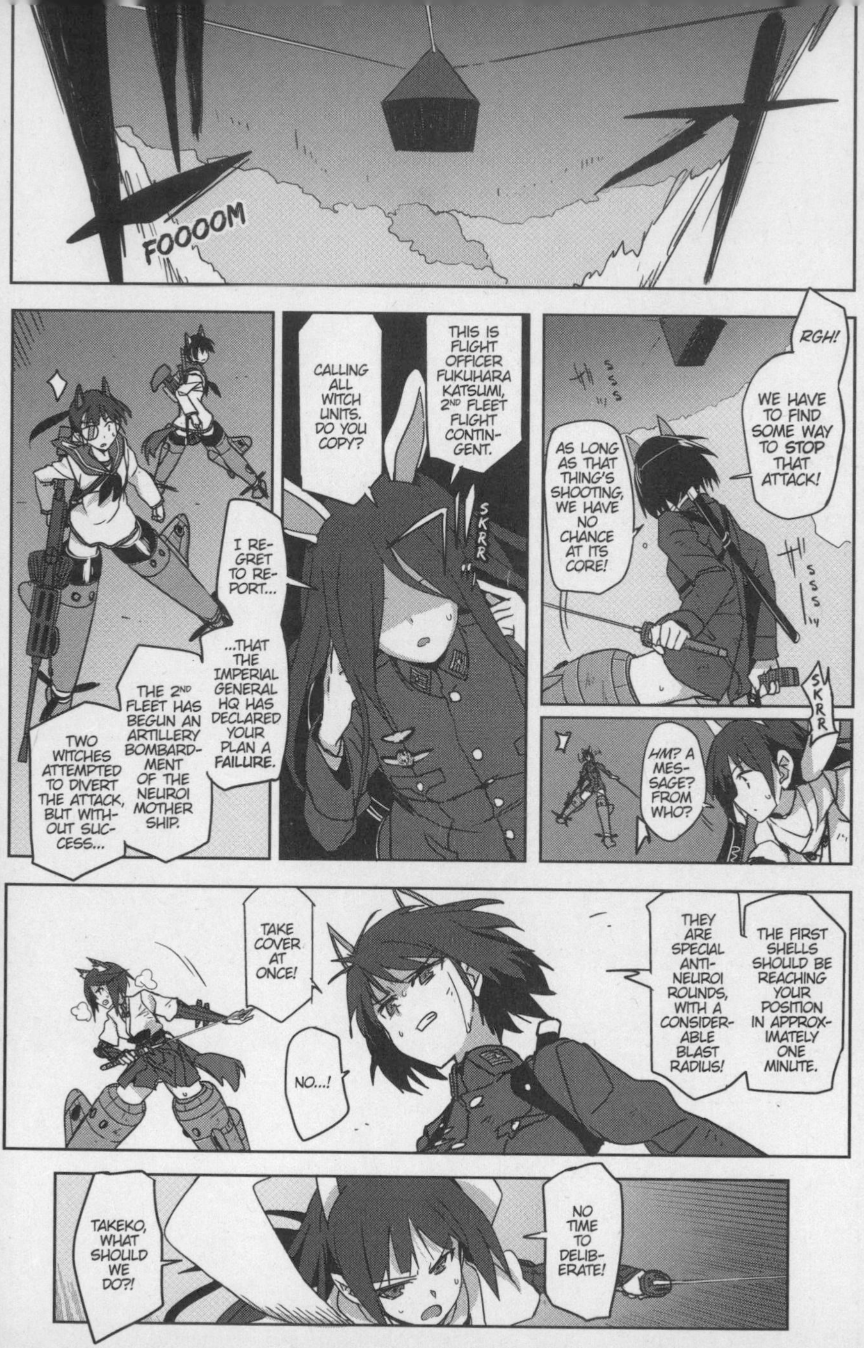
FOOOOM
RGH!
WE HAVE TO FIND SOME WAY TO STOP THAT ATTACK!
AS LONG AS THAT THING'S SHOOTING, WE HAVE NO CHANCE AT ITS CORE!
SSS
SSS
SKRR
HM? A MESSAGE? FROM WHO?
SKRR
THIS IS FLIGHT OFFICER FUKUHARA KATSUMI, 2ND FLEET FLIGHT CONTINGENT.
CALLING ALL WITCH UNITS. DO YOU COPY?
I REGRET TO REPORT...
...THAT THE IMPERIAL GENERAL HQ HAS DECLARED YOUR PLAN A FAILURE.
THE 2ND FLEET HAS BEGUN AN ARTILLERY BOMBARDMENT OF THE NEUROI MOTHER SHIP.
TWO WITCHES ATTEMPTED TO DIVERT THE ATTACK, BUT WITHOUT SUCCESS...
THE FIRST SHELLS SHOULD BE REACHING YOUR POSITION IN APPROXIMATELY ONE MINUTE.
THEY ARE SPECIAL ANTI-NEUROI ROUNDS, WITH A CONSIDERABLE BLAST RADIUS!
TAKE COVER AT ONCE!
NO...!
NO TIME TO DELIBERATE!
TAKEKO, WHAT SHOULD WE DO?!

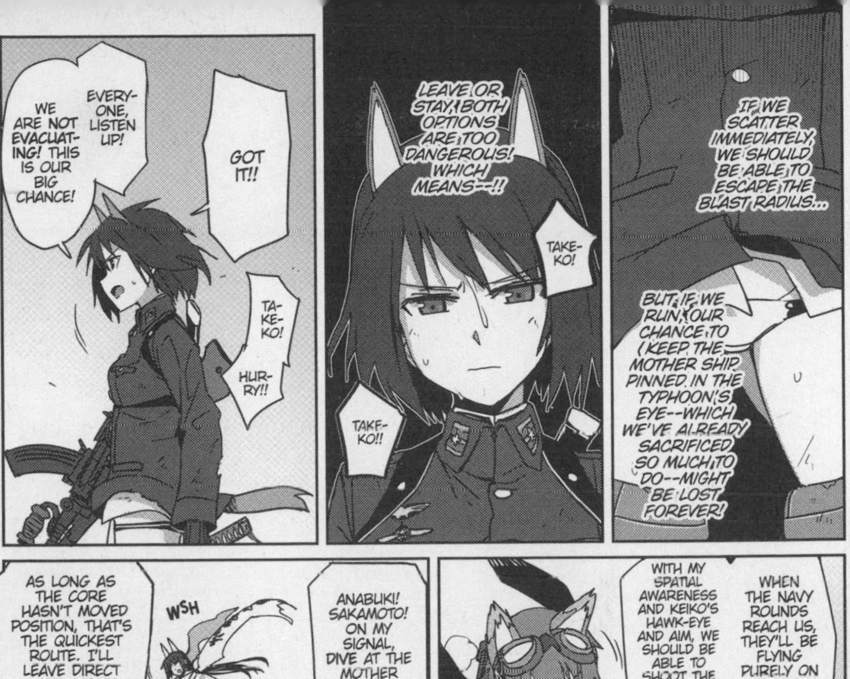
IF WE SCATTER IMMEDIATELY, WE SHOULD BE ABLE TO ESCAPE THE BLAST RADIUS...
BUT, IF WE RUN, OUR CHANCE TO KEEP THE MOTHER SHIP PINNED IN THE TYPHOON'S EYE--WHICH WE'VE ALREADY SACRIFICED SO MUCH TO DO--MIGHT BE LOST FOREVER!
LEAVE OR STAY, BOTH OPTIONS ARE TOO DANGEROUS! WHICH MEANS--!!
TAKE-KO!
TAKE-KO!!
EVERY-ONE, LISTEN UP!
WE ARE NOT EVACUATING! THIS IS OUR BIG CHANCE!
GOT IT!!
TA-KE-KO!
HUR-RY!!
WHEN THE NAVY ROUNDS REACH US, THEY'LL BE FLYING PURELY ON MOMENTUM, ALMOST IN FREE-FALL!
WITH MY SPATIAL AWARENESS AND KEIKO'S HAWK-EYE AND AIM, WE SHOULD BE ABLE TO SHOOT THE ORDINANCE DOWN BEFORE IT BURSTS!
KEIKO, HOW MANY MINENGESCHOS* DO YOU HAVE LEFT?
JUST A FEW ROUNDS.
SHOULD BE ENOUGH, DON'T YOU THINK?
ANABUKI! SAKAMOTO! ON MY SIGNAL, DIVE AT THE MOTHER SHIP'S CORE FROM DIRECTLY ABOVE!
WSH
AS LONG AS THE CORE HASN'T MOVED POSITION, THAT'S THE QUICKEST ROUTE. I'LL LEAVE DIRECT GUIDANCE TO YOU AND YOUR MAGIC EYE, SAKAMOTO!
NOD
BUT WHAT ABOUT THOSE BEAMS?
DO YOU HAVE SOME KIND OF PLAN FOR GETTING PAST THAT THING'S NASTIEST ATTACK?

*Mine shells, a type of autocannon ammo.

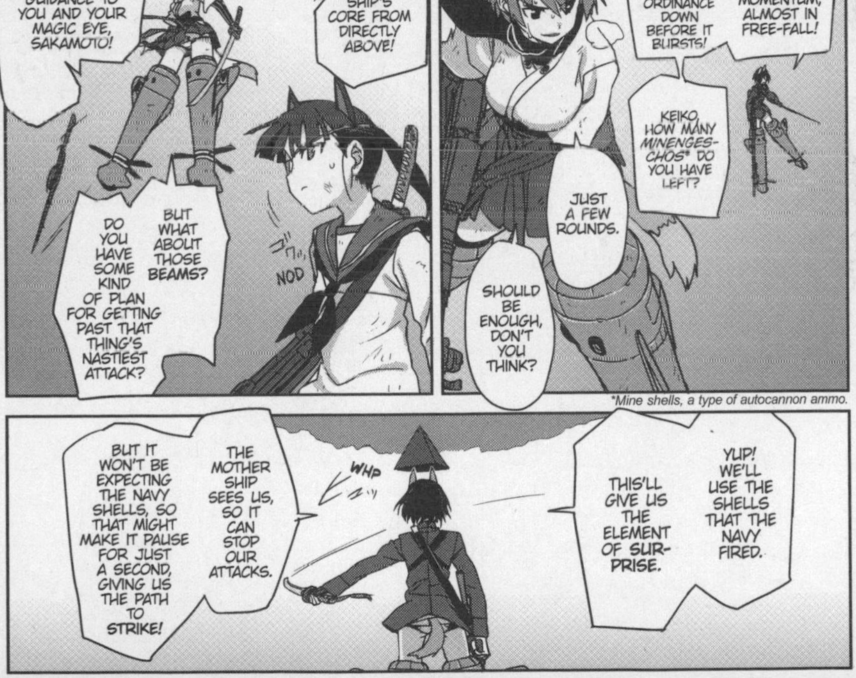
YUP! WE'LL USE THE SHELLS THAT THE NAVY FIRED.
THIS'LL GIVE US THE ELEMENT OF SURPRISE.
WHP
THE MOTHER SHIP SEES US, SO IT CAN STOP OUR ATTACKS.
BUT IT WON'T BE EXPECTING THE NAVY SHELLS, SO THAT MIGHT MAKE IT PAUSE FOR JUST A SECOND, GIVING US THE PATH TO STRIKE!

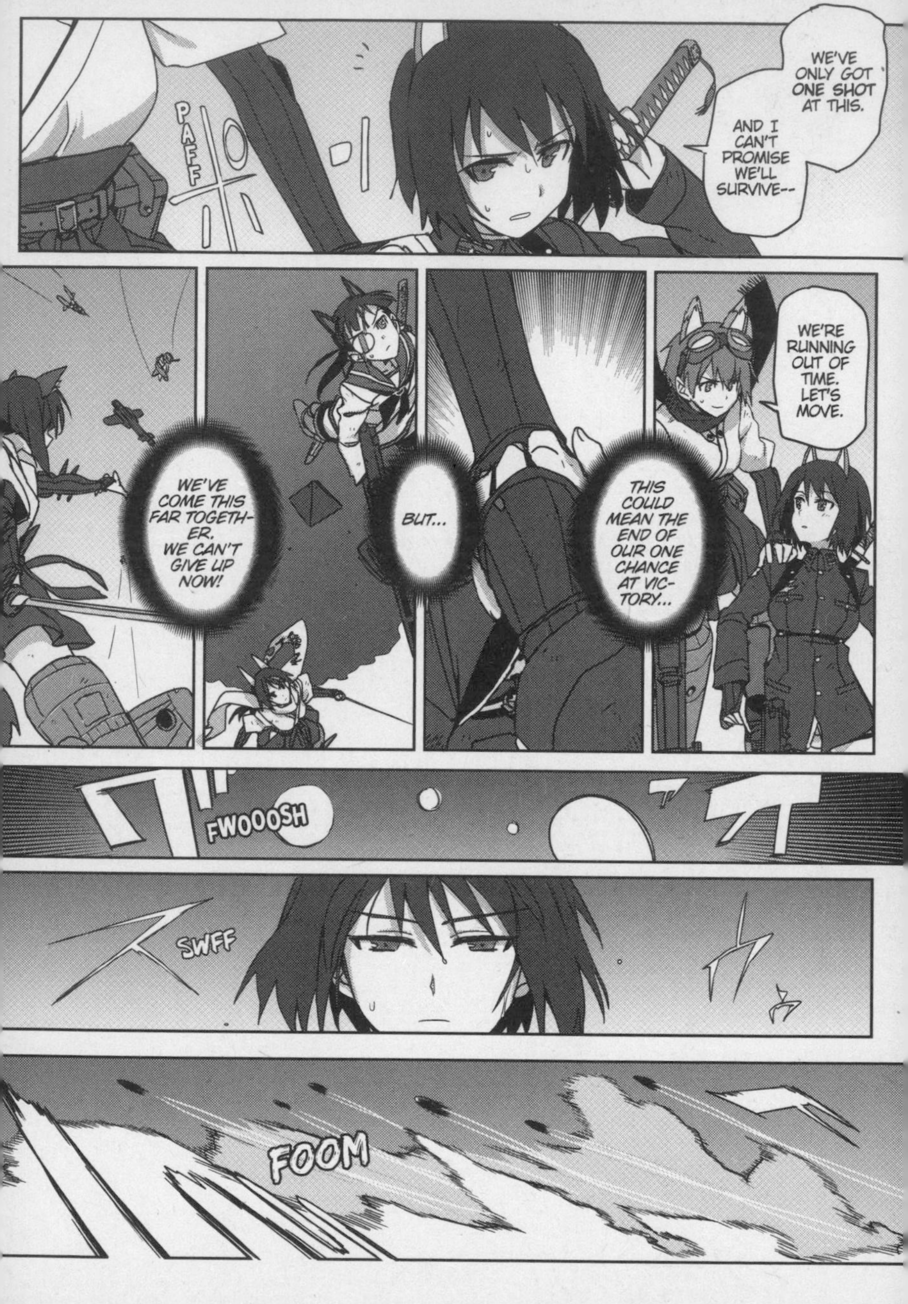
WE'VE ONLY GOT ONE SHOT AT THIS.
AND I CAN'T PROMISE WE'LL SURVIVE--
PAFF
WE'RE RUNNING OUT OF TIME. LET'S MOVE.
THIS COULD MEAN THE END OF OUR ONE CHANCE AT VICTORY...
BUT...
WE'VE COME THIS FAR TOGETHER. WE CAN'T GIVE UP NOW!
FWOOOSH
SWFF
FOOM

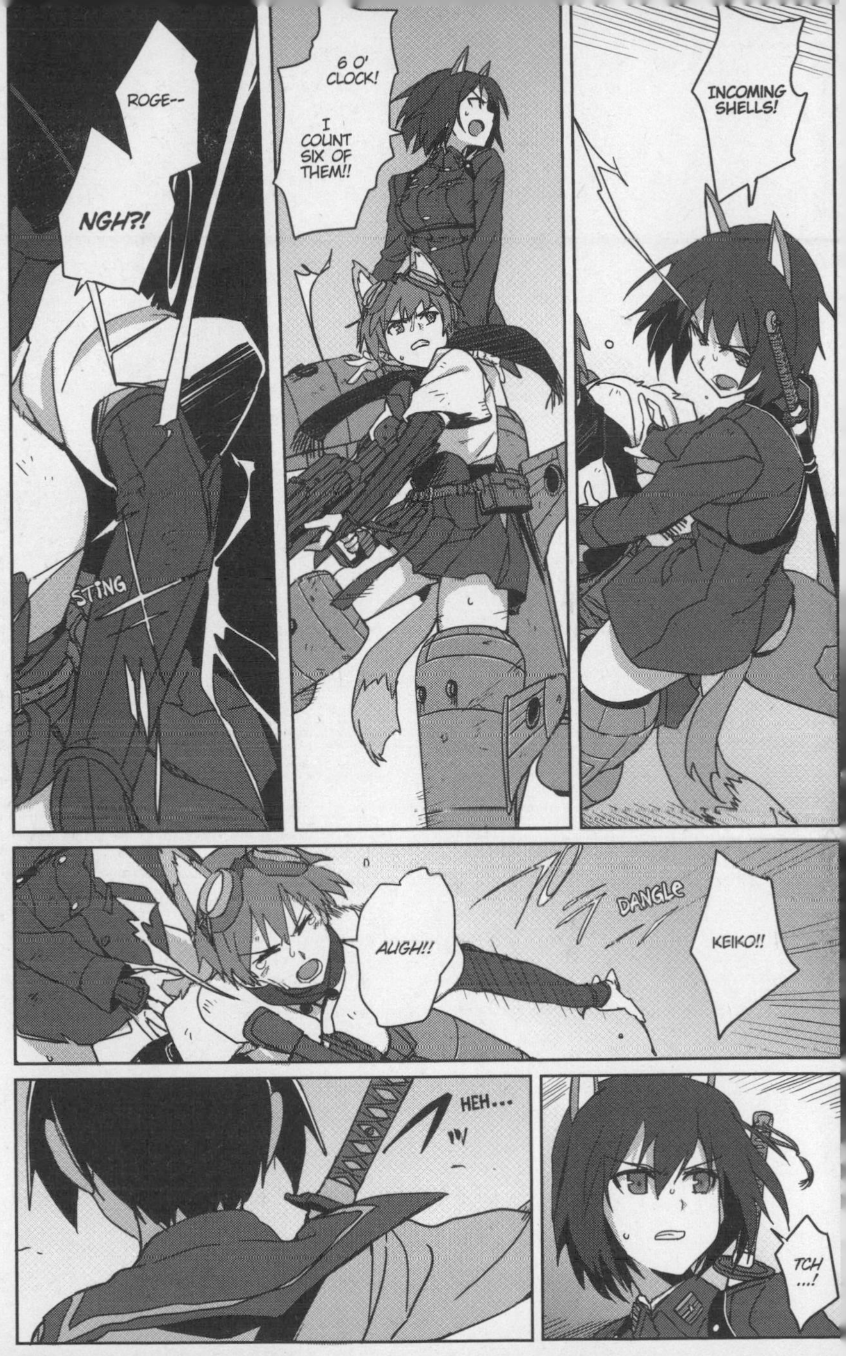
INCOMING SHELLS!
6 O' CLOCK!
I COUNT SIX OF THEM!!
ROGE--
NGH?!
STING
KEIKO!!
DANGLE
AUGH!!
TCH ...!
HEH...

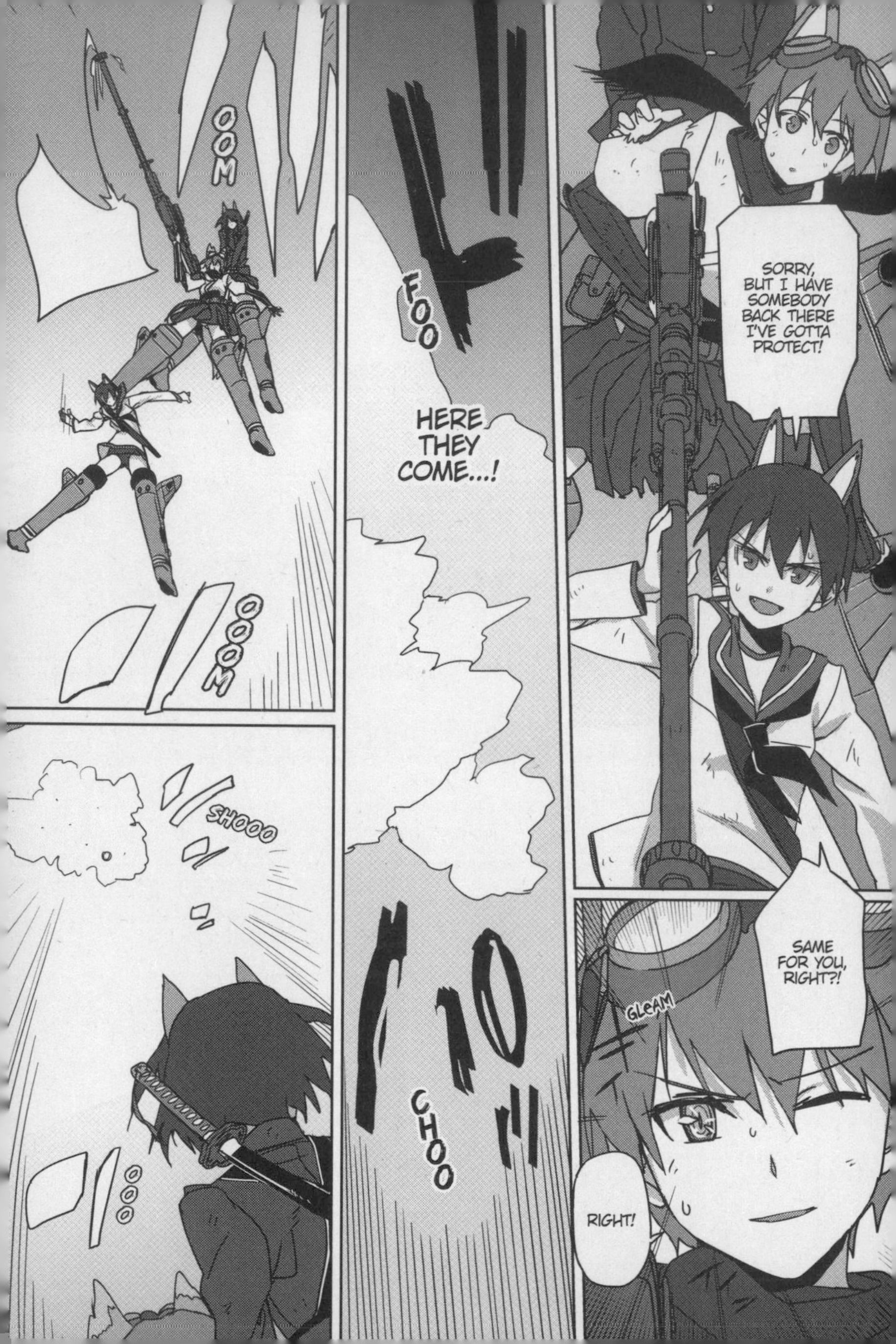
SORRY, BUT I HAVE SOMEBODY BACK THERE I'VE GOTTA PROTECT!
SAME FOR YOU, RIGHT?!
GLEAM
RIGHT!
FOO
HERE THEY COME...!
CHOO
OOM
OOOM
SHOOO
OOO

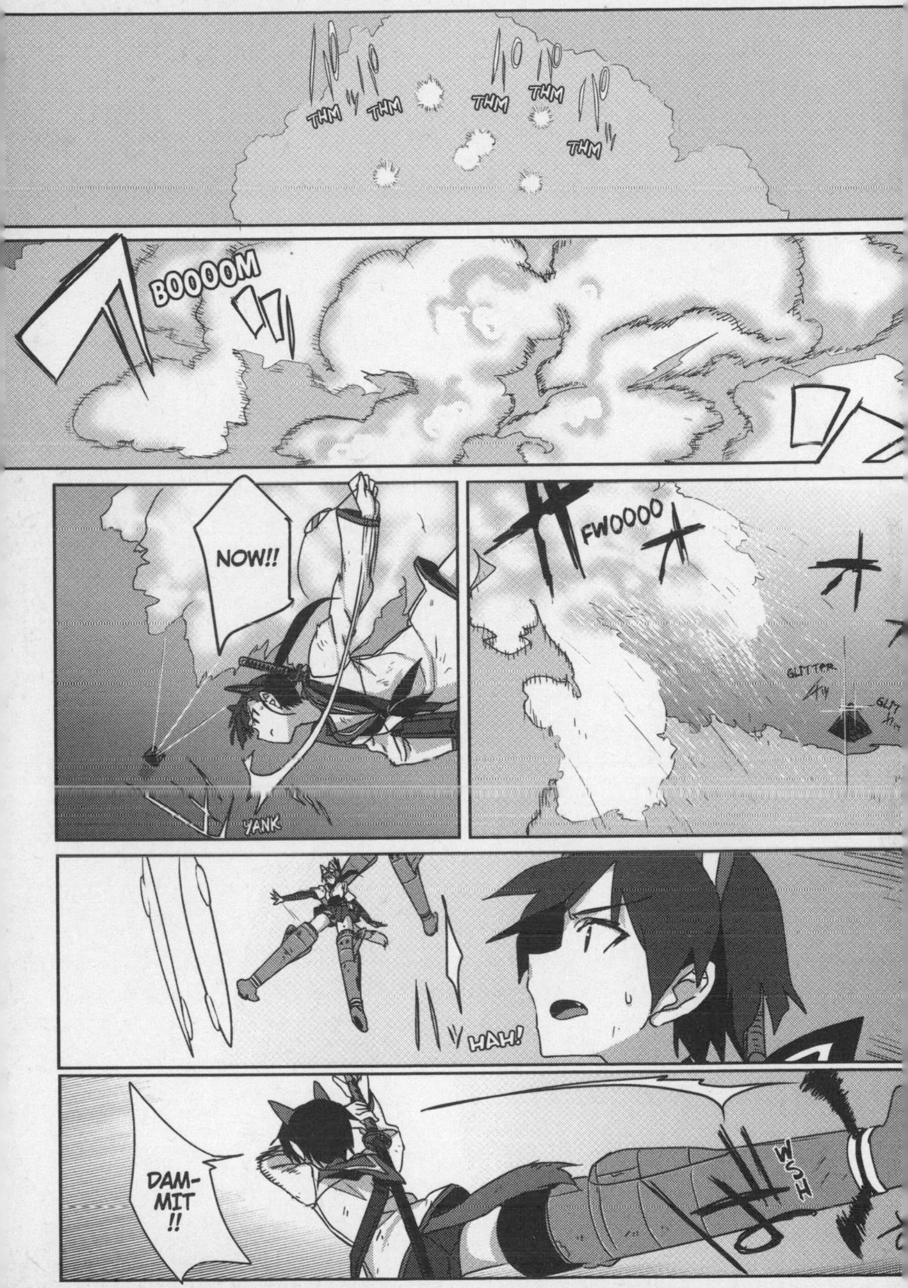
THM
THM
THM
THM
THM
BOOOOM
FWOOOO
GLITTER
NOW!!
YANK
HAH!
DAM-MIT!!
WSH

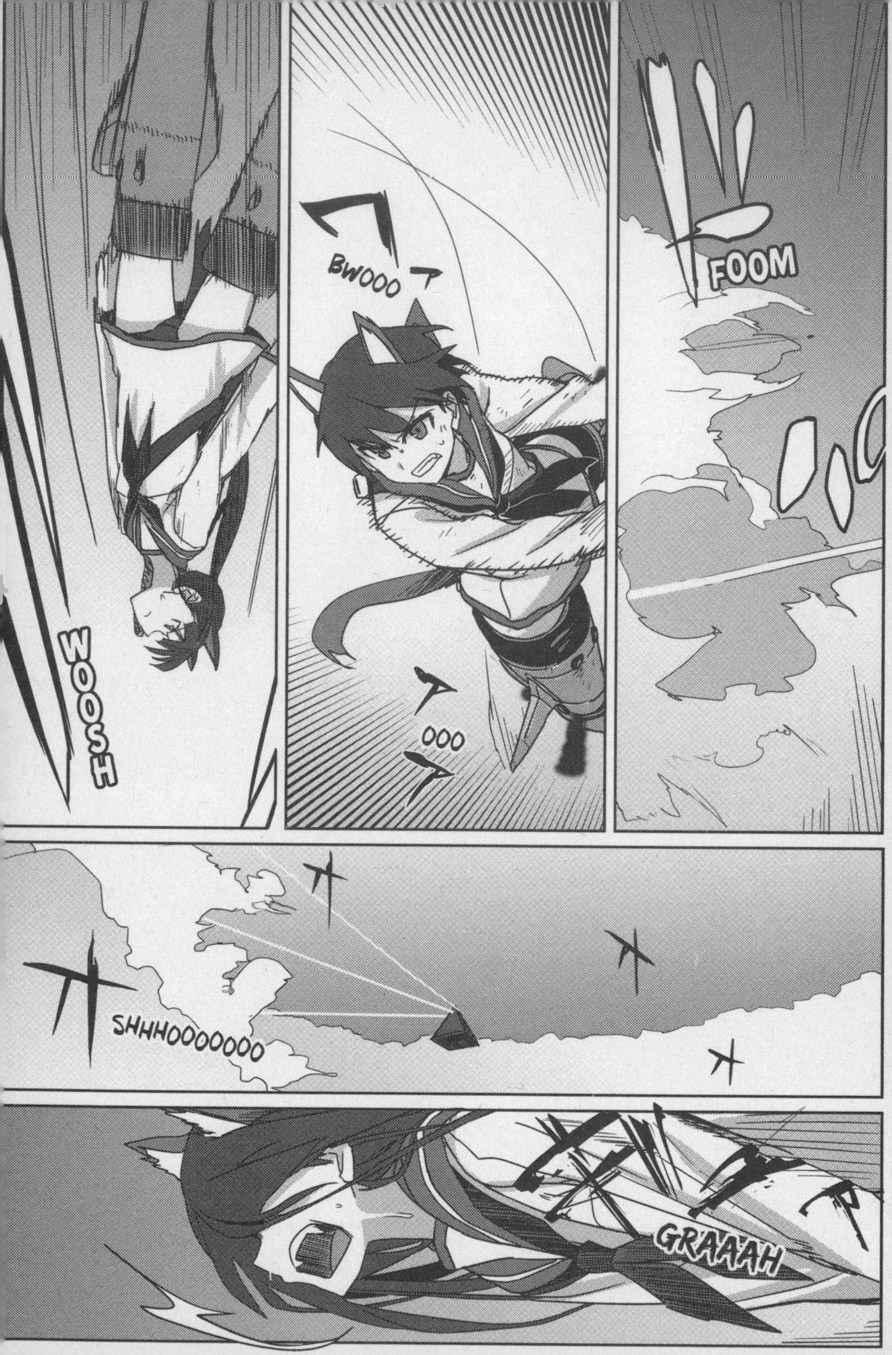
FOOM
BWOOO
OOO
WOOSH
SHHHOOOOOOO
GRAAAH

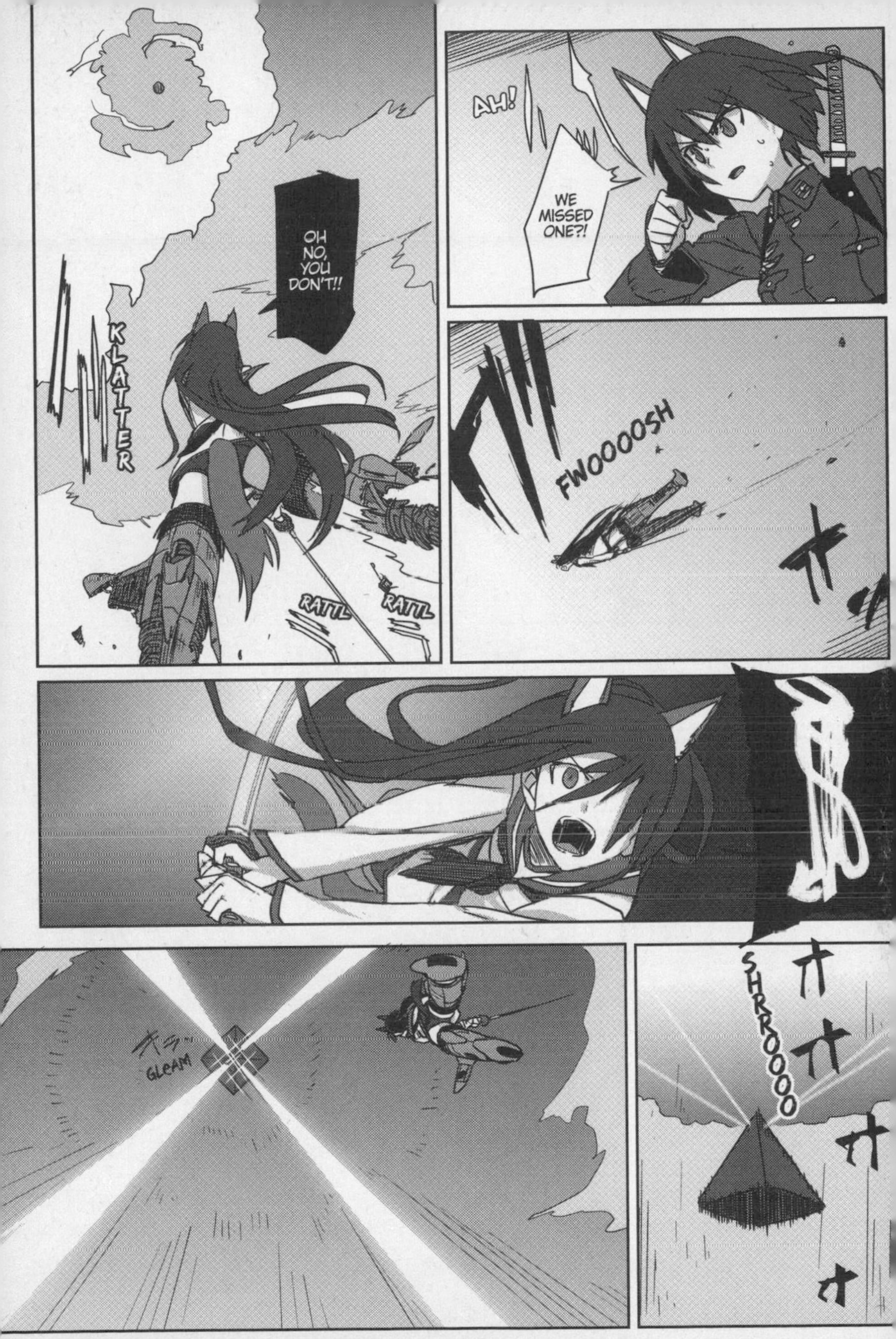
AH!
WE MISSED ONE?!
FWOOOOSH
OH NO, YOU DON'T!!
KLATTER
RATTL
RATTL
SHRROOOOO
GLEAM

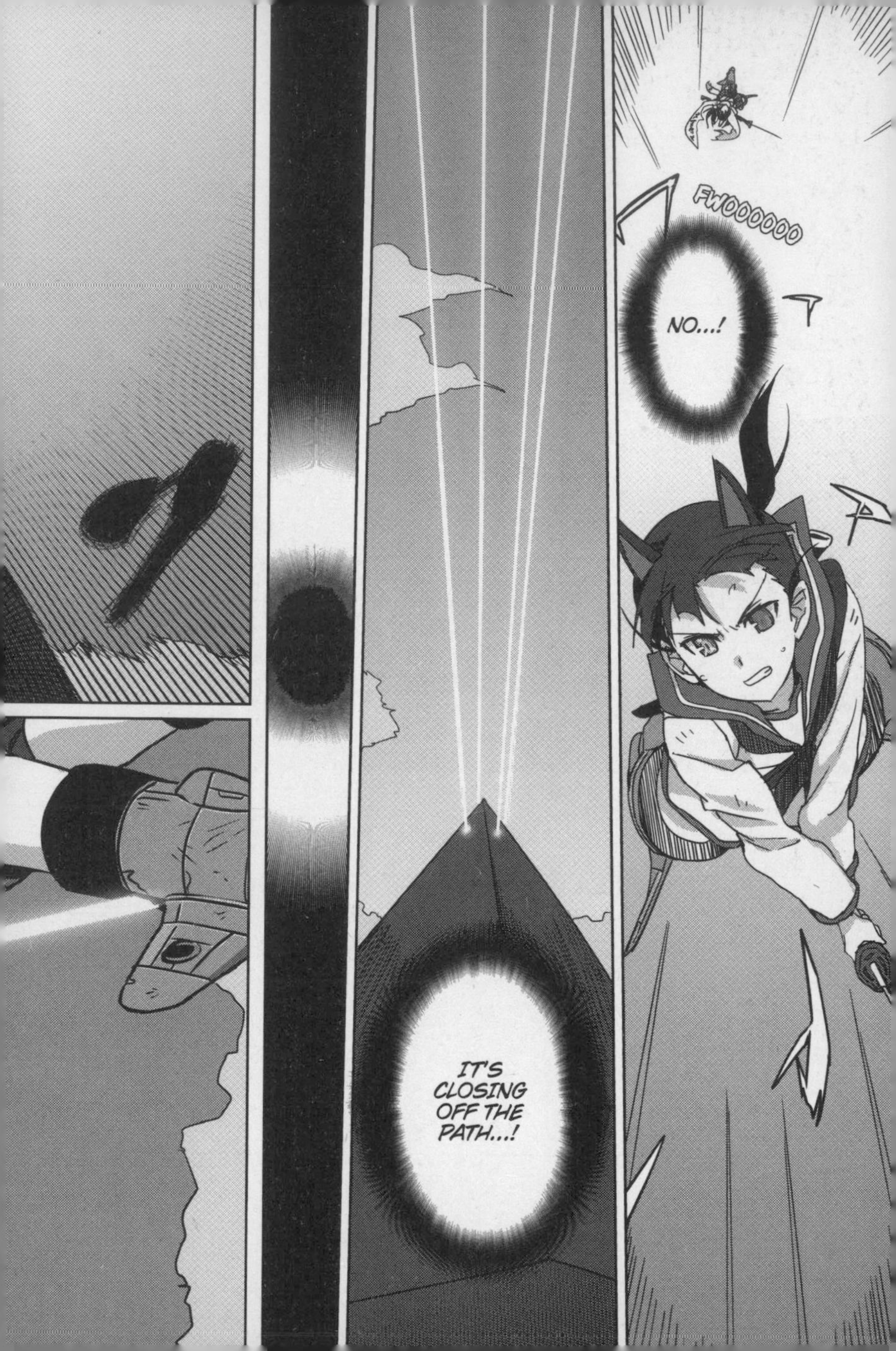
FWOOOOOO
NO...!
IT'S CLOSING OFF THE PATH...!

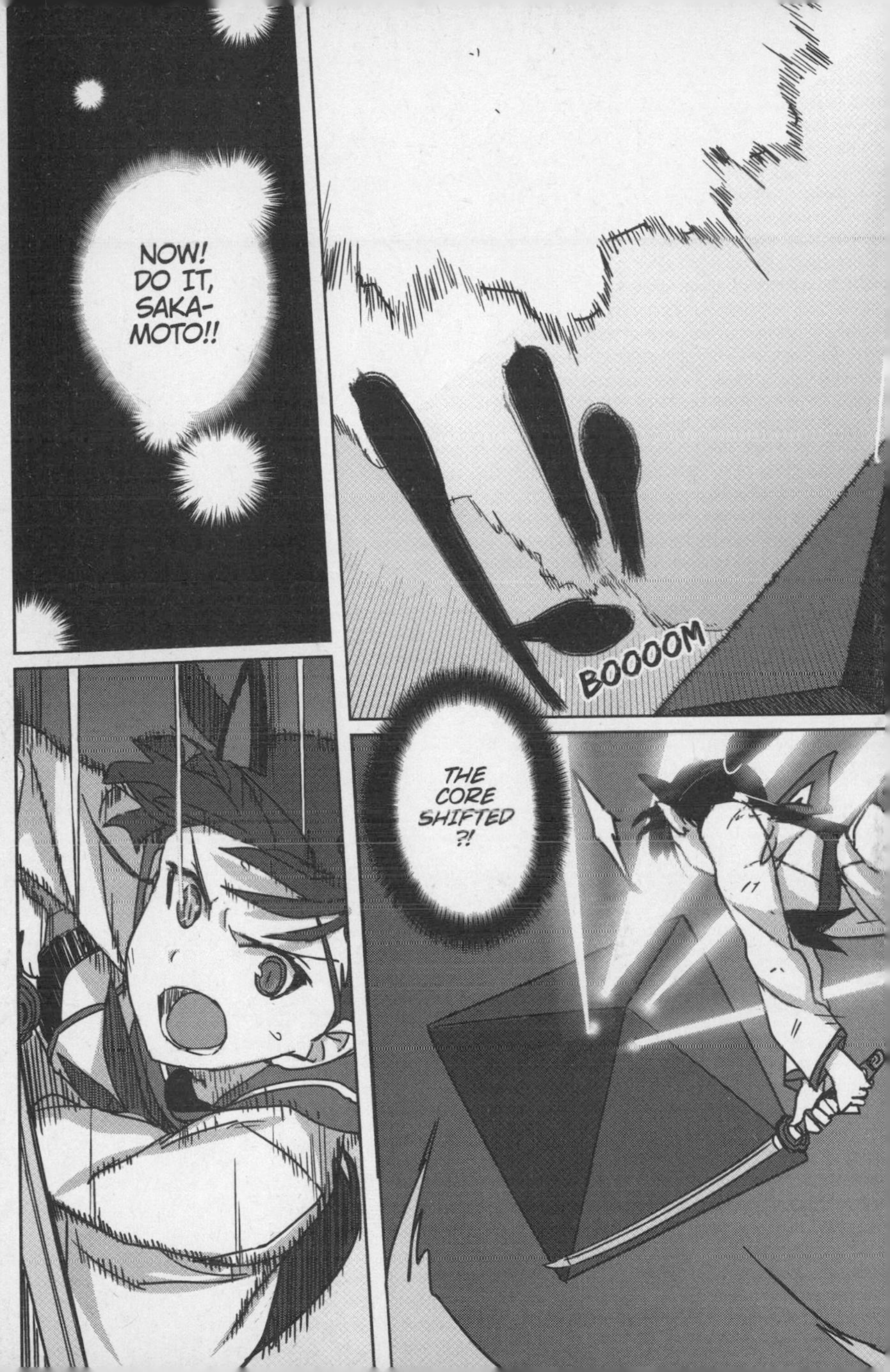
BOOOOM
NOW! DO IT, SAKA-MOTO!!
THE CORE SHIFTED ?!

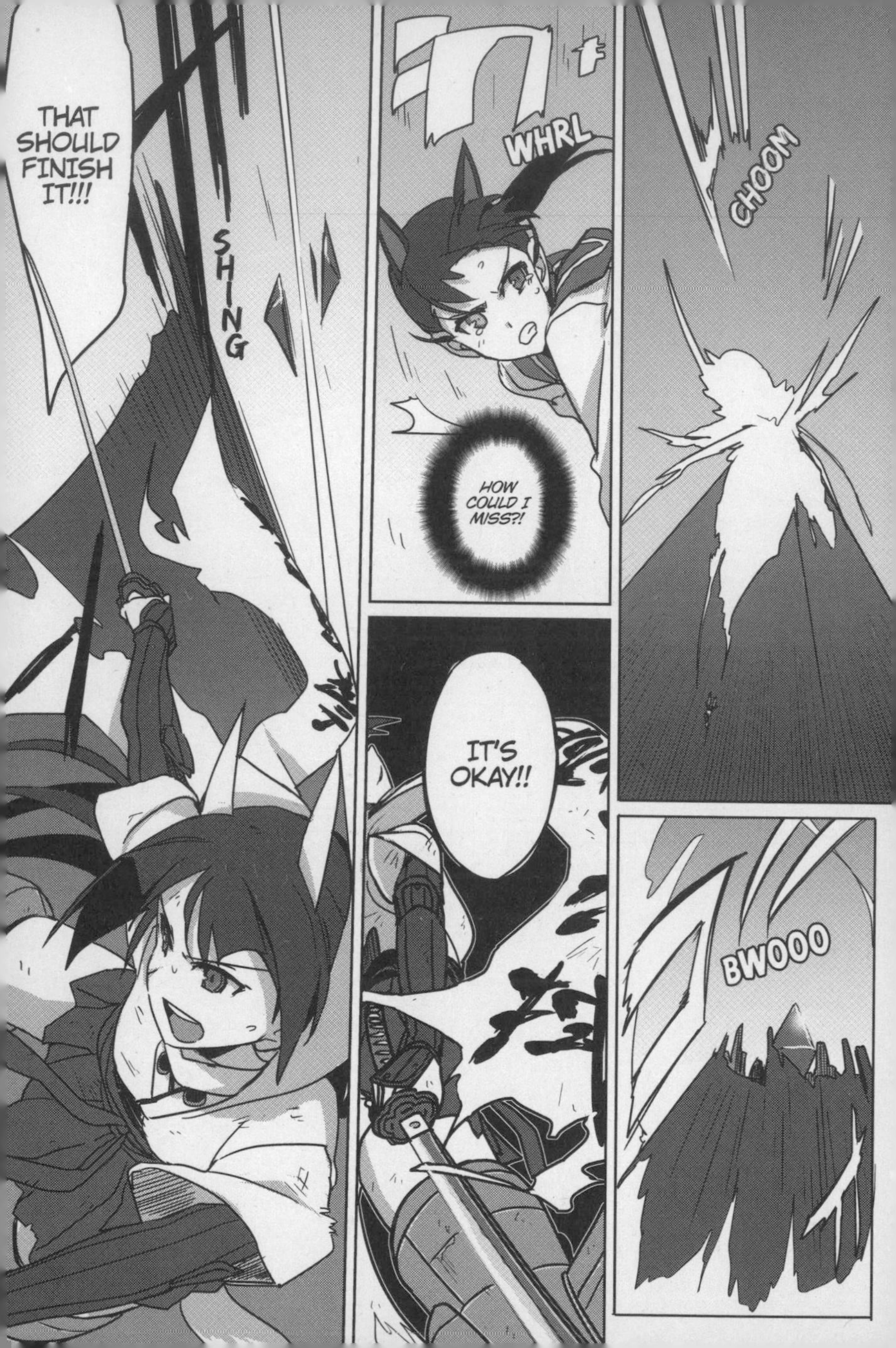
CHOOM
BWOOO
WHRL
HOW COULD I MISS?!
IT'S OKAY!!
THAT SHOULD FINISH IT!!!
SHING

What Witches are Made of
[Mission Complete]

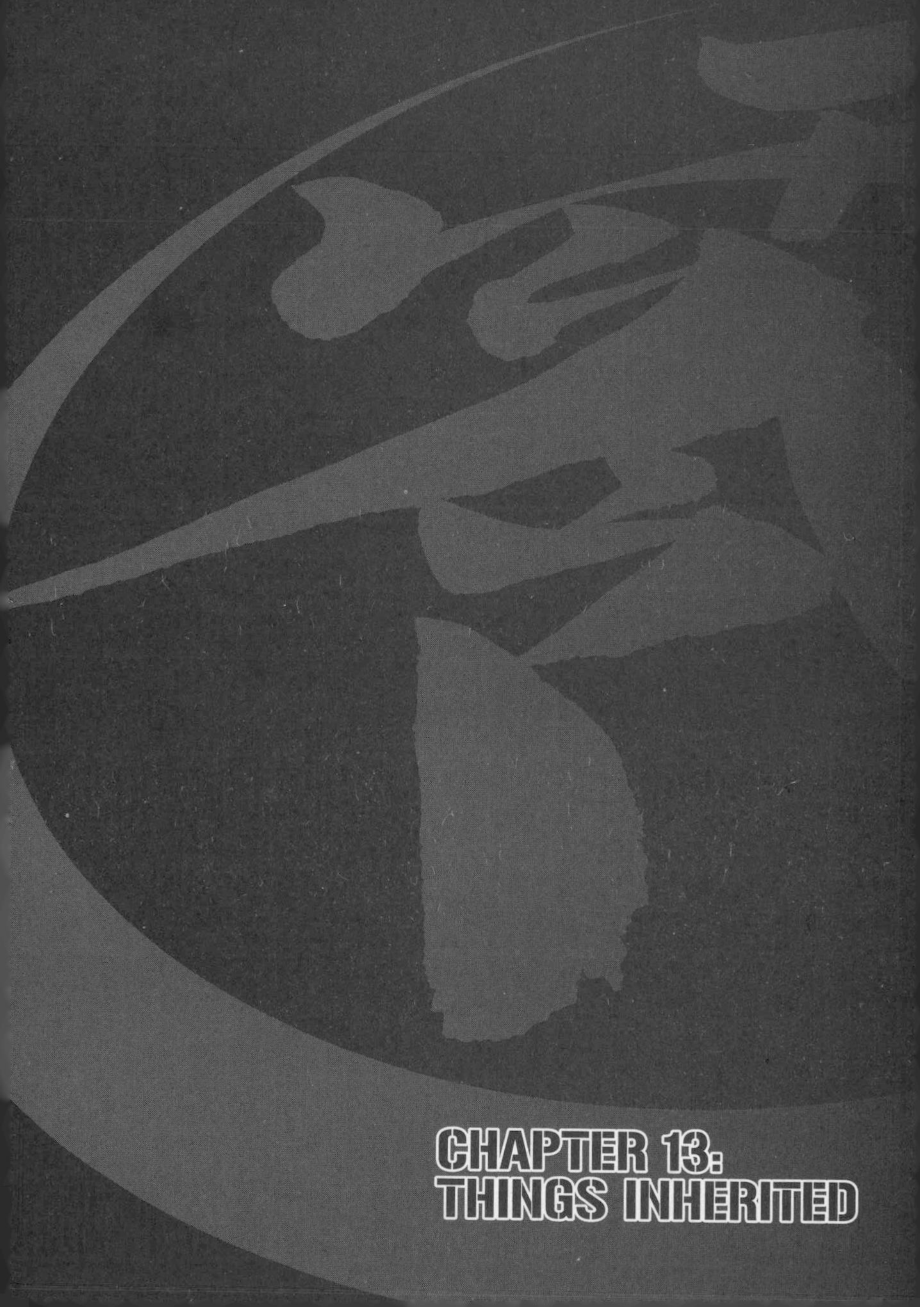

CHAPTER 13: THINGS INHERITED

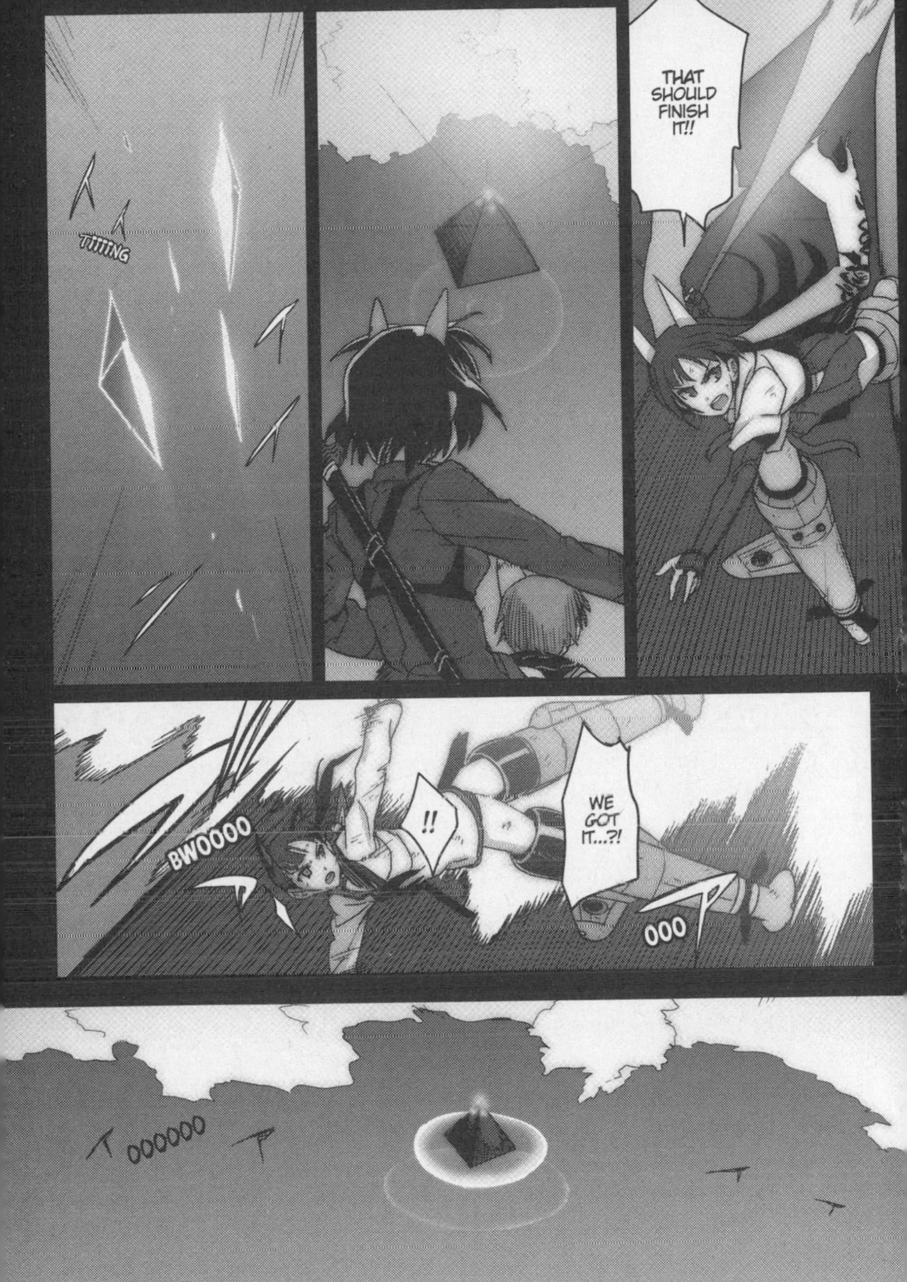
THAT SHOULD FINISH IT!!
TIIIING
WE GOT IT...?!
!!
BWOOOO
OOO
OOOOOO

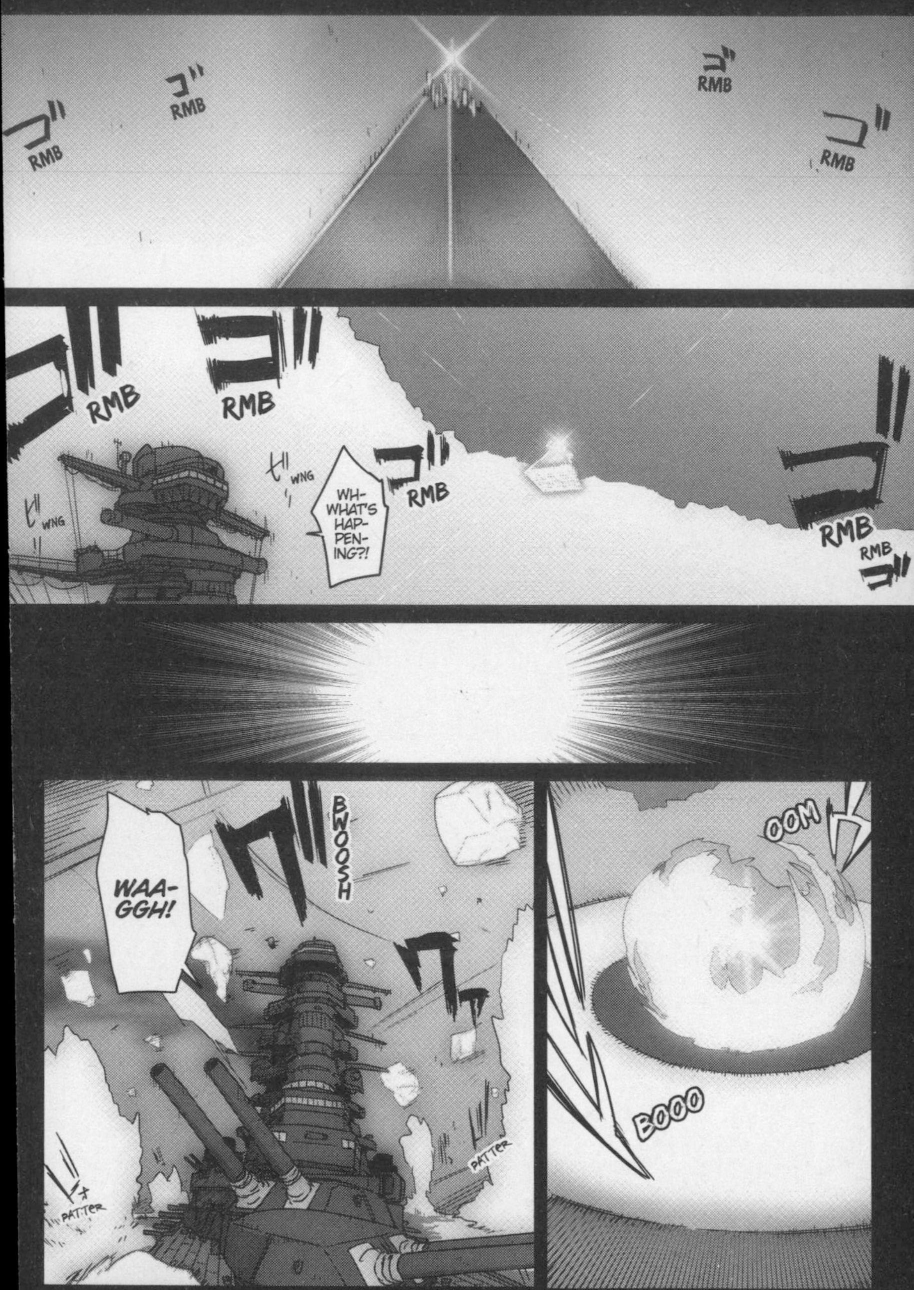

RMB
RMB
RMB
RMB
RMB
RMB
RMB
WH-WHAT'S HAP-PEN-ING?!
WNG
WNG
RMB
RMB
OOM
BOOO
BWOOSH
WAA-GGH!
PATTER
PATTER

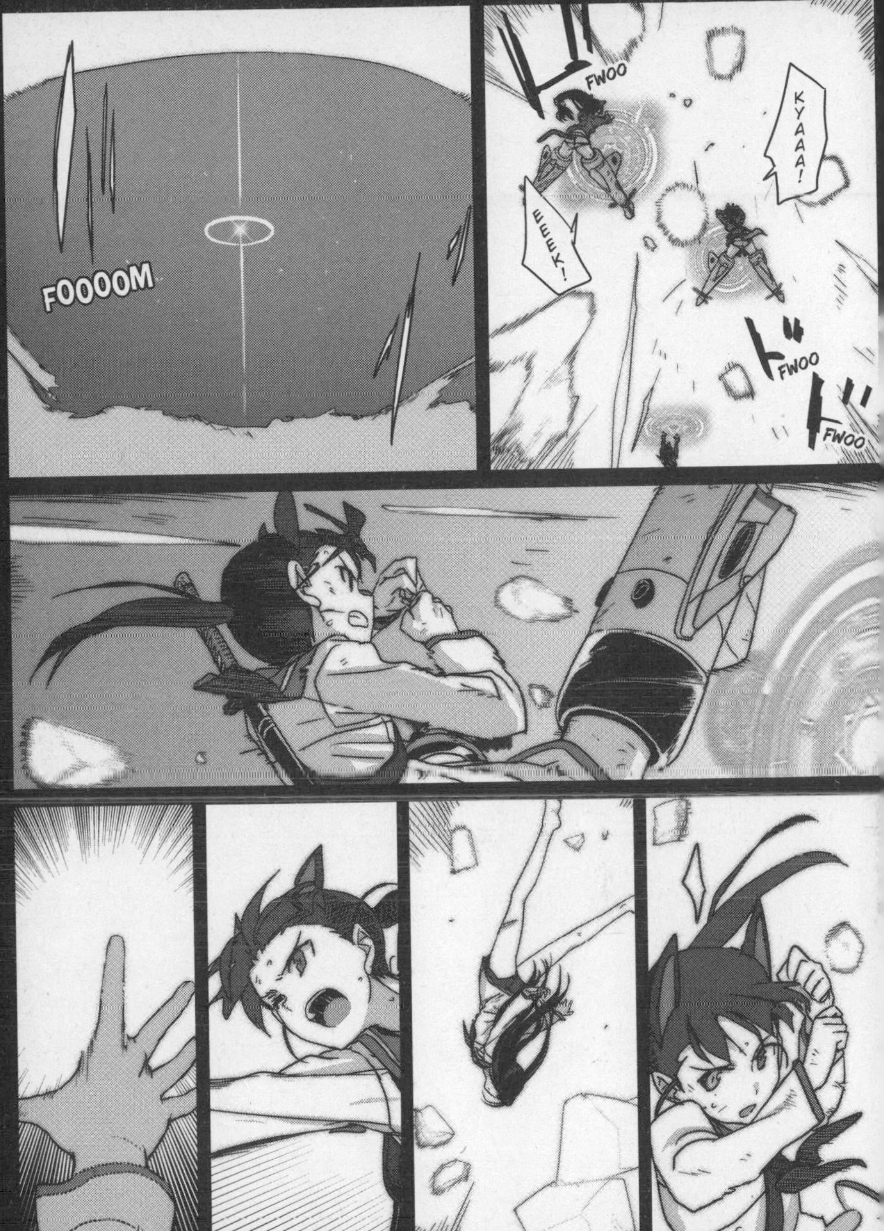
KYAAA!
FWOO
EEEK!
FWOO
FWOO
FOOOOM

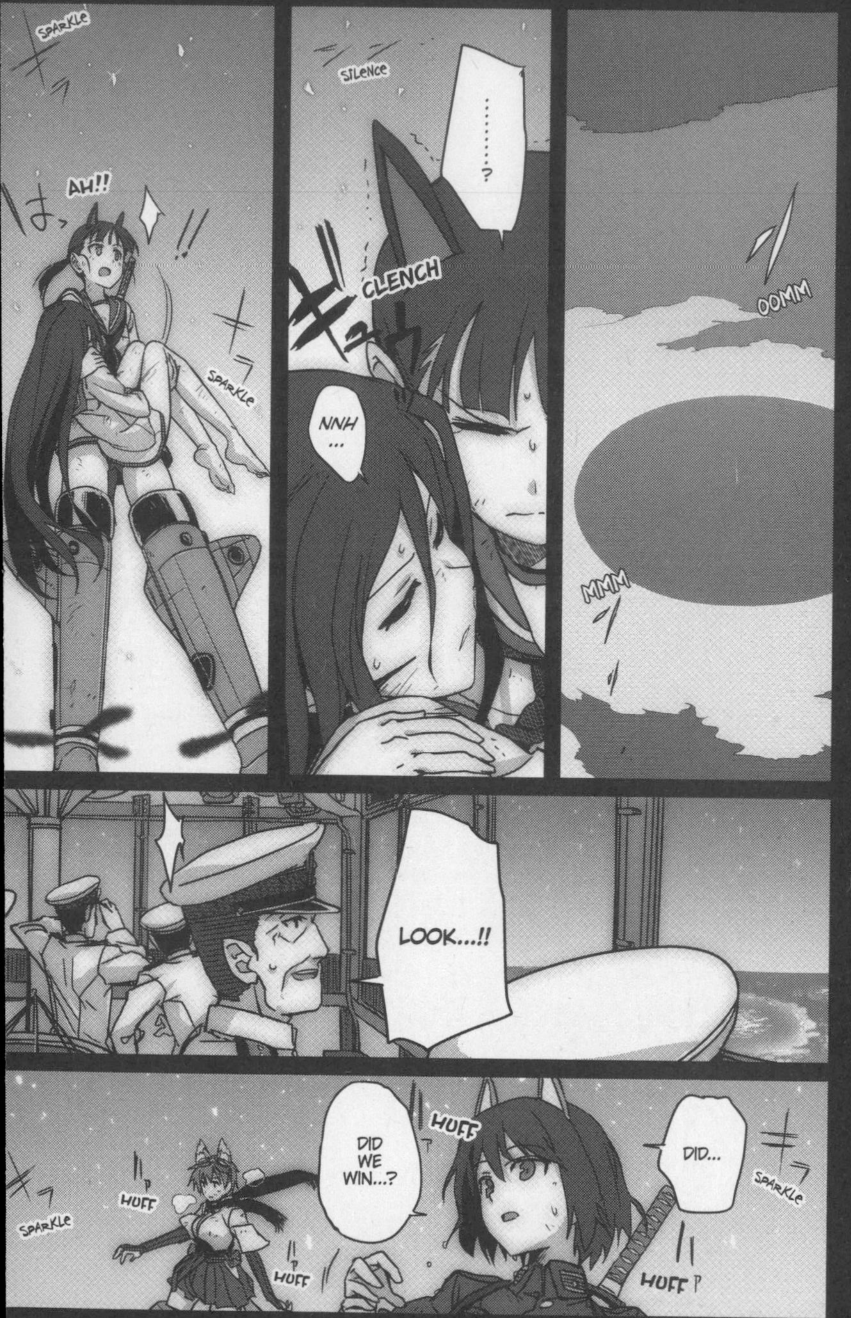
OOMM
MMM
SILENCE
......?
CLENCH
NNH ...
SPARKLE
AH!!
SPARKLE
LOOK...!!
DID...
SPARKLE
HUFF
HUFF
DID WE WIN...?
HUFF
HUFF
SPARKLE

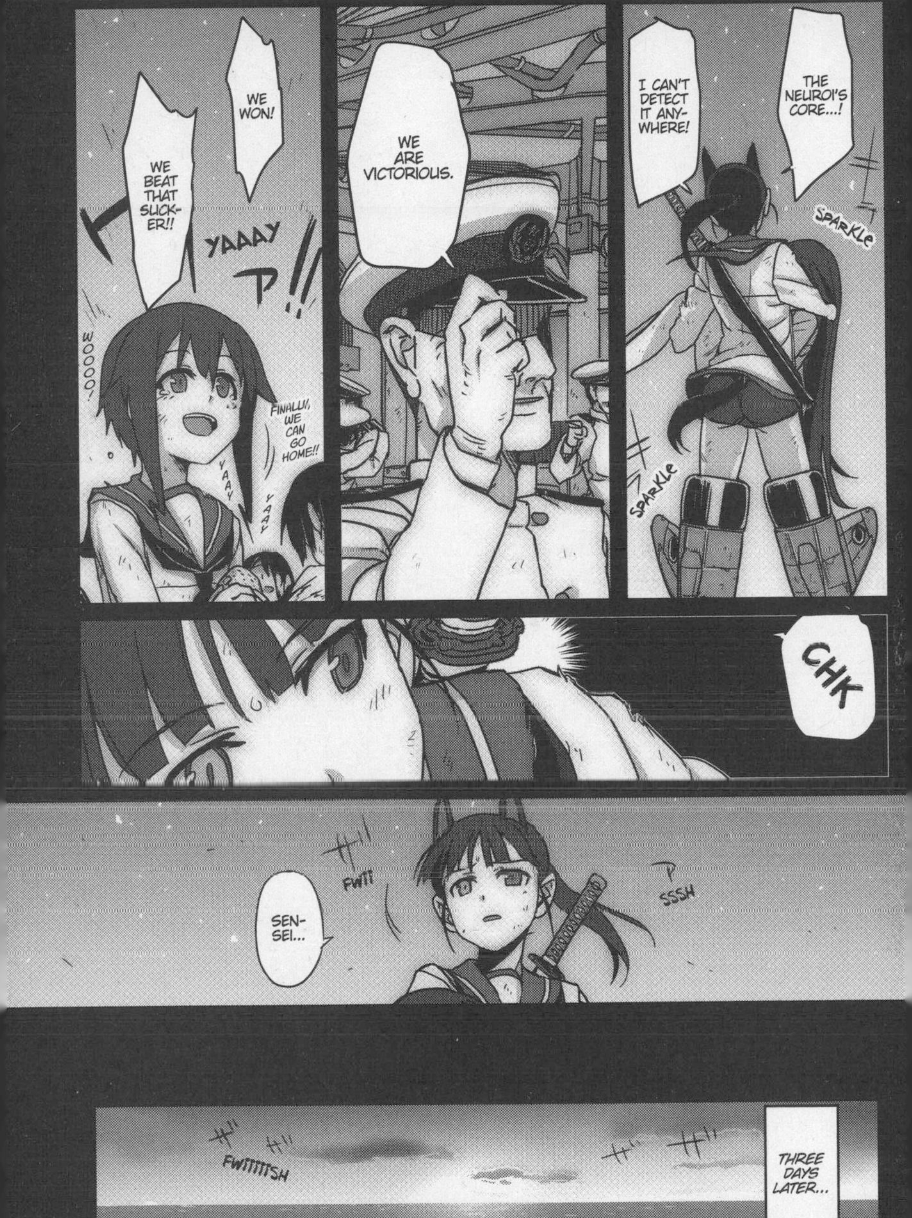
THE NEUROI'S CORE...!
I CAN'T DETECT IT ANYWHERE!
SPARKLE
SPARKLE
WE ARE VICTORIOUS.
WE WON!
WE BEAT THAT SUCKER!!
YAAAY
WOOOO!
FINALLY, WE CAN GO HOME!!
YAAY
YAAY
CHK
SSSH
FWIT
SEN-SEI...
THREE DAYS LATER...
FWITTTTSH

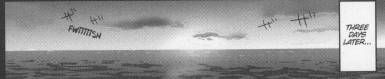

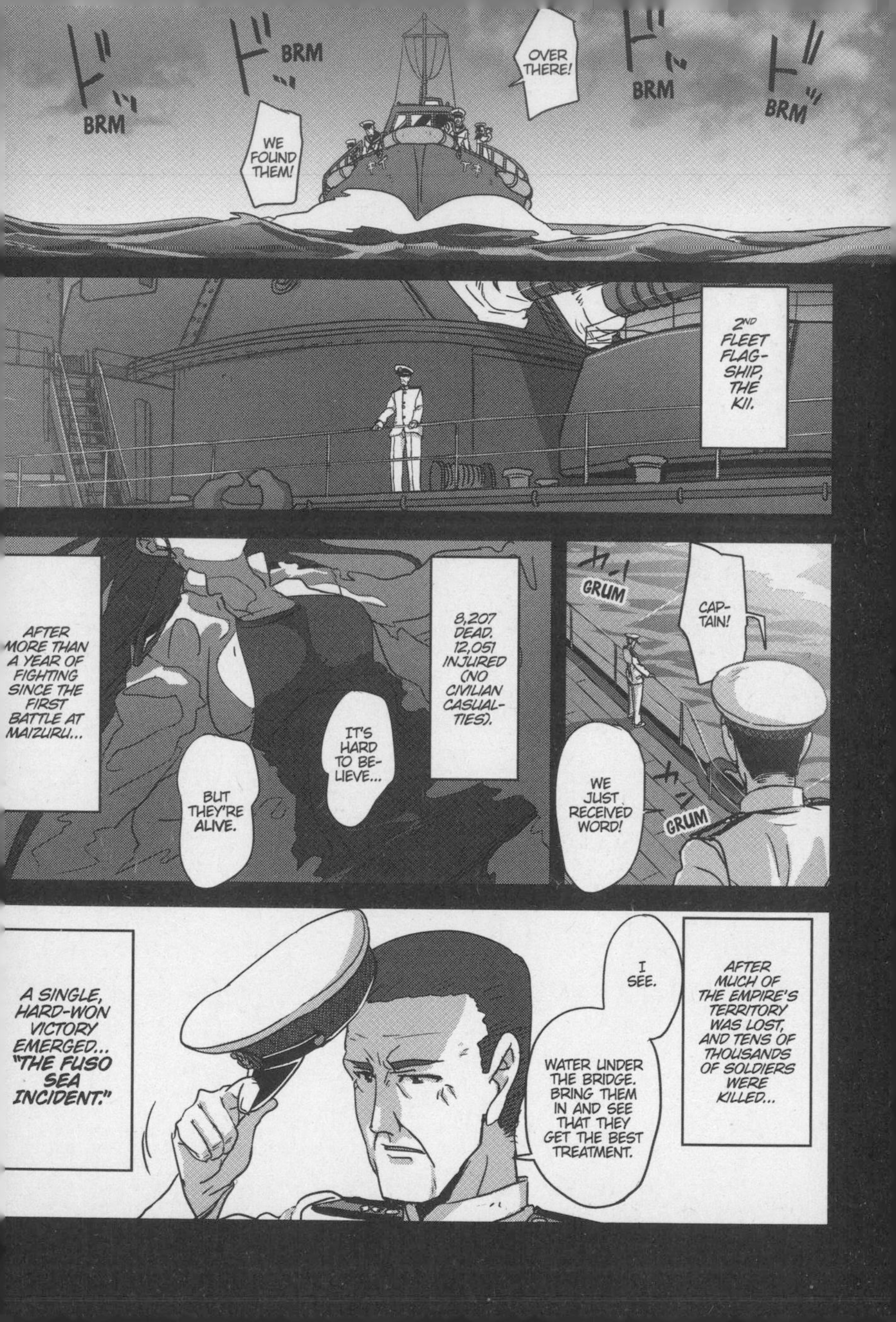
BRM
BRM
OVER THERE!
WE FOUND THEM!
BRM
BRM
2ND FLEET FLAGSHIP, THE KII.
GRUM
CAPTAIN!
WE JUST RECEIVED WORD!
GRUM
8,207 DEAD. 12,051 INJURED (NO CIVILIAN CASUALTIES).
IT'S HARD TO BELIEVE...
AFTER MORE THAN A YEAR OF FIGHTING SINCE THE FIRST BATTLE AT MAIZURU...
BUT THEY'RE ALIVE.
AFTER MUCH OF THE EMPIRE'S TERRITORY WAS LOST, AND TENS OF THOUSANDS OF SOLDIERS WERE KILLED...
I SEE.
WATER UNDER THE BRIDGE. BRING THEM IN AND SEE THAT THEY GET THE BEST TREATMENT.
A SINGLE, HARD-WON VICTORY EMERGED... "THE FUSO SEA INCIDENT."

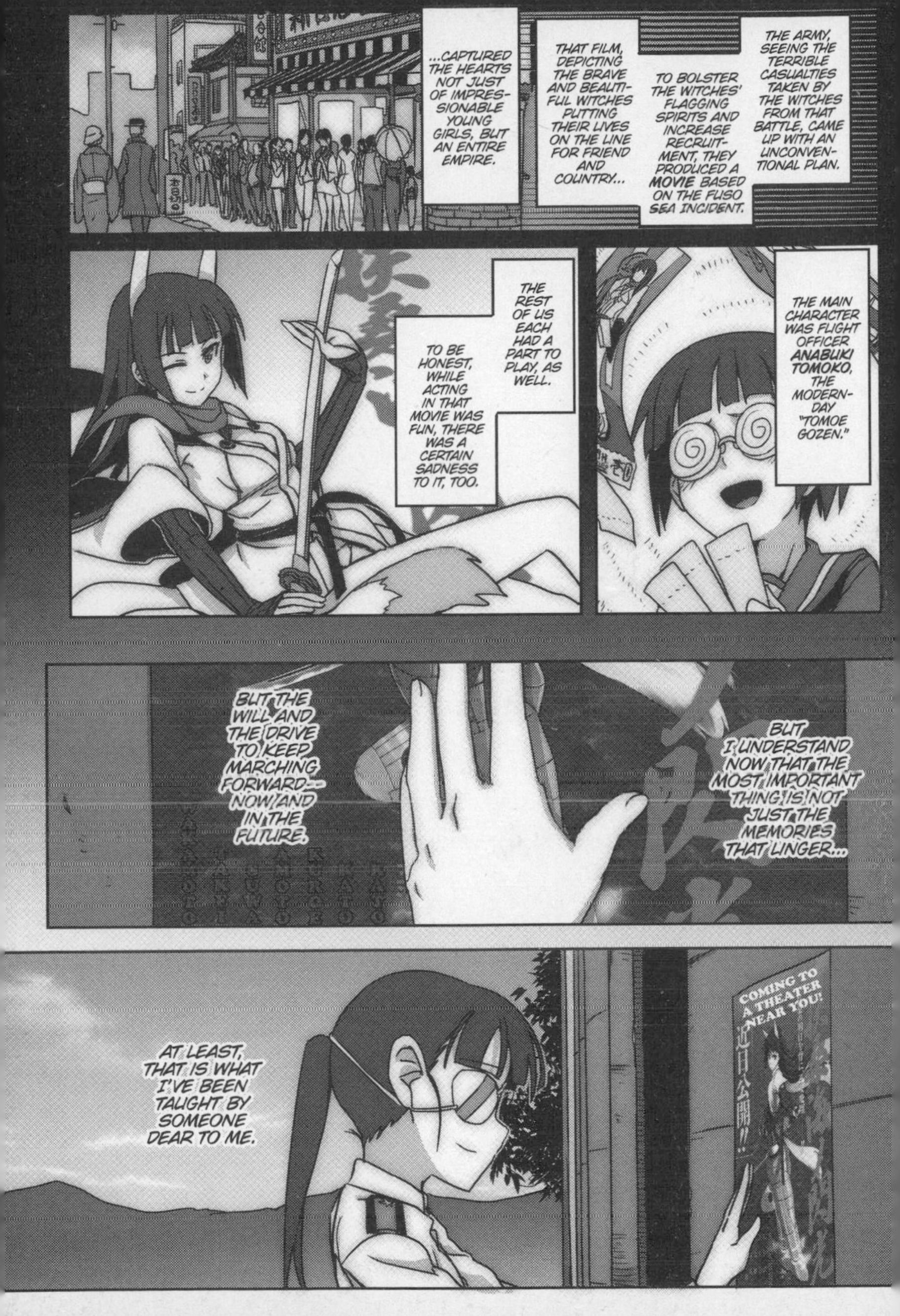
THE ARMY, SEEING THE TERRIBLE CASUALTIES TAKEN BY THE WITCHES FROM THAT BATTLE, CAME UP WITH AN UNCONVENTIONAL PLAN.
TO BOLSTER THE WITCHES' FLAGGING SPIRITS AND INCREASE RECRUITMENT, THEY PRODUCED A **MOVIE** BASED ON THE FUSO SEA INCIDENT.
THAT FILM, DEPICTING THE BRAVE AND BEAUTIFUL WITCHES PUTTING THEIR LIVES ON THE LINE FOR FRIEND AND COUNTRY...
...CAPTURED THE HEARTS NOT JUST OF IMPRESSIONABLE YOUNG GIRLS, BUT AN ENTIRE EMPIRE.
THE MAIN CHARACTER WAS FLIGHT OFFICER **ANABUKI TOMOKO**, THE MODERN-DAY "TOMOE GOZEN."
THE REST OF US EACH HAD A PART TO PLAY, AS WELL.
TO BE HONEST, WHILE ACTING IN THAT MOVIE WAS FUN, THERE WAS A CERTAIN SADNESS TO IT, TOO.
BUT I UNDERSTAND NOW THAT THE MOST IMPORTANT THING IS NOT JUST THE MEMORIES THAT LINGER...
BUT THE WILL AND THE DRIVE TO KEEP MARCHING FORWARD-- NOW AND IN THE FUTURE.
COMING TO A THEATER NEAR YOU!
近日公開!!
AT LEAST, THAT IS WHAT I'VE BEEN TAUGHT BY SOMEONE DEAR TO ME.

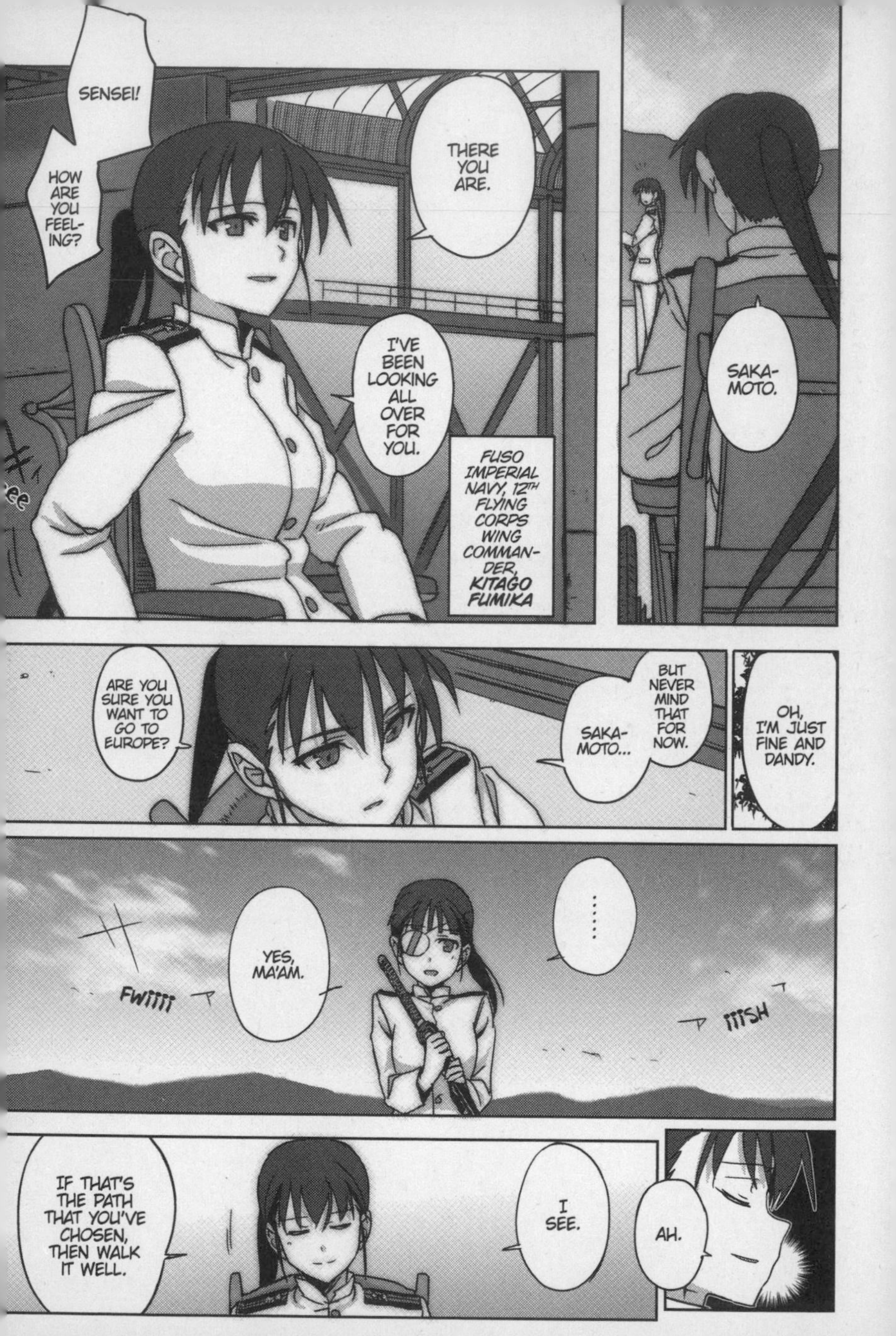
SAKA-MOTO.
THERE YOU ARE.
I'VE BEEN LOOKING ALL OVER FOR YOU.
FUSO IMPERIAL NAVY, 12TH FLYING CORPS WING COMMANDER, KITAGO FUMIKA
SENSEI!
HOW ARE YOU FEEL-ING?
OH, I'M JUST FINE AND DANDY.
BUT NEVER MIND THAT FOR NOW.
SAKA-MOTO...
ARE YOU SURE YOU WANT TO GO TO EUROPE?
......
YES, MA'AM.
FWIIII
IIISH
AH.
I SEE.
IF THAT'S THE PATH THAT YOU'VE CHOSEN, THEN WALK IT WELL.

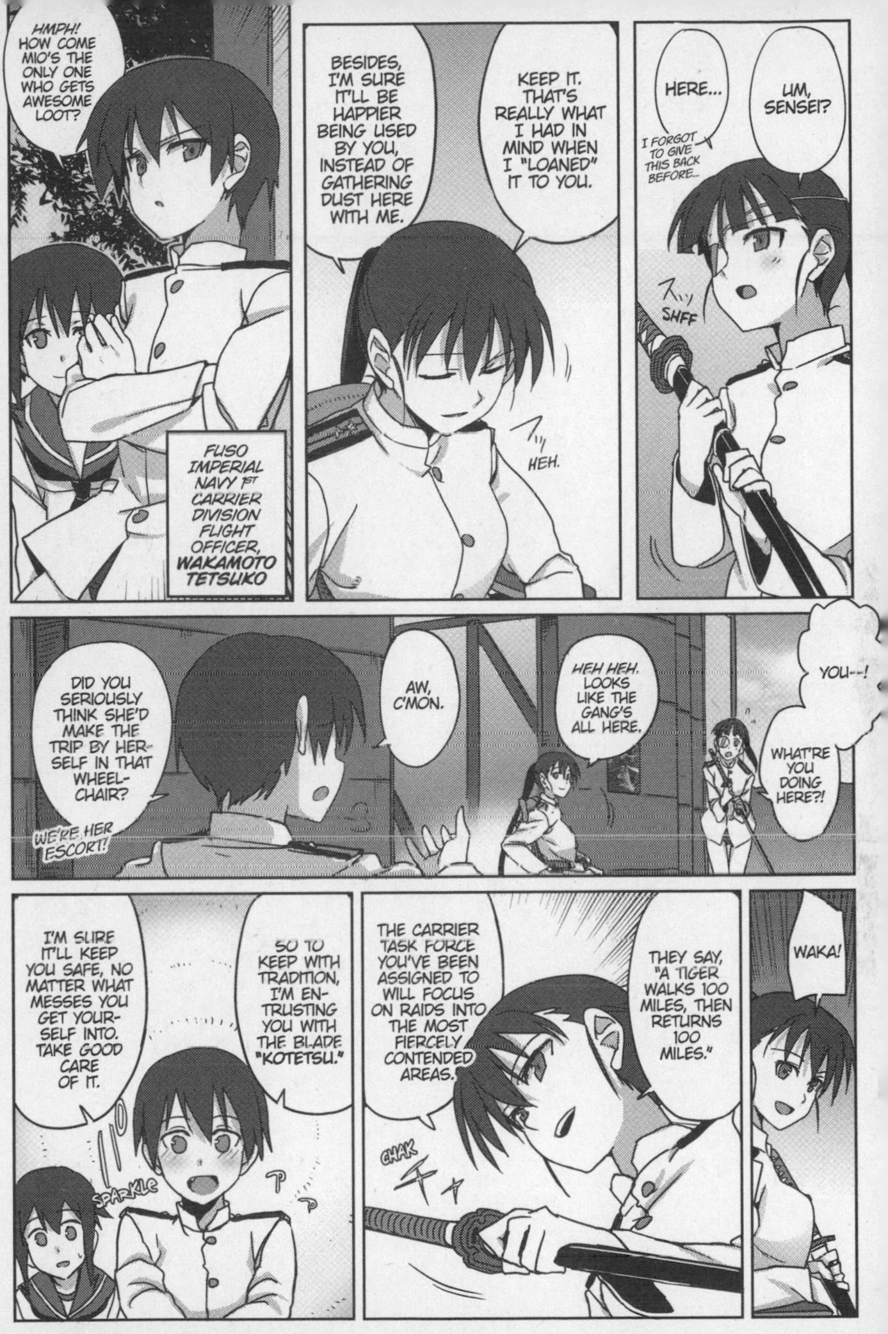
UM, SENSEI?
HERE...
I FORGOT TO GIVE THIS BACK BEFORE...
スッ
SHFF
KEEP IT. THAT'S REALLY WHAT I HAD IN MIND WHEN I "LOANED" IT TO YOU.
BESIDES, I'M SURE IT'LL BE HAPPIER BEING USED BY YOU, INSTEAD OF GATHERING DUST HERE WITH ME.
HEH.
HMPH! HOW COME MIO'S THE ONLY ONE WHO GETS AWESOME LOOT?
FUSO IMPERIAL NAVY 1ST CARRIER DIVISION FLIGHT OFFICER, **WAKAMOTO TETSUKO**
YOU--!
WHAT'RE YOU DOING HERE?!
HEH HEH. LOOKS LIKE THE GANG'S ALL HERE.
AW, C'MON.
DID YOU SERIOUSLY THINK SHE'D MAKE THE TRIP BY HER-SELF IN THAT WHEEL-CHAIR?
WE'RE HER ESCORT!
WAKA!
THEY SAY, "A TIGER WALKS 100 MILES, THEN RETURNS 100 MILES."
THE CARRIER TASK FORCE YOU'VE BEEN ASSIGNED TO WILL FOCUS ON RAIDS INTO THE MOST FIERCELY CONTENDED AREAS.
CHAK
SO TO KEEP WITH TRADITION, I'M EN-TRUSTING YOU WITH THE BLADE "KOTETSU."
I'M SURE IT'LL KEEP YOU SAFE, NO MATTER WHAT MESSES YOU GET YOUR-SELF INTO. TAKE GOOD CARE OF IT.
SPARKLE

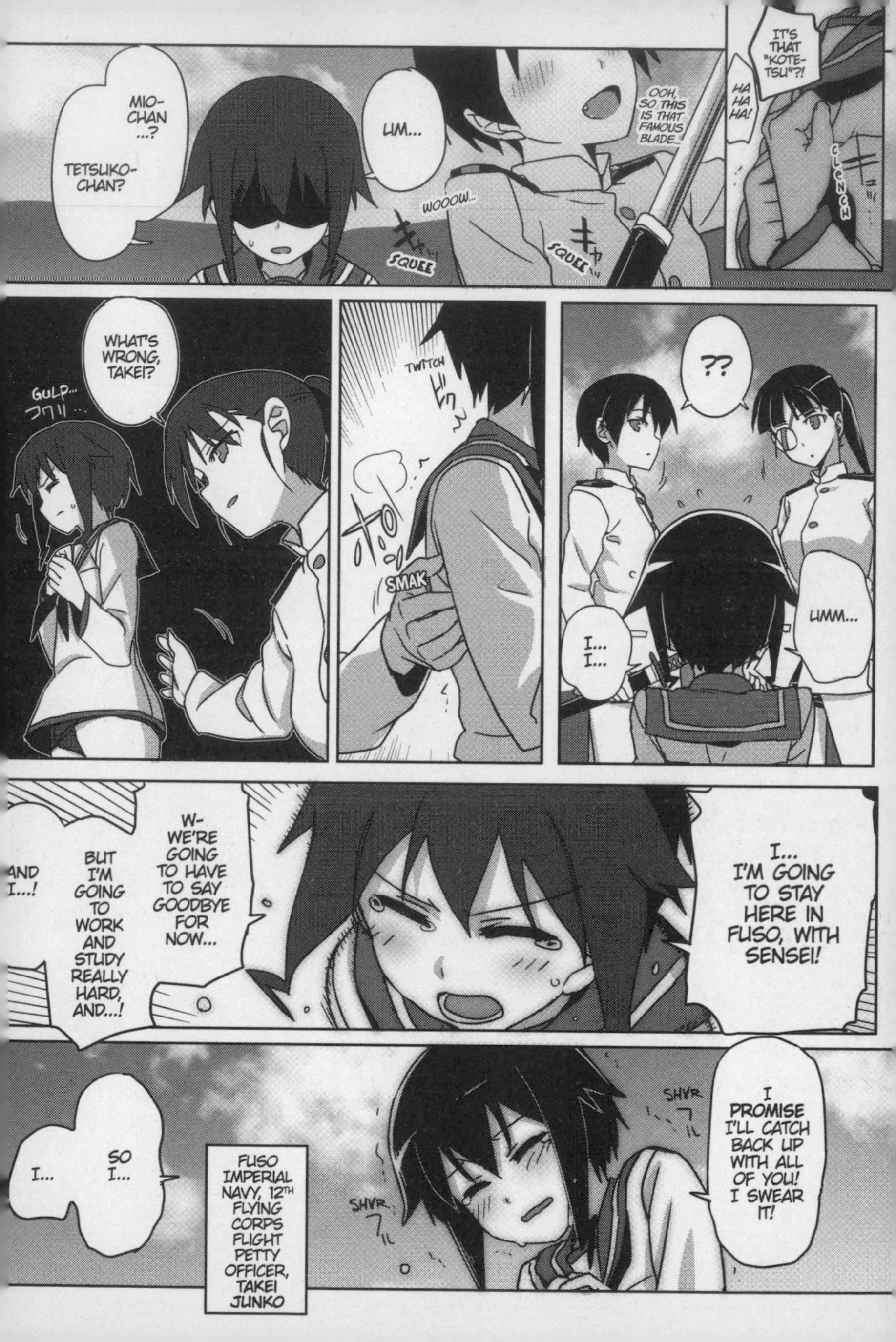
IT'S THAT "KOTE-TSU"?!
HA HA HA!
CLENCH
OOH, SO THIS IS THAT FAMOUS BLADE...
UM...
WOOOW...
SQUEE
SQUEE
MIO-CHAN ...?
TETSUKO-CHAN?
??
UMM...
I... I...
TWITCH
SMAK
WHAT'S WRONG, TAKEI?
GULP...
I... I'M GOING TO STAY HERE IN FUSO, WITH SENSEI!
W-WE'RE GOING TO HAVE TO SAY GOODBYE FOR NOW...
BUT I'M GOING TO WORK AND STUDY REALLY HARD, AND...!
AND I...!
I PROMISE I'LL CATCH BACK UP WITH ALL OF YOU! I SWEAR IT!
SHVR
SHVR
FUSO IMPERIAL NAVY, 12TH FLYING CORPS FLIGHT PETTY OFFICER, TAKEI JUNKO
SO I...
I...

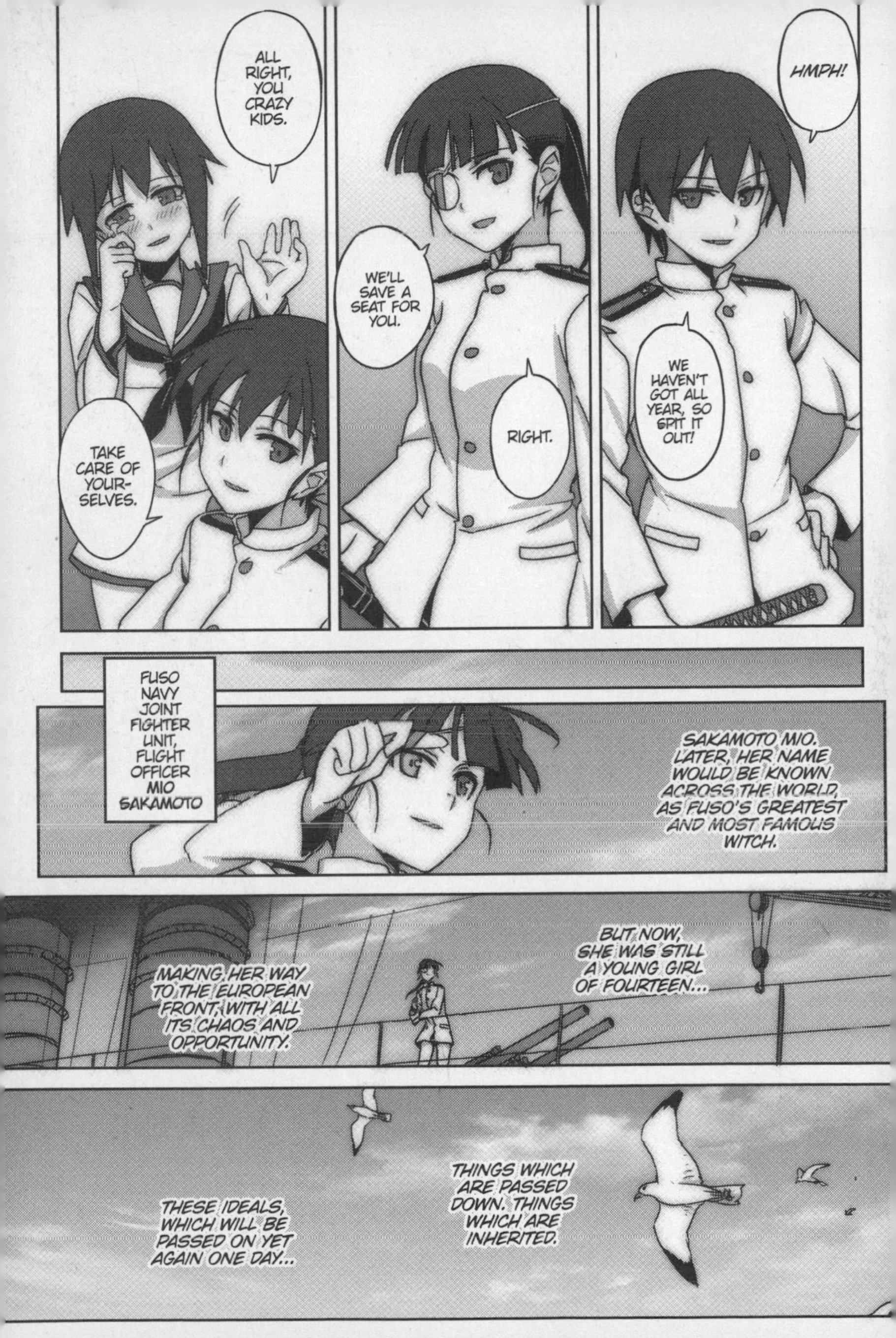
HMPH!
WE HAVEN'T GOT ALL YEAR, SO SPIT IT OUT!
WE'LL SAVE A SEAT FOR YOU.
RIGHT.
ALL RIGHT, YOU CRAZY KIDS.
TAKE CARE OF YOUR-SELVES.
SAKAMOTO MIO. LATER, HER NAME WOULD BE KNOWN ACROSS THE WORLD, AS FUSO'S GREATEST AND MOST FAMOUS WITCH.
FUSO NAVY JOINT FIGHTER UNIT, FLIGHT OFFICER MIO SAKAMOTO
BUT NOW, SHE WAS STILL A YOUNG GIRL OF FOURTEEN...
MAKING HER WAY TO THE EUROPEAN FRONT, WITH ALL ITS CHAOS AND OPPORTUNITY.
THINGS WHICH ARE PASSED DOWN. THINGS WHICH ARE INHERITED.
THESE IDEALS, WHICH WILL BE PASSED ON YET AGAIN ONE DAY...

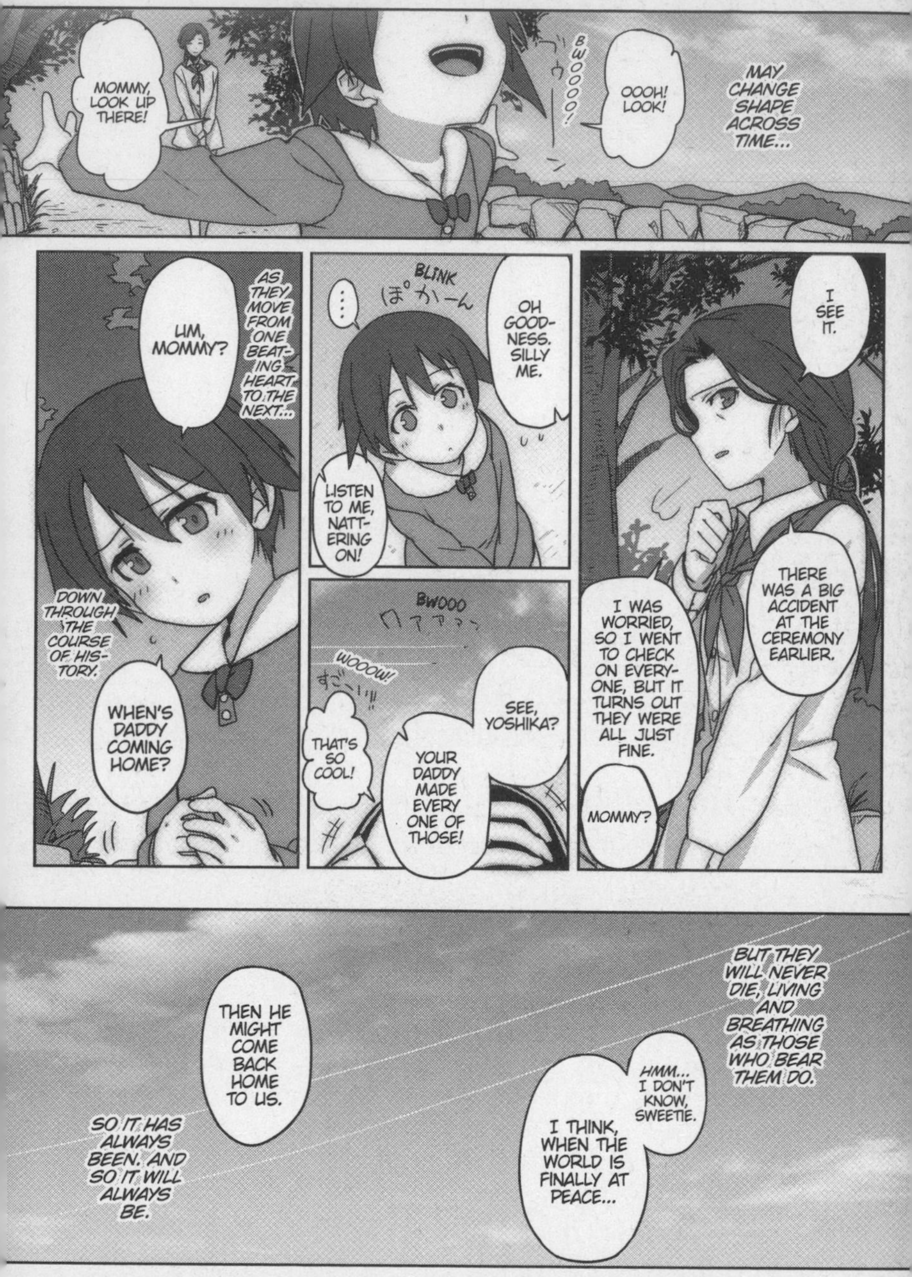
MAY CHANGE SHAPE ACROSS TIME...
OOOH! LOOK!
BWOOOOOO!
MOMMY, LOOK UP THERE!
I SEE IT.
THERE WAS A BIG ACCIDENT AT THE CEREMONY EARLIER.
I WAS WORRIED, SO I WENT TO CHECK ON EVERYONE, BUT IT TURNS OUT THEY WERE ALL JUST FINE.
MOMMY?
BLINK
ぽかーん
OH GOODNESS. SILLY ME.
....
LISTEN TO ME, NATTERING ON!
BWOOO
SEE, YOSHIKA?
YOUR DADDY MADE EVERY ONE OF THOSE!
WOOOW!
THAT'S SO COOL!
AS THEY MOVE FROM ONE BEATING HEART TO THE NEXT...
UM, MOMMY?
DOWN THROUGH THE COURSE OF HISTORY.
WHEN'S DADDY COMING HOME?
BUT THEY WILL NEVER DIE, LIVING AND BREATHING AS THOSE WHO BEAR THEM DO.
HMM... I DON'T KNOW, SWEETIE.
I THINK, WHEN THE WORLD IS FINALLY AT PEACE...
THEN HE MIGHT COME BACK HOME TO US.
SO IT HAS ALWAYS BEEN. AND SO IT WILL ALWAYS BE.

Strike Witches:
1937 Fuso Sea Incident
[Mission Complete]

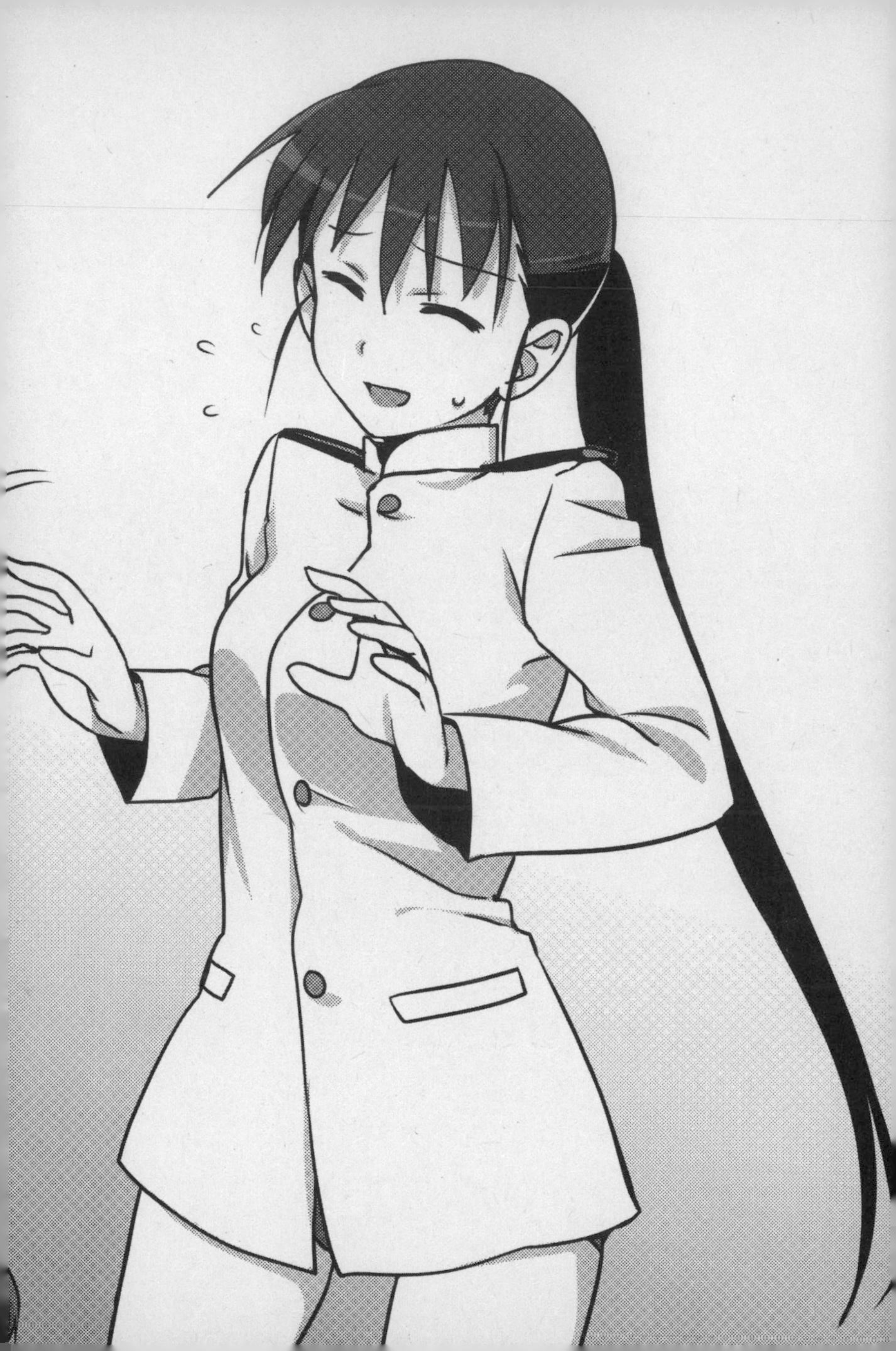

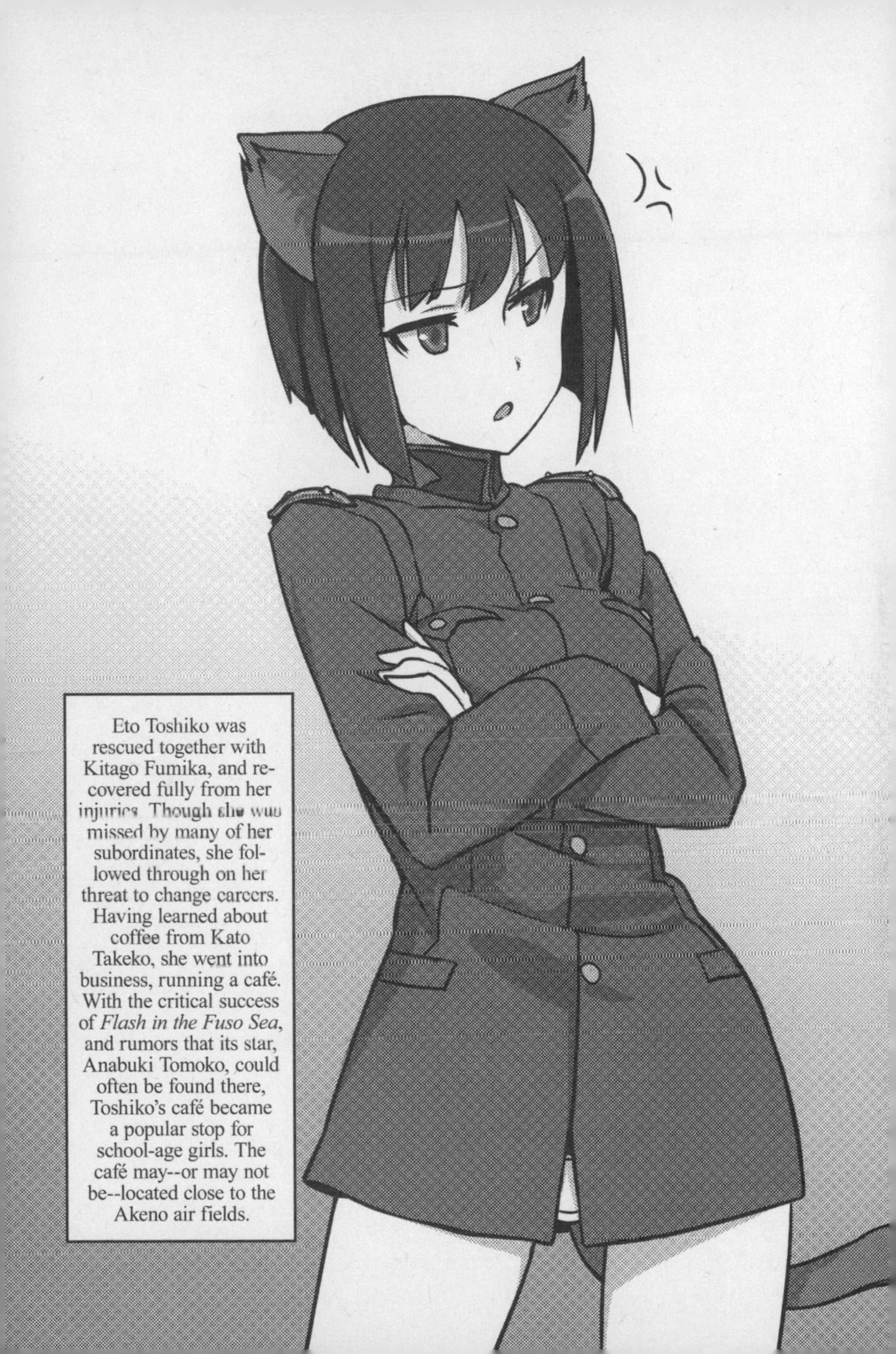

Eto Toshiko was rescued together with Kitago Fumika, and recovered fully from her injuries. Though she was missed by many of her subordinates, she followed through on her threat to change careers. Having learned about coffee from Kato Takeko, she went into business, running a café. With the critical success of *Flash in the Fuso Sea*, and rumors that its star, Anabuki Tomoko, could often be found there, Toshiko's café became a popular stop for school-age girls. The café may--or may not be--located close to the Akeno air fields.

By: Takaaki Suzuki

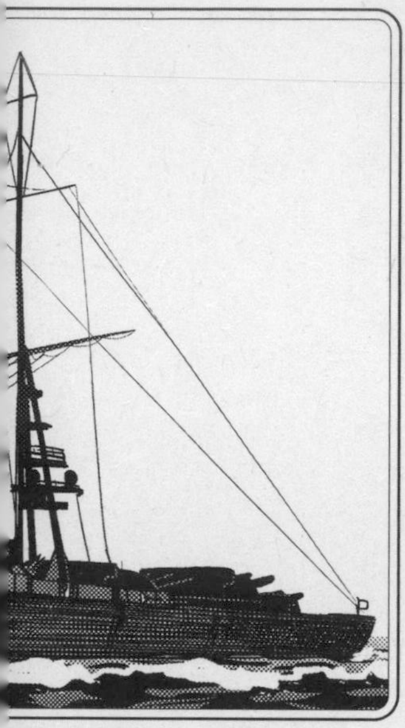

KII-CLASS BATTLESHIPS

At the close of the First Neuroi War, the Fuso Imperial Navy was constructing several warships of the new *Amagi*-class design. While they were originally intended to be high-speed battle cruisers, Fuso's experiences in the First Neuroi War, along with the advent of airplanes and airborne witches, convinced them to convert two of the cruisers, the *Amagi* and the *Akagi*, into aircraft carriers. Later, a third and a fourth *Amagi*-class ship made the conversion to carriers, but these were sold to Karlsland in exchange for advanced technology and machinery.

Reflecting on what they'd learned from the First Neuroi War, the Fuso Navy demanded new battleship designs that would be both fast and maneuverable, while retaining firepower heavy enough to bombard Neuroi land-installations from outside of Neuroi firing range. The *Amagi*-class cruisers were fast enough, but had lighter armor; and their base armament, the same 45-caliber 41cm guns as the *Nagato*-class, was thought to be insufficient. Thus, the *Amagi*-class was redesigned into the more powerful *Kii*-class.

At first glance, the exterior of the *Kii*-class was nearly identical to the *Amagi*-class. However, the *Kii*-class sported stronger, more strategically placed armor made from better materials. The ship's artillery magazine was strengthened, while additional armor plates protected the steam vents and funnel. The design also adopted advanced damage control technology from Karlsland and Liberion, such as watertight bulkheads, ballast tanks, stronger pumps, fire-resistant materials, and fire extinguishers. The original plans called for four triple-turret 50-caliber 46cm guns, but development of that weapon was behind schedule, as the triple-turret itself was still in the design stages. The next-best choice, five 50-caliber 41cm gun turrets, fell through as well, for the same reason. But the conversion of the *Amagi*-class cruisers into carriers had left a surplus of 45-caliber 41cm guns originally meant as their armament. So the original *Kii*-class design retained the same armaments as the

KII-class battleship

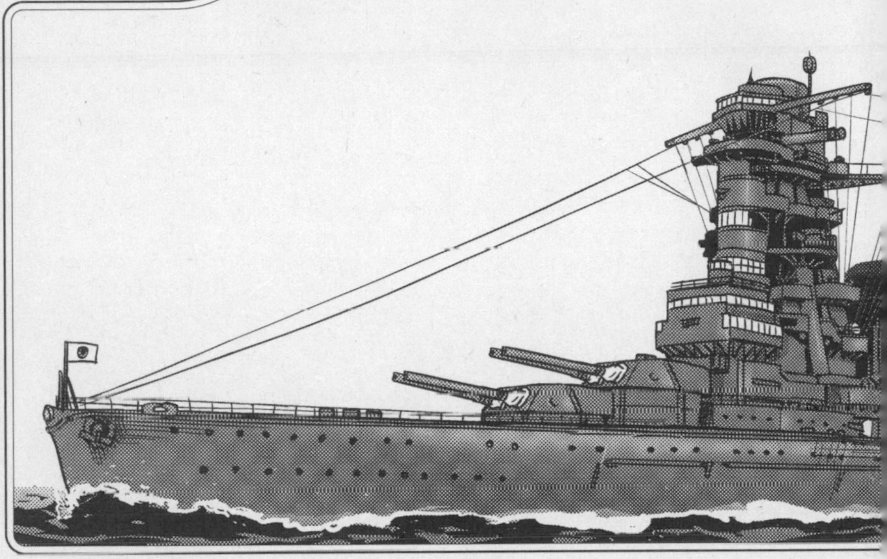

Amagi-class; however, the navy stipulated that these guns were to be replaced with the 50-caliber 41cm guns upon that weapon's completion. This led to major differences in weight distribution from the *Amagi*-class, as well as several other time-consuming adjustments to the design. In hindsight, this was generally agreed to have been a massive waste of time. Additionally, one proposal suggested that, instead of mounting the secondary guns by casemate directly into the superstructure, turret-guns should be installed along the broadsides. Since that would require yet more adjustments to the design, along with the need to prioritize manufacture of the new 14cm guns as main weapons for other battle cruisers, the proposal was shelved for use in later designs. Despite all this, the *Kii*-class design did manage to include several modifications that improved overall operation and use.

After that long and complicated development process, the final design for the *Kii*-class was set. Construction began on the first ship of the class, the *Kii*, in the Kure naval yard. At the same time, the Yokosuka naval yard began work on the second ship, the *Owari*. Two years later, both ships launched. Outfitting them took another year, then construction was finally complete. At that point, the original schedule called for construction on the third and fourth ships to begin right away. However, the navy put priority on developing the 50-caliber 41cm guns, and delayed the new ships by more than a year. Construction finally began on the third ship, the *Suruga*, at the Kobe Kawataki Shipyard; and the fourth ship, the *Konoe*, at Miyahishi's Nagasaki shipyard. The *Konoe* launched before the *Suruga*, but both ships were outfitted and completed in numerical order. This outfitting required an extra year over that of the *Kii* and the *Owari*, as the manufacture of the new main guns took longer than expected. (The *Kii* and *Owari* had simply used the ready-made guns from the *Amagi* and *Akagi*.) Some proposed that the *Kii* and *Owari* also upgrade their main guns to the newer models, but the time and cost required to manufacture the new guns, not to mention the difficulty of removing and replacing the old ones, tabled that idea. Furthermore, sudden advancements in Striker Units for the Witches led to an emphasis on the rapid construction of new and better aircraft carriers. The naval yards at Kure and Yokosuka were engaged in building new carriers, leaving no room to dock the completed battleships for re-outfitting.

Though the *Kii*-class battleships were Fuso's most advanced warship at the time, they were not included in the 1st Fleet, but relegated to the 2nd Fleet. Development on the 50-caliber 46cm guns and triple-gun turrets called for in the original designs continued apace. A working 45-caliber 46cm gun was completed first, which would later become the primary weapon on the *Yamato*-class battleship.

STRIKE WITCHES
1937
FUSO SEA
INCIDENT

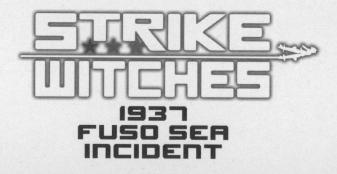

SPECIFICATIONS

Displacement:	46,860t
Overall length:	259.2m
Beam:	32.5m
Draft:	8.71m
Power:	161,000shp
Speed:	30.01kt
Armaments:	5x twin 41cm guns (*Kii, Owari/Suruga, Konoe* had 50cal. not 45cal. 41cm guns) 16x single 14cm guns 8x twin 12cm anti-aircraft guns
Armor:	Waterline Belt – 305mm Barbettes – 305mm Conning tower – 356mm
Range:	9,000nmi
Crew:	approx. 2,000

Afterword

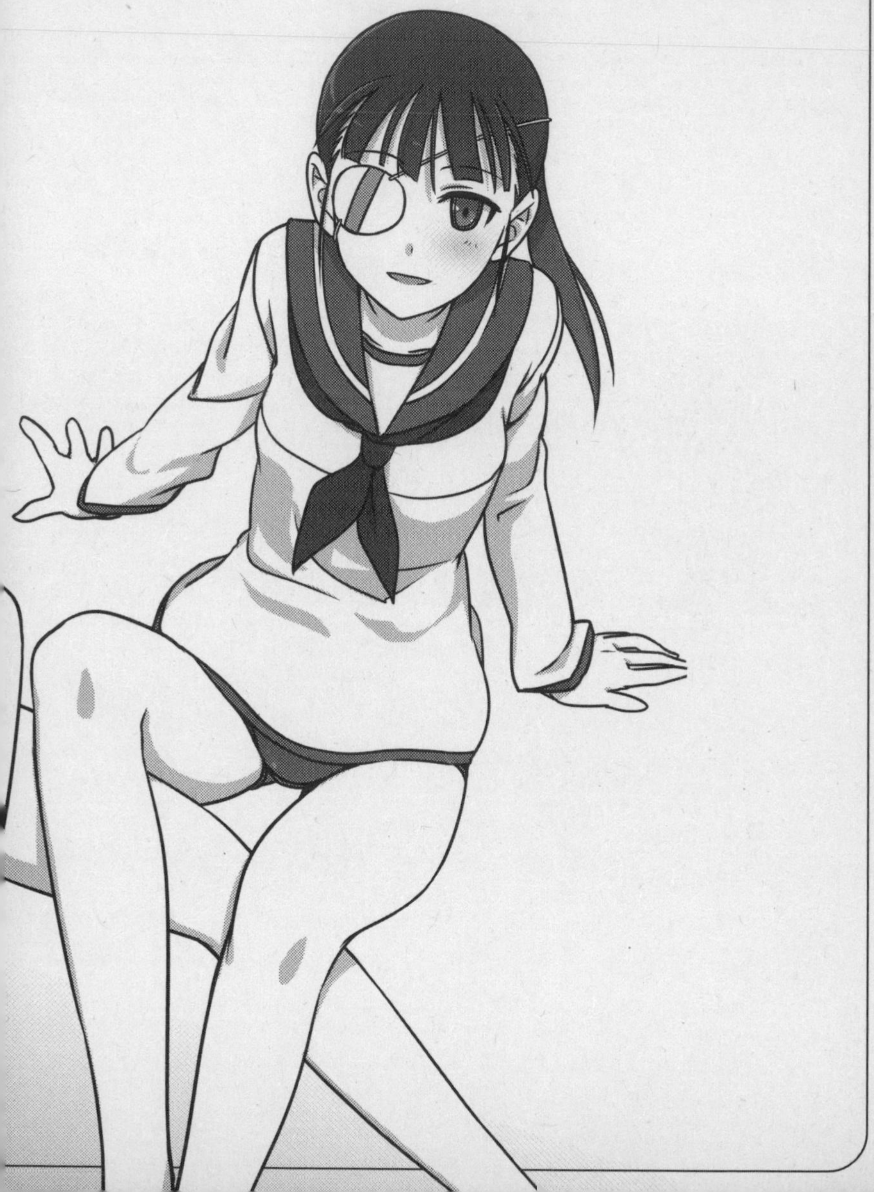

Thank you very much for reading volume 2 of *Strike Witches Zero: 1937 Fuso Sea Incident.* Time flies by so fast. It has already been over a year since I first began serializing this title. With even more help and support from many wonderful people, I was able to bring this second volume into the world. This may be the end of the "Fuso Sea Incident," but I am sure that the Strike Witches universe will continue to expand. I will be very happy if this series becomes yet another small step in that growth.

Finally, I would like to say thank you to Humikane Shimada-sama and Takaaki Suzuki-sama for their amazing world and characters, to the editors at *Nyantype* magazine for their diligent editing work, to Noboru Yamaguchi-sama for allowing me to use Tomoko, to my faithful assistant Tsukasa Shimada-sama for all of his help with various things in each chapter, and to all of the readers out there for their loving support. Again, thank you so much!

-NINGEN

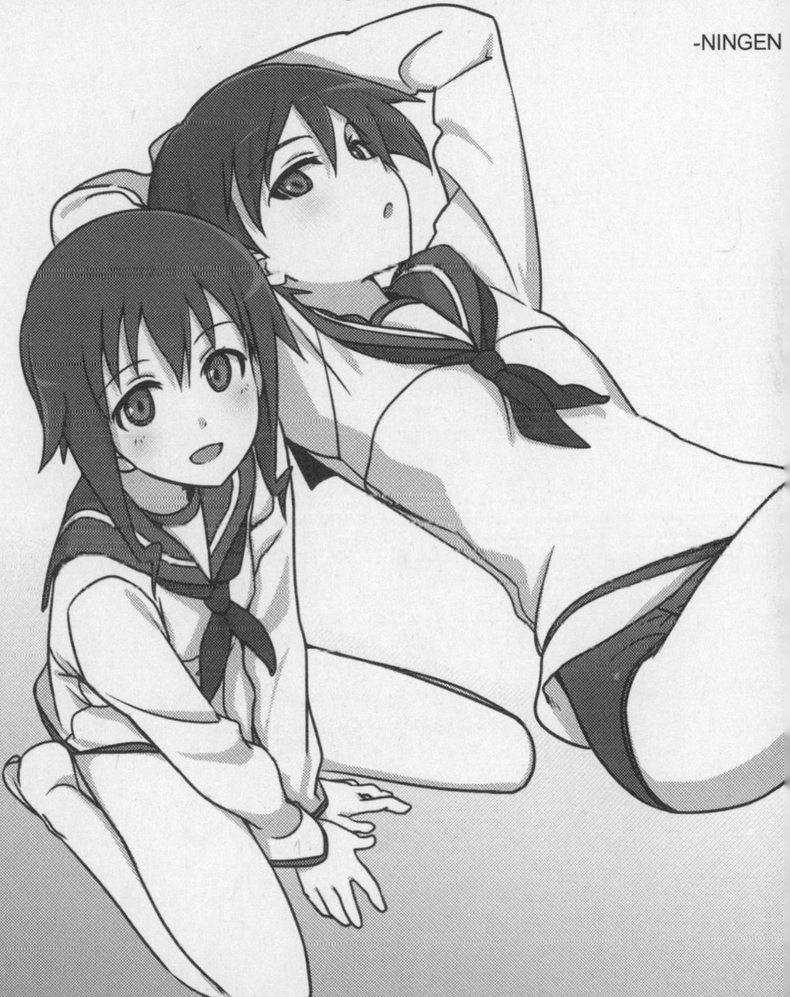

ストライクウィッチーズ零

STRIKE WITCHES ZERO

1937 扶桑海事変

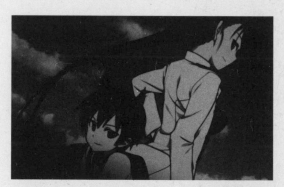

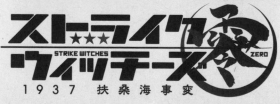

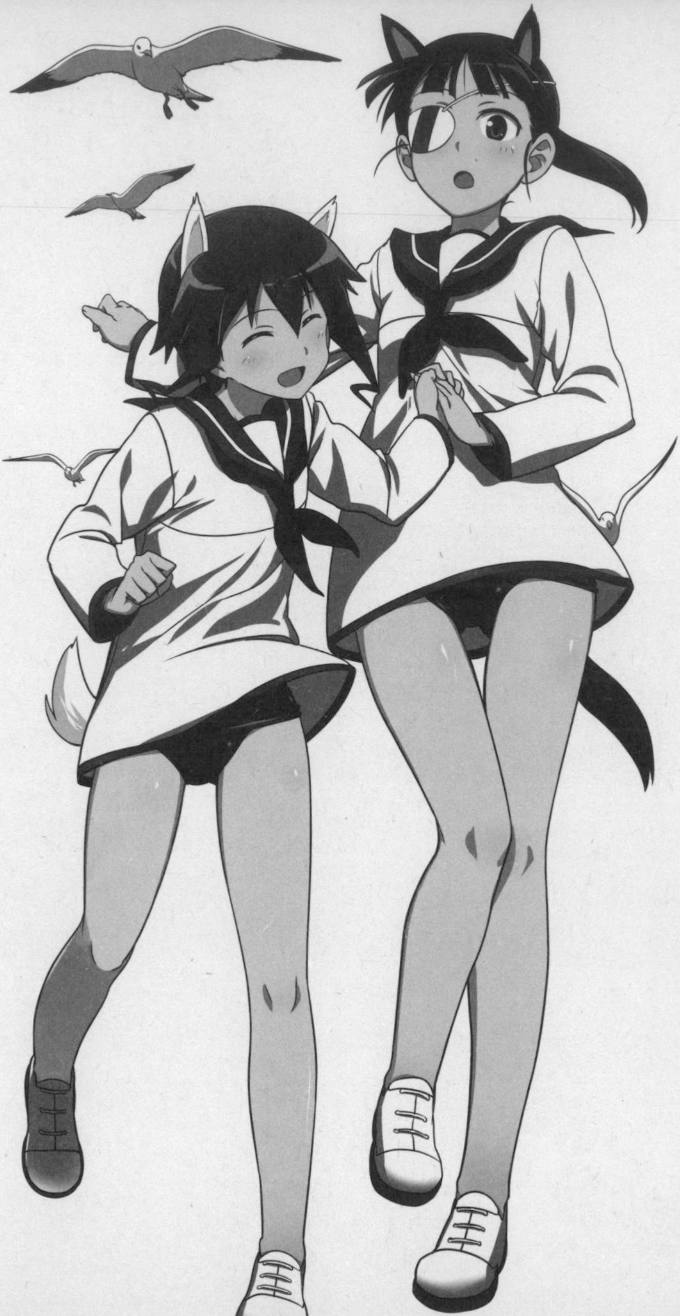

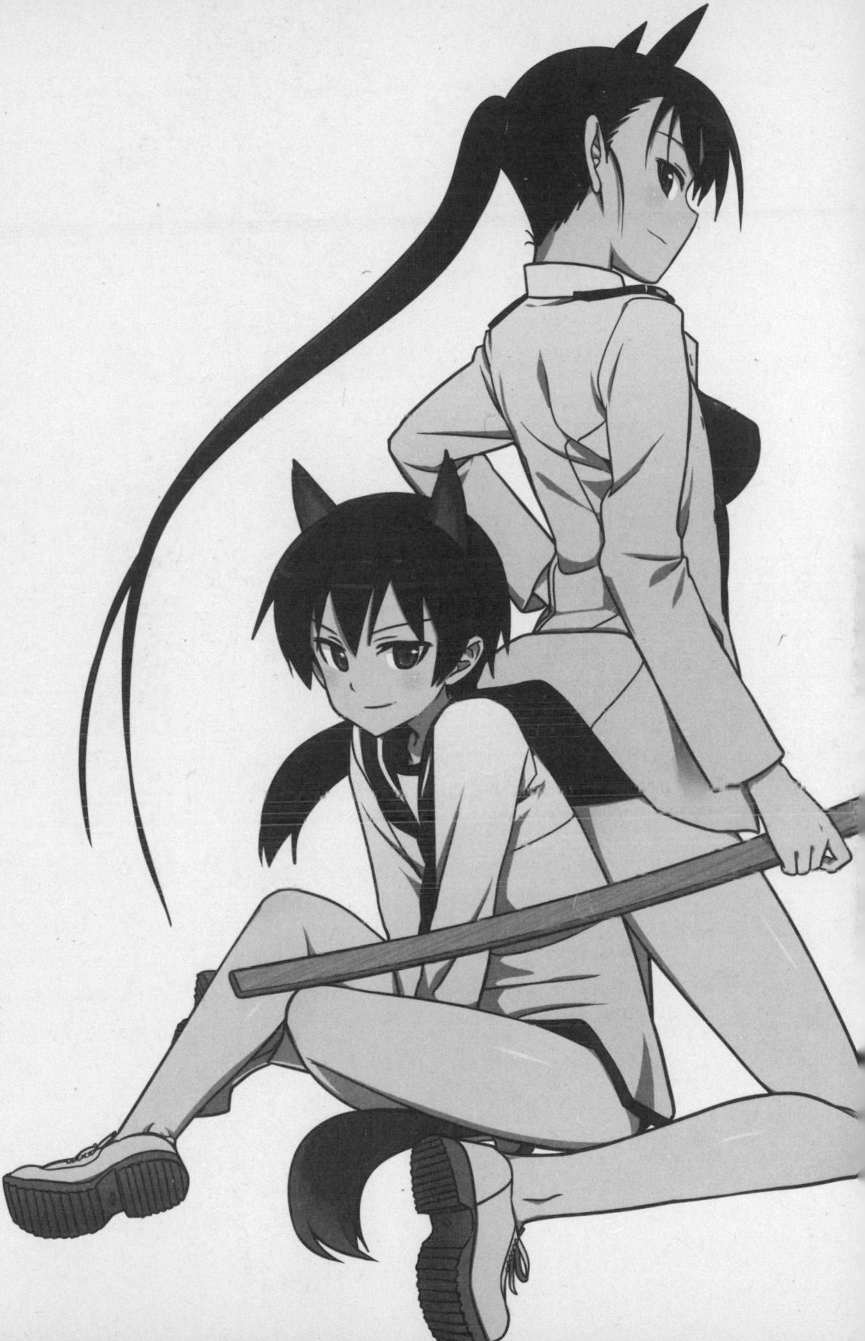

ストライクウィッチーズ零

1937扶桑海事変

第二巻

漫画 にんげん

原作 島田フミカネ&Projekt Kagonish

Kadokawa Comics A

SEVEN SEAS ENTERTAINMENT PRESENTS

STRIKE WITCHES
1937 FUSO SEA INCIDENT VOL. 2

art by **Ningen** / story by **Humikane Shimada** + **Projekt Kagonish**

TRANSLATION
Adrienne Beck

ADAPTATION
Shanti Whitesides

LETTERING AND LAYOUT
Alexandra Gunawan

COVER DESIGN
Nicky Lim

PROOFREADER
Janet Houck
Conner Crooks

MANAGING EDITOR
Adam Arnold

PUBLISHER
Jason DeAngelis

STRIKE WITCHES ZERO: 1937 FUSO KAIJI HEN VOL. 2
© Ningen 2012, © 2010 501st JOINT FIGHTER WING
Edited by KADOKAWA SHOTEN.
First published in Japan in 2011 by KADOKAWA CORPORATION, Tokyo.
English translation rights arranged with KADOKAWA CORPORATION, Tokyo
through TOHAN CORPORATION, Tokyo..

Seven Seas books may be purchased in bulk for educational, business, or
promotional use. For information on bulk purchases, please contact Macmillan
Corporate & Premium Sales Department at 1-800-221-7945 (ext 5442)
or write specialmarkets@macmillan.com.

Seven Seas and the Seven Seas logo are trademarks of
Seven Seas Entertainment, LLC. All rights reserved.

ISBN: 978-1-626920-80-4

Printed in Canada

First Printing: October 2014

10 9 8 7 6 5 4 3 2 1

FOLLOW US ONLINE: *www.gomanga.com*

READING DIRECTIONS

This book reads from *right to left*, Japanese style.
If this is your first time reading manga, you start
reading from the top right panel on each page and
take it from there. If you get lost, just follow the
numbered diagram here. It may seem backwards at
first, but you'll get the hang of it! Have fun!!

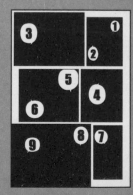